JESUSGATE

Other Books by Ernie Bringas

Going by the Book: Past and Present Tragedies of Biblical Authority

Created Equal: A Case for the Animal Human Connection

JESUSGATE

A History of
Concealment Unraveled

ERNIE BRINGAS

RAINBOW RIDGE
BOOKS

Unless otherwise stated, scripture herein was taken from the NRSV.

Cover and interior design by Frame 25 Productions
Cover photograph © Pattie Steib c/o Shutterstock.com

Published by:
Rainbow Ridge Books, LLC
140 Rainbow Ridge Road
Faber, Virginia 22938
434-361-1723

If you are unable to order this book from your local
bookseller, you may order directly from the distributor.

Square One Publishers, Inc.
115 Herricks Road
Garden City Park, NY 11040
Phone: (516) 535-2010
Fax: (516) 535-2014
Toll-free: 877-900-BOOK

Visit the author at:
www.jesusgate.net

Library of Congress Cataloging-in-Publication Data applied for.

ISBN 978-1-937907-04-4

10 9 8 7 6 5 4 3 2

Printed on acid-free recycled paper in the United States of America

This work is dedicated to:

Ginny, and in memory of Martha,
my two delightful sisters

WITH GRATITUDE

Here are some of the qualities I look for when I hand my manuscript to someone for review. First, I look for someone who has a sharp, educated mind, a willingness to help, and a strong backbone to express honest opinion. To that end, I wish to extend my sincere thanks to the following people. In alphabetical order: Dave Bourquin, Dr. Robert Erickson, and Al Gunby. The shortness of this message flies in the face of their many contributions and my immense gratitude for their help. An extended "thanks" to Dave, who fielded all my thorny grammar issues.

I should also reprise my deepest appreciation for Dr. Erickson's insightful suggestions regarding this work. For example, his counsel led to the WHAT TO EXPECT NEXT sections of this work, and also to a much more refreshed bibliography. His promotional advice was also most helpful, and I am grateful for his unwavering support.

I also want to thank my publisher, Robert Friedman, who would not allow this work to go unpublished. Not only does he reflect the qualities mentioned above, but he was also willing to put his initiative and expertise behind the publication of this work. Thanks, Bob.

Last, but not least, a special thank you to Jonathan Friedman for the creative layout design of this book's cover and content. I also appreciated his meticulous attention to my editorial concerns.

CONTENTS

Prologue:

THINGS YOU SHOULD KNOW

People say I look like Tom Cruise. That's what I tell my college students during lecture. Eventually they stop laughing. Truth is, I look more like Mayberry's Barney Fife. As for the Tom Cruise comparison, it's an obvious misstatement on my part, and an obvious no-brainer for my students. As I stand front and center, direct evidence proves me wrong. But not all statements and ideas can be so easily verified. When this occurs, as it often does, what method do we use to seek out the truth?

All branches of knowledge adhere to the stringent principles of the scientific method, including the religious field (known as biblical criticism or higher criticism). The scientific method is a rigidly controlled, analytical process that gave us antibiotics, a round trip to the Moon, and made Disneyland possible (okay, it also gave us AK-47s and nuclear bombs).

The practical value of the scientific method is that it can be applied across the board. From the study of quantum physics to the mating habits of the dung beetle, the scientific method reigns supreme. It is a system of methods, principles and calculated procedures, which brings reality (things as they really are) into focus. Although some religious questions rest outside the boundaries of science (for example, Does God exist?), many claims made by various religious groups can be investigated (for example, what evidence do we have that Jesus, Buddha, or Muhammad ever lived?).

Because scholars of religion utilize a scientific methodology, their fact-finding track record has proved remarkably productive. Obviously, they cannot deliver all of their findings with the same degree of "certainty" as normally associated with the laws of physics and chemistry. Accordingly, I agree with *The New Interpreter's Bible* (*NIB*)[1] that biblical criticism is not simply an objective science but is also an art. As the *NIB* notes, it has its scientific aspects (statistical and quantitative measurements). But it also has prominent subjective judgments even though they are based on substantial knowledge. In some cases, therefore, determinations are made on the basis of a "balance of probabilities."[2] *Although the dominant terms used herein will be biblical criticism or higher criticism, I take the following expressions to be synonymous with them: biblical scholarship, biblical analysis, biblical studies, and biblical science.*

Unfortunately, the expression "biblical criticism or higher criticism" gives the false impression of being negative or hostile—as though the Bible were going to be maligned. This impression is incorrect because the words "critic" and "criticism" derive from the Greek word *kritikos,* meaning "able to judge or analyze." *It is important for the reader to remember that the word "criticism" reflects a discipline of scholarly investigation, and should not be associated with the popular understanding as an expression of disapproval.*

Biblical criticism serves as a catchall expression that incorporates all the analytical processes of religious scholarship (such as textual criticism, historical criticism, source criticism, form criticism, redaction criticism, narrative criticism, and many more). Through harmonious interplay these disciplines help to determine the character, composition, authorship, historical authenticity, and origin of biblical documents; they also help to evaluate the influence of surrounding cultures on the development of Christianity in its early stages.

Be aware that this writing does not cover the many facets of biblical criticism. Although the writing herein may appear to be comprehensive, it isn't; it merely scratches the surface of a very complex discipline. It does, however, provide some basic and necessary information that may help create a more realistic understanding of our Christian heritage.

Incidentally, true scholars are not limited to the findings of biblical criticism. Scholars of religion traverse over a wide range of disciplines in their investigative journeys. In short, they will use any information that will help them to corral the truth (or at least a better approximation of the truth). This is not to suggest that all mainstream scholars and educators share identical viewpoints. Neither have they cornered the market on truth. That is not possible even under the best of circumstances, much less in a field of study where subjective interpretation of the evidence is often unavoidable. But I am confident that the information herein will fall well within the boundaries of mainstream scholarship; regarded as conventional by both religious and secular authorities in the field.

Furthermore, you can rest assured that the information herein is free from ecclesiastical control; that is, free from the Church's supernatural spin. Although many mainstream scholars are themselves Christian—as we shall see—they allow the facts to fall where they may. Of course, some spin is unavoidable but most mainstream scholars do not spin the potter's wheel so as to shape the information in accordance with the traditional teachings of Christianity.

THE WEAKEST LINK

It is important to know from which biased direction this book is written. Yes, I am biased. Everyone is biased or, at least, should be. If you disagree, put your car in neutral and see where it takes you. Before disclosing my preference, a cautionary word is needed.

To say one is biased, may convey the wrong impression. The word "bias" implies a predisposition either for or against something, usually based on opinion before there is good reason; a prejudicial leaning of the mind. But if one's opinion is shaped by education (as would be the case with doctors, lawyers, scientists and so forth) one might refer to it as a "professional judgment" rather than a biased opinion; assuming, of course, that one is commenting on one's field of expertise. All of this sounds fine. But what does it mean when two well-educated people in the same field disagree with each other's professional judgment? Whom should one believe?

Divergent views are apparent in all disciplines. But in the religious field, there is a divisional marker between scholars that cannot be ignored. It is the world's-apart difference between evangelical scholars (also known as fundamentalists)[3], and all other scholars of religion. I support the latter. I do not rely on fundamentalist scholars because they are considered by mainstream scholars to be the weakest link in the academic world. In fact, except for evangelical colleges and seminaries, no other seminaries or universities (from Stanford on the West Coast to Harvard on the East Coast) rely on evangelical publications for religious studies. The same holds true for the numerous community and state colleges across this nation (not to mention our European counterparts). The reasons for this exclusion are specific (see Appendix A). For the moment, suffice it to say, evangelicals usually won't accept data that doesn't tell them what they want to hear. For that reason, the information presented herein will not reflect their thinking. Rather, this work will reflect the knowledge disseminated by the majority of educational scholars worldwide. I do realize that all this may sound as exciting as a trip to the dentist. Yuck! But honestly, some of the findings of higher criticism are mind-boggling. "Hang on Sloopy, Sloopy hang on!"

CARTOONS

Our subject matter is serious. But I believe—and I'll bet my Mickey Mouse watch you do too—that life would be a drag if we couldn't have fun along the way. It's good for us to laugh, or at least crack a smile from time to time. So, aside from a *Non Sequitur* cartoon, enclosed are some original cartoons stemming from my funny bone. No, I can't draw—not even a crooked line. Therefore, a free-lance artist out of Phoenix, James Weeden, drew them for me.

A TAD OUTSIDE THE BOX by Ernie Bringas

Godzilla Goes To Heaven

BCE AND CE

What's this? The old familiar dating symbols BC (before Christ) and AD (in the year of our Lord)[4] are slowly being replaced—certainly within the academic community—with the symbols BCE (before the common era) and CE (the common era) respectively. This lettering has come into vogue as a sensitive response to the vast number of people (Hindus, Jews, Buddhists, Muslims, and so forth), who do not place Jesus at the center of history. This, then, is a less intrusive dating system that favors no special religious group (at least not as blatantly).

However, for the sake of clarity and practicality, I will use the old dating system. I know it's fashionable to go the other way, but I'm reluctant to impose it here. Furthermore, although I know that BC follows the date (for example, 33 BC), and traditionally AD precedes the date (AD 33), I choose to place AD following the date (33 AD); a style now used by many academic authorities.

[NOTE: c. or ca.—an abbreviation that means "about," or, "around." For example: The Greco-Roman era ran from ca. 300 BC to 400 AD.]

A DEFINING MOMENT

I will try to define in parentheses many of the words that I feel might not be understood by some readers. For many of you, this approach will appear to be somewhat condescending (the author coming across as superior to the reader). Rest assured, I have no such delusions. I realize that most of you reading these pages are not in need of these definitions. Nevertheless, bear with me. Through this overly cautious approach, the attempt will be made to keep everyone on the same page, so to speak (especially some younger readers). Also, this approach will be helpful if the words I use have multiple meanings or are esoteric (obscure; not well known). I will, however, try to avoid esoteric language whenever possible.

[NOTE: A minimal amount of material from my former writings will be found herein. However, rest assured that any minimal duplication is rewritten by necessity. For the most part, it has also been revised and expanded. The opening theme may be similar, but the closet's full of new clothes.]

A FINAL COMMENT

Before I launch into the Jesusgate syndrome, rest assured that I do not come to this table as an outsider. I have been in the Church since childhood. After receiving my B.A. degree from California State University, Long Beach, I spent three years at United Theological Seminary in Dayton, Ohio, where I obtained my M.Div. (Master of Divinity degree). Thereafter, I served the Church as a United Methodist minister for almost twenty years.

Presently, as an adjunct faculty member, I teach World Religions, and have taught Introduction to the New Testament, at Glendale Community College in Arizona. Under their auspices I have also taught these courses at Arizona State University.

JESUSGATE, AN INTRODUCTION

This is not a religious book; it is a book about religion. Specifically, this work seeks to assess and unravel the Jesusgate phenomenon. The term Jesusgate, used herein, indicates that Christian leaders, by acts of commission and omission, have seriously neglected their responsibility to share with churchgoers, vital information about the origins of Christianity and the Jesus tradition. As a result, people have been rendered religiously illiterate. An incredible knowledge gap has ensued between what scholars of religion now know, as opposed to what lay people have been led to believe (be they parishioners in the pew, or persons on the street). Welcome to the gap. (The phenomenon I call Jesusgate will be fully explained in the early chapters of this work.)

For the past three centuries, scholars of religion have sounded the clarion call hoping to reduce this knowledge disparity. But most of society remains unaware or misinformed (some important exceptions to be noted later). Having served as a minister in the United Methodist Church, I can definitely attest to the dominating influence of religious illiteracy. When I speak of religious illiteracy, I am not referring to what laypersons may or may not know about biblical content. Someone may well be able to quote you chapter and verse and yet be totally unaware about the findings of biblical criticism. Clearly, the information accruing from religious scholarship over the past few centuries has not trickled down to the general population.

Mass ignorance about this informational divide floats the illusion that everything is perfectly normal. Sadly, people everywhere are caught in a lockstep procession of antiquated beliefs; oblivious to vital information that would liberate them from many of the obsolete notions they presently hold to be sacred. They remain unaware of the findings from religious, academic studies begun as long ago as the Enlightenment of the seventeenth century, especially in the area of New Testament scholarship. Shockingly, then, people today possess the religious mentality of those living prior to the seventeenth century. This all sounds unbelievable, but it's true.

As we shall see, the gulf between scholar and layperson has created much more than religious illiteracy. It has also fostered many serious problems on all levels of human interaction (be it familial, social, religious, political, scientific, you name it).

The signs and dangers of antiquated belief could easily be detected in other disciplines, such as medicine (beware of the doctor who suggests bloodsucking leeches to alleviate your headache). This type of discernment is sorely lacking in the religious arena and society as a whole. How could it be otherwise when most individuals are thinking at a level of religious understanding that predates the seventeenth century! No other field of thought has suffered such a prolonged, arrested condition within the general population.

The responsibility for this outdated mind-set must rest primarily with the clergy. The dialogue from the movie, *Cool Hand Luke*, sums it up nicely: "What we have here is the failure to communicate." The Jesusgate phenomenon—the clergy's inability or unwillingness to inform, and the subsequent rise of religious illiteracy—is the starting point for everything that follows in the main body of this work.

In an effort to help abate the Jesusgate influence, this work will describe the clergy's role in creating and maintaining this informational chasm. More importantly, it will showcase the numerous findings from biblical scholarship that have accrued over the past several centuries, findings that make the beliefs of most people indefensible.

As noted earlier, this deficiency of knowledge is not restricted to any one group; it permeates all segments of our society. This is not to say that all Christians and non-Christians are religiously illiterate. Indeed, there are pockets of lay people who are well-informed about the findings of mainstream scholarship that have emerged over the past three centuries.

Nevertheless, the number of informed, versus those who are uninformed, is dramatically lopsided in favor of the latter. There are over two billion Christians worldwide, and I would estimate that less than one percent of them know much about the findings of higher criticism.

Thus, the lack of understanding within the ranks of the laity remains unchecked.

For the record, this is not an anti-Christian work, nor is it pro-Christian. It may seem anti to many readers because the knowledge being presented is almost the direct opposite of everything believers and nonbelievers have ever heard about Christianity. As humanly possible, however, this data is presented from a fact-based, academic viewpoint. The approach is primarily historical, not religious. I am drawing from the concrete knowledge that scholars have at hand. For example, scholars know to a certainty that we do not possess any of the original biblical writings. However, as we noted in the opening segment, not all issues are so easily discerned.

Accordingly, there are some issues of belief that remain outside of the scholar's reach. Was Jesus really the Son of God? Is there life after death? Are angels real? Is God on the side of Muslims or Christians? The foregoing questions are prime examples of metaphysical (beyond the physical) issues. Biblical scholars who stay within the constraints of their discipline cannot make these determinations. This does not mean that scholars are without opinions about these topics. But when they do offer opinions on these abstract or "supernatural" matters, it is only within their capacity as believers or unbelievers, not as scholars.

Christianity is still my religion of choice even though my efforts to convey "new" knowledge may be misconstrued in the opposite vein. My goal is to diminish religious illiteracy, so that we may continue into the twenty-first century with intellectual integrity when contemplating the substance of religious teaching. But I do confess that popular Christianity (what most people believe) no longer speaks to me or for me. If I call myself Christian, it is simply because I believe—as one example—the perceptive teaching of the New Testament to "love the neighbor," which I might add is not exclusive to Christianity. I should also say that I do not embrace all of Christianity in the literal sense (the Virgin Birth, for example). The following pages will make it plain as to why.

Intro to Chapter 1

HOLLYWOOD DAYS

It's December of 1962. I'm in studio A at Columbia Records in Hollywood, the largest recording company in the world (today it is owned by Sony). On my right is future recording star, Glen Campbell. Glen, a super guitarist and studio musician, is one of several musicians who have just laid down the instrumental track for our first Rip Chords' release, called *Here I Stand*. This song will be our first hit on the national charts, albeit a moderate success. Glen gave the song a great lift with his lead guitar. Recent remix attempts have watered down his contribution, but on the original release, the imprint of his lead guitar is indelible. (In June of 2011, I was so sorry to hear when Glen announced that he was at the beginning stages of Alzheimer's disease.)

To my left is our twenty-year-old record producer, Terry Melcher (1942-2004). (From a creative standpoint, record producers are the equivalent of film directors; the former shapes a song into its final form, the latter shapes a screenplay into its final form.) Terry became a producer at Columbia through the megastar influence of his mother (actress/singer, Doris Day). But his ensuing success he owes only to himself. He became one of Columbia's most creative and successful rock 'n' roll producers. Aside from his initial triumph with the Rip Chords, Terry went on to produce the Byrds, Paul Revere & the Raiders, and, in 1988, he earned a Golden Globe nomination for co-writing and producing a #1 hit, *Kokomo*, for the aging Beach Boys. But let's get back to my group.

Unless you're an avid fan of early rock 'n' roll, you probably don't remember us. I was one of the two original Rip Chords (the other being my high school buddy, Phil Stewart). Later, our group expanded to four when, Columbia producers, Terry Melcher and Bruce Johnston joined us (Bruce joined the Beach Boys after our group disbanded).

The Rip Chords recorded from 1962-65. We placed five singles in the TOP 100: *Here I Stand*, *Gone*, *Hey Little Cobra*, *Three Window Coup*, and *One Piece Topless Bathing Suit* (don't worry, that last song is not what you think). We also produced two albums for a total of 33 recordings. But we are best known for our chartbuster, *Hey Little Cobra*, which was fully layered by Terry Melcher and Bruce Johnston. Ironically, no one in any of these groups I have mentioned would have made it on the TV show, *American Idol*. Our success was not based on the superstar quality of a soloist. It was based on the ability to create a particular "sound." It was a different genre altogether.

Unfortunately, from the very start, misinformation about the Rip Chords was widespread, especially in terms of who constituted our group and who did the vocals on our body of work. Information on the Internet, as one example, is riddled with errors and misrepresentation. When you Google the Rip Chords, a number of websites will pop up that blatantly mislead. Case in point, there is a so-called official website that passes off several individuals as the original recording Rip Chords. Although these individuals did tour with the group as performers, that was the extent of their involvement. Subsequently, they do not appear vocally on any Rip Chords' recordings. But they imply the opposite. This falsehood reappears on other websites as it snowballs across the Internet.

Is it any wonder that music buffs today are still guessing about who did the actual singing on the original recordings? Outsiders continue to incorrectly tweak the Rip Chords' story into numerous scenarios, while insiders continue to distort the facts for personal gain. It wasn't until Sundazed Music released *SUMMER U.S.A.! THE BEST OF THE RIP CHORDS* in 2006 that the CD booklet and jacket finally corrected many of these errors. Nevertheless, misinformation continues unabated. (If you want an eyewitness account about the Rip Chords, see my website at www.ripchords.info.)

These comments I have laid out may seem ho-hum. After all, the Rip Chords were not the Beatles (as if I had to remind anyone). And yet, if one stops to contemplate, there is something very troubling here. This anecdote illustrates how the historical record can become so convoluted even when modern technology is at hand. We can't seem to set the record straight, not even for the recent past (shades of 2004 presidential contender John Kerry and the swift boat controversy). And when all the principal parties are dead, what then? Who will sort out the mess? Would that even be possible?

And what do you do when two reliable sources have different versions of the same story? For example, just the other day I was listening to NPR's *Diane Rehm Show*, where her interview with Christopher Plummer (who played the role of Captain Ritter von Trapp in the *Sound of Music*) led to a conversation about the once famous actor, Tyrone Power. Power died of a massive heart attack at the age of 44 while making the film epic, *Solomon and Sheba* (he died in route to the hospital). According to Plummer, who was a friend of the handsome swashbuckler, Tyrone had to carry the well-endowed actress, Gina Lollobrigida, up a flight of stairs. Unfortunately, it took several "takes" before they got the scene they wanted. At that point, Power took a break and retired to his bungalow where the heart attack ensued. But according to Wikipedia (a somewhat reliable internet source), Power had his heart attack while filming the dueling scene with his co-star and friend, George Sanders. Here we have two different sources with two very different versions. (I'll side with Plummer on this one because I heard the details directly from him, but I really can't say for sure).

This never-ending mix-up brings me to my point: How does truth, or what we might call the best approximation of the truth, get clarified? What is truth? Unfortunately, I think Tommy Smothers (of the Smothers Brothers) nailed it at the 2008 Emmy Awards when he said: "Truth is whatever you get people to believe."

As for the historical record, can the stories of antiquity be reliable when we can't even sort out modern day happenings? Perhaps the following, partial, definition—ironically taken from the TV hit *Desperate Housewives*—carries more weight than one might care to admit: "History is a set of lies agreed upon."

Of course, that last sentence is only partially true because the historical record is not devoid of accuracy. It simply means that one needs to be wary of sources, and how the historical details are interpreted.

WHAT TO EXPECT NEXT

This chapter will begin the process of unraveling the Jesusgate phenomenon. It will help the reader understand, (1) the fog of religion, (2) the role of the clergy in creating Jesusgate, (3) the consequences thereof.

Chapter 1

PREPPING FOR JESUSGATE

SEMINARY: Usually a minimum three-year graduate school beyond college for training students to be priests, ministers or rabbis; leads to a M. Div. (Master of Divinity, degree). Other degrees may be earned.

THEOLOGY: The study of God and "His/Her/Its" relationship to humanity and the universe; anything that pertains to religion or religious beliefs (theological, theologian). Greek origin, theos (god); ology (a subject of study or branch of knowledge

PREP #1: THE FOG OF RELIGION

It is widely known that truth is the first casualty of war. We call it "the fog of war." But the fog of war is thin when compared to the fog of religion.

The title of this book should serve as a warning that the Church has not been straightforward in its presentation about Jesus. Throughout history Christian leaders, by acts of commission and omission, have failed in their responsibility to share with the laity vital information about the origins of Christianity and the Jesus tradition. The failure to inform originates within the first few centuries of the Christian movement, but even more so since the Enlightenment of the seventeenth century. As a consequence, an incredible knowledge gap has developed between what religious scholars (or scholars of religion) now know about Christianity and what Christians have been led to believe. Thus, laypersons find themselves in a state of religious illiteracy, albeit unknowingly. The problem comes to us SOA (supersized on arrival).

It can't be overemphasized: The knowledge gap between religious scholar and parishioner is enormous. (What scholars of religion have discovered will be examined later.) Scholars fully armed with the findings of biblical criticism, and other disciplines, are now cruising down the informational highway in their hot-rod Cobras, while the majority of laypersons continue to ride the horse and buggy (so to speak). And similar to the proverbial "fork in the road," this damaging disconnection—between scholar and layperson—continues to widen with each passing day. This expanding knowledge gap means that communication between these two estranged groups is virtually nonexistent.

PREP #2: WHAT DO THE MINISTERS KNOW, AND WHEN DID THEY KNOW IT?

Suspended betwixt these polarized and unevenly matched groups are the clergy. They serve many functions; education is one. Even as the college science teacher serves as the conduit between scientist and student, so should the minister serve as the conduit between scholar and layperson. In other words, the clergy are—or should be—the go-betweens. They are the indispensable pipelines.

But clergy are in serious default as regards this critical function. The pipelines are clogged! (Exceptions to be noted later.) In the words of the late theologian, James D. Smart: ". . . the findings and resources of biblical scholars have remained largely limited to seminary classrooms and libraries. Only a minute fraction of this learning has been shared with congregants, and most Christians to this day are unaware that it even exists."[1]

Not even with the Enlightenment of the seventeenth century and the subsequent rise of mass education have the clergy been willing to widen this systemic bottleneck. It was the late scholar, Robert W. Funk (1926-2005), who also echoed this concern:

> It is difficult to avoid the conclusion that the churches have failed to educate their constituencies; that pastors have failed to inform their parishioners . . . . Clergy have decided that what they learned in seminary

is a secret to be kept . . . . The pulpit has become the
locus of the soft assurance rather than the source of hard
information.[2]

Most recently, it was the world-famous scholar, Bart D. Ehrman, (in
his 2009 publication, *Jesus, Interrupted*) who brought it home this way:

> . . . many pastors who learned this material in semi-
> nary have, for a variety of reasons, not shared it with
> their parishioners once they take up positions in the
> church. (Churches, of course, are the most obvious place
> where the Bible is—or, rather, ought to be—taught and
> discussed.) As a result, not only are most Americans
> (increasingly) ignorant of the *contents* of the Bible, but
> they are also almost completely in the dark about what
> scholars have been saying about the Bible for the past
> two centuries.[3] [Parenthesis and italics his]

Perpetuating this predicament is the fact that many of these clergy are
themselves undereducated. Unlike other professions—lawyers, nurses,
doctors, and engineers—there are no set legal standards required to practice ministry. Each religious body sets its own educational requirements.
They range widely. Although many religious groups adhere to strict educational standards (university and seminary degrees), others may not
require any degree. Of course, higher education doesn't guarantee that
any particular clergyperson will be well versed in biblical criticism.

Here's the gist of it. Many ministers are in the know, but, for a flood
of reasons, won't speak out; others can't speak out because they're not in
the know. In either case, the layperson loses. Fortunately, a few forthright
ministers are making their congregants aware of this disturbing situation,
and sharing with them the findings of biblical scholarship. So, let's be
clear from the start: not all of the clergy—be they Catholic, Protestant,
or Eastern Orthodox—will be part of the Jesusgate equation. However,
they are definitely in the minority.

As a former pastor, I can tell you that it is very difficult to keep from
getting sucked into the Jesusgate whirlpool. No one is immune from this
pervasive influence and all of my colleagues have probably been there
at one time or another. Again, from the distinguished scholar, Robert

W. Funk, as he reflects on his personal struggle to share his educational knowledge with his congregants:

> Why had I not thought to share those things . . . with people in my church? Instead I do what many clergy do and that is dissemble [to hide one's true feelings and beliefs]. And I dissembled as much by what I didn't say as by what I did say.[4] [Brackets mine]

PREP # 3: THE CONSEQUENCES THEREOF

If anyone believes that the failure to inform is inconsequential, they've got more beans than Taco Bell. This informational divide has left the masses theologically anemic; that is, people are oblivious to even the most elementary data we now have about the historical development of the Bible, the Jesus tradition, and Church history. For instance, most Christians assume that the Gospels—Matthew, Mark, Luke, and John—were written by the disciples of Jesus or some other eyewitnesses to his ministry. But the overwhelming majority of scholars no longer accept this view. This grain of sand that I highlight here is only a miniscule sampling of the theological beach that lies ahead—a beach littered with the fading traces of theological, faith-based sandcastles that have been swept away by the rising tide of knowledge.

I repeat: The clergy's failure to inform—whatever their reasons—has created a vast knowledge gap between what churchgoers believe about the Jesus story and what scholars now understand about the Jesus story. Clearly, the present day image of Jesus as promoted by what scholars call popular Christianity (or, pre-critical Christianity), is not in accord with the scholar's understanding of Jesus. This dichotomy (division) does not bode well for either side. But laypeople bear the brunt of this separation as they are left to splash around in the stagnant backwaters of religious naiveté.

As previously declared, laypersons today are trapped within the confines of a religious worldview more appropriate to those who lived prior to the Enlightenment of the seventeenth century! However unbelievable that may seem, the Christian masses are literally trapped in the archaic thought patterns of the ancient world. They hold antiquated religious beliefs which are no longer reasonable, defensible, or helpful to the twenty-first century mind. The obsolete concepts I refer to are the embedded religious myths, doctrines, and beliefs of an earlier age, conceived and developed in response to superstitions and misconceptions that modern disciplines no longer entertain.

No field of study outside of religion—biological evolution runs a close second—has suffered such a prolonged arrested condition in the general population. I contend that this appalling setback is a direct result of what I have termed Jesusgate: a clerical practice that continues to withhold the findings of biblical analysis from the unsuspecting laity.

We must not gloss over the horrendous Jesusgate influence. The consequences are far-reaching. Without trying to sound melodramatic, I'll paraphrase it in terms of Rod Serling's[5] introduction to the *Twilight Zone*, with a slight shift in emphasis.

> There is a world of knowledge, beyond that which is known by most people. It is a dimension as vast as space and as timeless as truth. It is the ground between light and shadow, between biblical criticism and popular Christianity.

The above three preps have incorporated many elements of the Jesusgate syndrome. But a broader description is now necessary.

Intro to Chapter 2

BASKING IN THE LIMELIGHT

During my short stint in Hollywood circles, I was fortunate enough to meet the likes of Doris Day, Dick Clark, Andy Williams, Glen Campbell, Bobby Darin, Tommy Dorsey, and a few other notables. I must admit that most of these encounters were brief and accidental. Nevertheless, these chance meetings were quite revealing.

Although most celebrities handle their vaulted status with modesty, some go ballistic. Success, coupled only with a modicum of fame, can put one's head into orbit. It's not hard to zip ahead of yourself when the hype is ripe. Dag Hammarskjold, former secretary-general of the United Nations (1953-61), put it this way: "Around a man who has been pushed into the limelight, a legend begins to grow as it does a dead man. But a dead man is in no danger of yielding to the temptation to nourish his legend, or accept its picture as reality. I pity the man," Hammarskjold continues, "who falls in love with his image as it is drawn by public opinion during the honeymoon of publicity."[1]

I'll be the first to admit that I was not immune to the blinding glare of my celebrity status (however little there was). But fortunately, I was well grounded by family and friends; my delusional moments of grandeur were quickly crushed. I can still hear my mom yelling: "Ernie, take out the trash!"

Conceit and arrogance are odious markers in the human personality. These traits often lead to obnoxious behavior. I remember one Tinseltown encounter that frames this issue: it was a somewhat unexpected collision with Phil Spector.

In the 1960s, Phil Spector was a rock 'n' roll phenom. He was a record producer that specialized in girl groups; that is, vocal groups of young women. Who can forget those blockbuster hits by the Crystals, *He's A Rebel,* and *Da Doo Ron Ron?* Let's not forget the Ronettes and their mega hits of *Baby I Love You* and *Walking in the Rain.* Spector backed their vocals with his *Wall of Sound,* a production technique that utilized reverberation, echo chambers, and a multiplicity of musicians. His Wall of Sound can be clearly heard in the huge hit, which he produced for the Righteous Brothers—*You've Lost That Lovin' Feeling* (according to industry sources [BMI], the most played song in radio history).

Many of Spector's hits were recorded at a little studio called Gold Star, located on Santa Monica Blvd., in Hollywood. The studio had an exceptional echo chamber that helped produce the Wall of Sound. Gold Star was the recording Mecca of many early rock legends. For example, Sonny and Cher, Tijuana Brass, Eddie Cochran, Brian Wilson, Jimi Hendrix, Art Garfunkel, Neil Young, Iron Butterfly, John Lennon—the list is extensive. Between 1950 and 1984, Gold Star generated more Grammy Hall of Fame winners than any other independent studio in America (see: www.goldstarrecordingstudios.com).

I was well acquainted with Gold Star. I had been recording there since the age of seventeen. This was the place I would run into Phil Spector. Here's what happened.

In the summer of 1965, I was back in California for a well-deserved rest from my second arduous year at United Theological seminary (Dayton, Ohio). One day I happened to be at Gold Star. I was in the hallway when this thin looking character (whom I didn't recognize) scurried up to me, barking as he approached. "I hear you guys" (meaning the Rip Chords), "have been hitting on my girls while you all were on tour!"

"Is he yelling at me?" I thought to myself. When it became clear that he was, I responded firmly: "I don't know what you're talking about. I don't know you, and I don't know your girls."

"I'm Phil Spector!" he shot back angrily, apparently more agitated because I had failed to recognize him.

"Listen," I said sharply, "I'm a seminary student home for the summer. I haven't even been on tour with the Rip Chords because I've been cloistered away all year studying, and I resent your accusation. What's your problem?"

I think I startled him. Without a word he spun around and scurried off in the same direction from which he had approached. That confrontational scene was bizarre but evidently not uncommon for Spector. I later learned that he had a nasty reputation for being eccentric and unpredictable. At least that was the scuttlebutt back then, so, aside from my own encounter, I really can't say. Nevertheless, in 2003, he drew media attention when he was accused of shooting to death a young woman who was visiting at his mansion. On April 14, 2009, a jury convicted him of second-degree murder. It's likely that he will spend his remaining years in prison.

My personal encounter with Spector helps to illustrate what can happen to people when they accept as true an exaggerated sense of their own importance. This type of arrogance is easy to spot. But conversely, there are times when arrogance can disguise itself as legitimate, albeit equally offensive and destructive. The religious arena, strangely enough, would be such a place. But why and how does this happen?

WHAT TO EXPECT NEXT

This chapter provides a complete rundown on the distasteful characteristics of Jesusgate, and Jesusgaters. It will further define this Jesusgate element and the two-party theological chasm it has created between scholar and layperson. It also exposes the driving forces that shaped the Jesusgate movement.

Chapter 2

JESUSGATE

WATERGATE: A political scandal in which an attempt to bug the national headquarters of the Democratic Party (in the Watergate building in Washington, D.C.), led to the resignation of President Richard Milhous Nixon (1974). [Oxford American Dictionaries]

HERESY: belief or opinion contrary to religious teachings.

We've heard of Watergate, Monicagate, Travelgate, Skategate, and other "gates," but what is Jesusgate? Jesusgate is the term I use to describe a religious whitewash. It started in the first century AD when the early church leaders resorted to underhanded tactics in an effort to protect the Jesus persona. These questionable practices continue down to the present day, albeit in a different manner (as we shall see). The clergy have methodically suppressed, concealed, denied, ignored—I'm just getting started—downplayed, marginalized, distorted, rationalized, sanitized, or eliminated vital information about the Jesus tradition; hence, the term Jesusgate (or Jesusgaters).

The reader can rightly assume that Jesusgate and Watergate (the forerunner of all "gates") share common ground; that is, negative ground. But to ensure the integrity of this usage, distinctions and similarities between the two must be drawn.

Our first distinction is one of time and numbers. Watergate transpired over a short period of time, and involved only President Richard Nixon and a few high-powered advisors. In contrast, Jesusgate involves thousands of church leaders over a span of 2000 years and stretches across the entire theological and geographical breadth of the Christian movement.

A second variance between these gates is that Watergate violates societal law whereas Jesusgate does not. The term Watergate now symbolizes a formalized conspiracy concocted by a few politicians who sought to conceal illegal activity (the breaking and entering of the Democratic offices at the Watergate complex). In a futile effort to avoid prosecution, President Nixon and company tried to lie about the sordid mess. This in itself was an obstruction of justice, not to mention the original crime of the failed Watergate burglary. Thus, Watergate came to represent the violation of both societal law and personal ethics.

Although Jesusgate does lower the ethical flag, it does not violate any written laws established by a legislative body. Therefore, Jesusgate is strictly a moral (or ethical) problem, not a legal one.

A third difference between these gates is that the Watergate conspirators, by trying to obstruct the truth, sought to create a false political landscape. They failed. This failed effort was not only an attempt to avoid incrimination, but to also preserve Nixon's political life by misleading the American people. But they got caught! That is why today there is widespread recognition of Watergate as a negative term, based on the actual facts that finally saw the light of day (thanks to informant "Deep Throat" and some aggressive reporters). As a consequence, President Nixon resigned in dishonor and some of his advisors served jail time. The Watergate conspiracy was a bust.

In vivid contrast, Jesusgaters have not incurred suspicion because no legal laws have been broken and because their ethical offense is subtle and well camouflaged (it always has been). Thus, the clergy have, consciously or subconsciously, woven a successful web of deception that remains largely unnoticed. By neglecting to share the findings of biblical criticism with their congregants, they have created a biographical portrait of Jesus that lacks authenticity. And because this is the only portrait that the Church has hung on the theological wall, it gives the unsuspecting observer the false impression that there's nothing else to see. All other sketches (views about Jesus) have been removed from the gallery, creating the illusion that no other renditions of Jesus exist.

This also explains why the Church's black-and-white portrayal of Jesus goes unquestioned (not only by Christians, but most people in general). People are unaware of how their beliefs about Jesus have been shaped by the enduring Jesusgate influence. Everything seems perfectly normal as the masses continue to swallow and follow. That is why the term Jesusgate—aside from conveying the hint that something is amiss—makes little sense.

As one can see, Watergate and Jesusgate have generated different results under different circumstances. Other differences could be raised but we'd be spinning our wheels. Speaking of wheels, I now turn to the twin-like similarities that bind these gates together.

ON A BICYCLE BUILT FOR TWO

There are two distasteful characteristics of Watergate that are equally central to Jesusgate. These two troublesome features, like the riders on a tandem bicycle, journey together in quick succession as one almost always follows the other. The front rider is called, *presumption* (an idea that is held to be true, although it is not known for certain). Religious presumption is characterized by the belief that one has the ultimate God, the ultimate Good, the ultimate Way, and the only keys to the Kingdom. This dogmatic presumptuousness (emphatic assertion of opinion) often leads to unpleasant or arrogant behavior. Under the right circumstances of authoritative control, it can also become quite dangerous.

Pedaling right behind in tandem sequence, we find our second rider—*expediency*. The word "expediency" needs clarification because it carries both a positive and negative nuance. In the positive sense it is defined as: wise, beneficial, sensible and helpful. In its negative sense it is defined as: a means of attaining an end, especially one that is convenient but considered improper or immoral. In other words, seeking personal advantage that is based on self-interest without regard for what is just and fair. Obviously, it is the negative side of expediency that, along with presumption, brings Watergate and Jesusgate into juxtaposition (side-kicks of a sort).

We know the Watergate story. We know it started with Nixon's presumption of self-importance. This led the President and his cohorts down the nasty path of expediency; a path that led to burglary, denial, lies, shame and, ultimately, to Nixon's resignation and, for others, imprisonment.

What about Jesusgate? How did, and how does, presumption and expediency interplay within the religious personality? What are the consequences? Before we proceed to answer these questions, two quick points are warranted.

First, keep in mind that not all Christians are presumptuous. Second, not all presumptuous Christians are negatively expedient. Nevertheless, whenever presumption does hop onto our metaphorical tandem bicycle, expediency is almost always right behind. Notice that I said, "almost always." But more often than not, both riders are on board; they're soul mates, so to speak. Wherever presumption abides, expediency lurks nearby. Therefore, it's almost impossible to speak about one without including the other in the same breath. This will become evident as we allow Winnie the Pooh's friend, Tigger, the one and only, to run along side our tandem bike. I love mixing metaphors.

THE TIGGER SYNDROME: "I'M THE ONLY ONE!"

If you're familiar with Winnie the Pooh (who isn't), then you're familiar with Tigger too (my favorite cartoon character). I was first introduced to Tigger at Disneyland in 1969, through an animated Disney film called *Winnie the Pooh and the Blustery Day*. That's when I heard the Tigger song for the first time, *The Wonderful Thing About Tiggers* by Richard and Robert Sherman and sung by Paul Winchell. The song highlights Tigger's uniqueness. He's the only one! And that's precisely what he declares when he sings his catchy little tune. He croons about how wonderful Tiggers are, and unabashedly claims that he's the only one! He's the only one? That sounds very presumptuous, doesn't it?

Even so, those last four words that Tigger belts out fit him just fine. But these are arrogant and misguided words when they come from anyone who assumes that their "holy" book or religious leader is the only one or the only way. Sadly, the Tigger syndrome (I'm the only one) appears to be the main ingredient of most religious brews.[2] Common sense, however, should tell believers of these various faiths that they all can't be right in their assertions of possessing God's ultimate truth, especially when they contradict each other. But I guess common sense is no match for the "voice" of God that they all claim to be hearing. After all, once they have God in their pocket, there's nothing left to discuss.

The failure to question or challenge religious belief is a perpetual dysfunction that afflicts most devotees, especially those associated with the world's two largest religions, Christianity and Islam. Be they clergy or laity, the failure to critique provides the impetus for presumption. Once they presume to possess God's word, they cannot—by virtue of this presumption—engage the world objectively. Any effort to alert these Tiggerites to the basic weakness of their position becomes instantaneously hopeless. Even the old cliché, "you can lead a horse to water but you can't make him drink," fails to encompass this no-win situation. When it comes to religion, you can't even get the horse near the water. And even if you could, the cliché might better be stated: "You can lead a person to knowledge, but you can't make him think."

This lack of discernment, as already noted when I spoke about some evangelical scholars (see Appendix A), is encouraged by an oversimplified understanding of what is called *divine revelation* (such as the Bible or Qur'an). The underlying assumption is that God has intervened directly into human affairs so as to render the message unalterable and indisputable. This "I'm the only one" presumption is easily seen in the popular slogan "The Bible said it! I believe it! That settles it!" Mainstream scholars no longer have this straitjacketed view of the Bible.

Aside from the literalist minded ones, neither do many clergy; they do not regard the Bible as uncontestable. Nevertheless, they tend to view it as a God-given document to which all other authorities must yield, and their congregants are taught to think along those same lines. In either case, where does this magisterial view of the Bible take us? We're back to presumption and expediency, the main aspects of Jesusgate mentality and behavior—characteristics that are totally inappropriate.

YOU DON'T TUG ON SUPERMAN'S CAPE

Super heroes anyone? Recently, I took my 9-year-old niece to see *The Avengers*. The 2012 film featured the favorite Marvel Super Heroes Iron Man, the Hulk, Thor, and Captain America. They save the earth from alien forces, of course. Most enjoyable was hearing my little niece burst out laughing when the Hulk pulverized one of their so-called gods. The movie reminded me of an old 1972 Jim Croce blockbuster hit called *You Don't Mess Around With Jim*. The melodious chorus warns that one shouldn't tug on Superman's cape, spit into the wind, pull that mask off the old Lone Ranger and, last but not least, one shouldn't mess around with Jim.

Those sentiments reaffirm what we already know—you don't mess around with tough guys or, more importantly, with the sacred. This hands-off policy would certainly apply to the Bible and, of course, Jesus.

There is no one more exalted in the Western world than Jesus. If approached with disrespect, he becomes the third rail of Christianity. In 1966, Beatle John Lennon made the offhanded remark that the Beatles were more popular than Jesus. Although his ill-conceived words harbored no ill will, Christian retaliation was swift; Beatle records and memorabilia were tossed into bonfires across the nation. (Prior to the freedom of speech, Lennon himself would have been tossed into the fire.) Wisely, Lennon apologized.

You touch the third rail at your own peril. In 385 AD, the Spaniard Priscillian learned this lesson the worst way. He was charged with heresy because he disputed the doctrines of the Trinity and Resurrection. He then became the first Christian to be murdered by other Christians. Priscillian and six of his followers were decapitated,[3] an *expedient* purge against dissent. It would seem that without the separation of Church and State, you end up with the separation of head and shoulders. This is still the case in some Muslin countries.

Our two-seater has taken us down many shameful and destructive roads. History is replete with other examples. It has led Christians not only to the murder of Priscillian but to the persecution of Jews and other non-Christians; it has led to genocide and terrorism, the oppression of women, the suppression of sexuality, censorship, homophobia, and the stifling of medical and other scientific inquiry (everything from astronomy to stem cell research).

No one can deny that the redeeming side of religion is love and kindness, and that it has made enormous contributions to Western society. But its dark side is fueled by presumption and expediency. Indoctrinated to believe that one possesses the God-given truth, or ultimate savior, one can easily be driven to irrationalism and fanaticism. The Inquisition from Medieval times is a great, but horribly sad, example.

The Inquisition was a court system established in 1231 by Pope Gregory IX in order to prosecute those who were charged with heresy; it was put in place to hunt down anyone who was out of step with Christian belief. It was an evil, monstrous, reprehensible instrument of terror. Those who were accused of deviant belief faced unimaginable torture. Many were burned at the stake. St. Thomas Aquinas (1225-74), arguably one of the most intelligent Christian scholars of the Middle Ages, was apparently supportive of the Inquisition. He presumptuously had no doubt about its harsh measures to crush descent. "Heresy," he said, "is infidelity to God and is more abominable to God than other sins and therefore should be punished more severely than any other sin."[4]

Of course, presumptuous rhetoric is well embedded within the very beginnings of Christianity. The high watermark of NT presumption—if interpreted literally as most Christians are prone to do—can be found in the Gospel of John. It is here that the Gospel writer sternly warns: "Whoever believes in the Son has eternal life; whoever disobeys the Son will not see life, but must endure God's wrath." (John 3:36) To bolster this ultimatum, he pens to the lips of Jesus this well-known declaration: "I am the way, and the truth, and the life. No one comes to the Father except through me." (John 14:6) This one-way stance that Jesus allegedly takes, is magnified by other NT writings. For example, the author of Luke-Acts boldly declares: "There is salvation in no one else, for there is no other name under heaven given among mortals by which we must be saved." (Acts 4:12) These few verses I have quoted (there are others), inevitably create a mind-set of exclusivity that usually leads to an attitude of intolerance.

We have already seen what happened to Priscillian and six of his followers in 385 AD. In 447 AD, Pope Leo I presumptuously stated: "If the followers of heresy so damnable were allowed to live there would be an end of human and divine law." Pope Innocent III (served 1198-1216) followed suit by declaring that heresy was treason against God and more shockingly evil than treason against a king."[5] I've already mentioned St. Thomas Aquinas, but there were many others who fostered these naïve and narrow attitudes.

This brings us back to the Inquisition, the poster child for the one-two punch of presumption and expediency. Unbelievably, the Inquisition lasted for nearly 500 years! During this period (1231-1700s), the Court and its henchmen, persecuted, prosecuted and executed not only Christians accused of heresy, but also Jews, Muslims, pagans and, most of all, women (the latter on the ludicrous charge of witchcraft). Indeed, the women had their own holocaust. We don't have exact numbers, but some estimate that millions of women were tortured and burned at the stake.[6]

We Christians were responsible for this human catastrophe. We jumped up on that tandem bike. Those who *presumed* the Bible to be

God's word relied on scripture as a justification for their heinous behavior. The Bible not only told them that witches existed, but also gave instructions on what to do with them:

> You shall not permit a female sorcerer to live. (Exodus 22:18)

> A man or a woman who is a medium or a wizard shall be put to death; they shall be stoned to death, their blood is upon them. (Leviticus 20:27)

Martin Luther, founder of the Protestant Reformation (1517), was equally misguided by presumption and expediency. Upholding the Bible as the supreme authority, he had no reservations about burning so-called witches. He sanctioned four executions at Wittenberg (Germany).[7] "I should have no compassion on these witches," he wrote. "I would burn all of them."[8]

Similarly, in 1545, John Calvin, French theologian and influential reformer, personally led a campaign against thirty-one persons accused of witchcraft. They were all executed.[9] Calvin declared, "The Bible teaches us that there are witches and that they must be slain . . . this law of God is a universal law."[10] He also wrote, "The fact that the Word of God has been declared by men's lips in no way lessens its nature; it is still the Word of Christ, of God."[11]

Nobody was safe. Even the clergy couldn't dodge their own colleagues who rode that tandem bike. Although the Inquisition was headed up by the pope and consisted of other priests, they sometimes persecuted their own peers. John Wycliffe, for example, was a priest condemned by the Church because he spoke out against clerical authority and questioned certain aspects of Holy Communion. He also translated the Latin Bible into English. The pope was so infuriated by his translation, that many years following the death of Wycliffe, he had the body exhumed (unearthed). His bones were crushed and thrown into the river. (You couldn't make this stuff up.)

Another example of peer persecution was Jan Hus, an ordained priest who was burned at the stake in 1415, for denying the supreme authority of popes and councils (denials that Catholics, on their way to becoming Protestants, did in mass numbers a 100 years later). Charges of heresy also befell Bishop Ridley and preacher Hugh Latimer who, together, were martyred at the stake in 1555.

Further comment on the Inquisition is not necessary. Ample sources prevail on this subject.

Unfortunately, our two-seater is more characteristic of monotheistic religions (Judaism, Christianity, and Islam) since their followers believe that they possess unquestionable God-given revelation. This divine disclosure is generally crystallized in the form of a canon (any recognized collection of sacred writings) generally believed to be without error. Belief in the canon's ultimate authority can take its leaders and followers alike, into the darkest corners of hell. It should also be noted that during the Middle Ages, Church authority and doctrine could not be questioned without serious consequence.

Looking back on the examples I have presented, one can recognize presumption and expediency throughout: Kill or persecute anyone who disagrees with your religious view; kill anyone who does not consider the Bible, Jesus, or Church to be God's infallible instruments; kill or persecute anyone who appears peculiar, mysterious, heretical, or from another faith such as Jews, Muslims, and other different believers. Do it in God's name—it's what He wants; it's for man's own good; God wills it. Slay those innocents as echoed in the song, *One Tin Soldier*. It is here, in heaven's name, and thereby justified in the end, that we are given permission to kill the neighbor and cheat the friend.

Whatever is contrary to love is usually driven by ignorance, which influences people in a way that is seldom benign. From the 1950 movie, *Born Yesterday,* William Holden says to Judy Holliday: "A world full of ignorant people is too dangerous to live in."

WHAT A DIFFERENCE A DAY MAKES (Yes and No)

Today, violent acts against free thinkers and religious dissidents are no longer tolerated in free societies. In America, First Amendment Rights, along with the separation of Church and State, have provided a safe haven for religionists and free thinkers alike (otherwise I'd be dead). Also, any rational Christian will view the above bloody recounts with horror and regret. Furthermore, we Christians would argue that it's all in the past. That was then, this is now. Let's forget it.

Not so fast. Although we can no longer exercise violence against others without being punished, religious presumption and expediency continue unabated. There is no doubt that blind devotion to the Bible and Jesus, more often than not, creates a *presumptuous personality* (PP). Are you afflicted with a PP? You are if you can answer yes to any one of the statements below. Take the quiz. "COME ON DOWN!"

The PP is characterized by the following attitudes: (1) feeling that those who have different beliefs are wrong and out of step with God; (2) needing to convince others to accept the Bible and Jesus as ultimate beacons of truth, or they will suffer God's condemnation; (3) feeling superior to anyone (Christian or not) who believes differently than you (Catholic, Mormon, Baptist, United Methodist, Buddhist, Muslim, conservative, liberal); (4) an attitude of impending certainty about the Second Coming, Armageddon, and so forth; and (5) feelings of anger or hostility toward the findings of biblical criticism or any knowledge that challenges traditional beliefs.

As stated earlier, presumptuous Christians can no longer express their misguided devotion to God through the physical persecution of others. Yes, we have seen examples today where a few Christian extremists have taken their PP to the ultimate level (killing, for example, abortion doctors under the absurd assumption that God wills it). In general, however, believers no longer run amuck. If they do—they do so under the penalty of the law. This societal restraint has all but eliminated many of the expedient measures that Christians were once at liberty to take. Those days are gone, at least in the West, and we can be thankful that they are. Pity our Muslim counterparts.

Presumption, however, has a way of bleeding out from physical abuse into mental and emotional abuse. As I stated in my first publication, *Going by the Book*—"This aura of presumption slowly divides people, even parents and their children, husbands and wives, brothers and sisters, and long-time friends. Few people have escaped its destructive effects. To maintain peace and avoid hurting loved ones, those Christians and non-Christians who do not share this presumptuous attitude must either pretend to accept it, ignore it, remain uncomfortably silent, or avoid contact with those who take this obstinate posture. It is ironic that Christians, whose guiding principles spur them to be amiable, loving, and selfless, can simultaneously evoke oppressive attitudes of exclusivity, arrogance, and intolerance."[12]

The underlying cause of these past and present problems I have cited, originated with the inception of Christianity. I refer, of course, to the never-ending Jesusgate phenomenon. It is an influence that creates mayhem, and impedes the progress of humankind both socially and spiritually.

JESUSGATE PAST AND PRESENT

Originally, Jesusgate was a conspiracy by design (formalized and organized). In its early stages—the first 500 years of Christianity—this is a story about overzealous clerics who, driven by presumption and expediency, took whatever measures necessary to preserve their slant on Jesus. They "... forged documents in the names of apostles to provide authorization for their own points of view," and ..."falsified writings that were in circulation in order to make them more acceptable for their own purposes...."[13] They not only cooked the historical record, but they went so far as to kill people in order to safeguard their theological bias. They also obliterated pagan religions in order to hide their apparent similarities to Christianity. This will clearly be demonstrated in subsequent chapters.

Much later, during the Scientific Revolution of the 1500s and the Enlightenment of the 1600s, Jesusgate morphed (slowly transformed itself). It lost its transparency. Jesusgate became not so much a conspiracy by design (the sin of commission), but a conspiracy by default (the sin of omission); that is, clergy inaction. They failed to inform the laity.

I say this because over the past few centuries, the clergy have stymied millions of trusting Christians by failing to alert them to the crucial discoveries of biblical criticism. As a minor example, the majority of scholars now agree that the description of Jesus' birth as portrayed in the New Testament (Matthew and Luke) is not to be taken literally. But the majority of people (Christian or otherwise) are oblivious of this consensus. According to an *NBC Dateline* poll (11-10-05), almost 70 percent of Americans believe Jesus' birth story to be historically accurate. Why? What happened to the pipeline between scholar and layperson? It's obvious: the clergy have failed to step up to the plate. As a result, Jesusgate has become a story of malfeasance (the violation of public trust or duty).

In its present configuration, however, it would be a mistake to view Jesusgate as a plot conjured up by conspiring clergy. The clergy are not sitting around in their church basements smoking stogies while plotting to pull one over on the public. That would certainly be collusion (a secret conspiracy in order to deceive). That's not even possible given the multiple divisions within the Christian body. Today, Jesusgate is more accurately defined as an unspoken capitulation amongst most clergy to keep silent about the findings in academia for fear of offending or losing the laity. Jesusgate is a minister's personal failure of conscience, the loss of courage to inform. Although Jesusgate is no longer an organized conspiracy as it was during the first 500 years of Christianity, it nevertheless still mimics Watergate in terms of *presumption and expediency.*

Again, keep in mind that not all ministers fall into the Jesusgate category. There are some ministers who openly write about, or discuss with their congregants, the findings of biblical criticism, and yet maintain their faith in the central doctrines of Christianity. They simply draw different conclusions based on the information that others interpret differently. In so doing, they cannot be classified as Jesusgaters as they do not restrict the flow of mainstream scholarship to their congregants. Nevertheless, as I have already noted, these ministers are highly outnumbered by their Jesusgate colleagues.

I will add that some clergy fail to inform because they choose, for a variety of reasons, to be disengaged. On the other hand, there are ministers who are well-meaning but they unwittingly promote the Jesusgate phenomenon by being misguided, uneducated or undereducated.

To be clear, most clergy have become Jesusgaters by their own choosing. They continue to project Christianity in traditional mode; they serve it up to the laity with little regard for even the most widely accepted findings of biblical studies. That's because many of those findings conflict with the long-held doctrines of the Church. That makes the educational lift much too heavy for some ministers who, by their assumed commitment, are unavoidably wedded to the beliefs of their congregants. It's almost impossible to buck the layperson's party line.

That is precisely why the laity are very much part and parcel of the Jesusgate equation. Their role, however, is not so much the suppression of biblical criticism since the knowledge gap I claim the clergy have created renders them unlikely to have that information anyway. No, I think they are more likely to be the victims of traditional hype: they have been taught to believe in sacred revelation—be it Jesus, the Bible, or Church—as ultimate truth. In effect, they are taught to be presumptuous. Such indoctrination by the clergy inevitably backfires as laypersons become immune to any new information that might challenge the religious status quo.

Be that as it may, laypeople are the victims of clergy deficiency or, clergy unwillingness to battle the dragon of ignorance. As a consequence, most everyone unknowingly gravitates to the lowest common denominator. People simply follow the clergy's simplistic lead and remain unaware of scholarship that would help to bring them into the 21 century.

Having said this, I must restate that many of the clergy honestly believe in the certainty of their religious path. But that's part of the problem. Along with their followers, these people presume to have the better holy book, the better savior, and the better way. This dogmatic posturing permits them to comfortably brush away any new knowledge that might alter some of those beliefs. Once again, it is obvious that presumption forms the very nucleus of the Jesusgate condition. A condition so strong and pervasive, it does not allow Christians to escape the outmoded thought patterns of popular Christianity.

THE GIST OF IT

Unfortunately, Jesusgaters dominate the current scene. They continue to withhold, suppress, or ignore, the findings of biblical criticism. This allows them to promote faulty and unrealistic beliefs about Jesus. Although lay people are partly to blame for their uninformed situation, it is obvious that the clergy are primarily responsible for the knowledge gap that has developed between scholars of religion, and the laity. This is no accident.

In sequential predictability, our tandem riders steer one to the conclusion that one's cause is so important (presumption) that "the ends justify the means" (expediency). In other words, one does whatever one deems necessary in order to preserve what one believes to be the supreme good (or truth)—no matter what! In Nixon's case, he and his associates believed that winning his reelection was the best thing for the nation and, perhaps the world. This presumption—right or wrong—led them straight into the dark side of expediency. They sought to increase Nixon's odds by illegally spying on the Democratic Party. Although Nixon had not initiated the Watergate break-in, he became involved with the cover-up. His denial of that concealment is a classic example of what happens when one rides that tandem bicycle. Of course, these men were also protecting their basic self-interests (such as power, status and, later on, the hope of not going to jail or, in Nixon's case, not getting impeached).

In similar ways, most clerics exhibit these same Watergate missteps. Presumption takes the lead when clergy are prone to consider their religion to be God's ultimate message to humanity (identical to what many Muslims and other devotees believe about their own religion). This makes their cause one of supreme value; the greatest good which must be championed and protected at any cost. Here comes expediency, right behind—doing whatever it takes to preserve their religious narrow-mindedness, and that of their congregants.

Of course there are many reasons why the clergy continue to suppress or ignore the findings from biblical criticism, especially when it pertains to Jesus. But whatever the reason, they have made every effort to shield Christians from anything that might create ripples in the "holy water;" that is, anything that would undermine the laity's sacred beliefs and, subsequently, undermine their own role and status. After all, as was the case with the Watergate players, the clergy are not only expediently guarding their presumptuous beliefs, but also their self-interests (jobs, authority, image, and so forth). *It is with this mirrored correlation (presumption and expediency) that I embrace the Jesusgate usage.*

Be it Watergate or Jesusgate, these "gaters" have exaggerated their cause and trivialized their wrongdoing in order to justify what they believe is in everyone else's best interest. It is an argument of convenience based on a distorted view of reality. And I believe that Jesusgate, when properly understood, will expose a much more serious problem than that of Watergate.

Before closing this chapter, three brief comments are warranted. I'm adding this sentence here because I know that a paragraph needs at least two sentences. Here's another one for good measure.

First, I do not believe that Jesusgaters (past or present) intended any malice aforethought (the intention to harm). On the contrary, most of the time they are faithful believers trying to champion a noble cause. Nevertheless, whenever that tandem bike is ridden, someone is going to get hurt. That's because the ride is usually prompted by a very narrow and self-serving interest. Therefore, 99 percent of the time, when one hops onto that tandem bike, it's at the expense of one's good judgment and, unfortunately, the welfare of others.

Second, in the case of some clergy, presumption is not always the tip of the spear. As I suggested earlier, some of these Jesusgaters are simply afraid to offend. Others are complacent, jaded, uncaring, undereducated or, just unwilling to rock the boat. But whatever their motivation—or lack thereof—the end result has been the intellectual and spiritual crippling of their parishioners.

Third, if anyone should think that Jesusgate is a figment of my imagination (or an exaggeration), the upcoming information should prove beyond a reasonable doubt that laypersons—by virtue of being kept out of the informational loop—are totally out of sync with scholars of religion and the discipline they call biblical criticism.

Intro to Chapter 3

IQ + KQ = RQ

During the mid-1980s, while working with a church youth group in Lubbock, Texas, I devised an equation (IQ + KQ = RQ) in order to help these youth grasp the significance of acquired knowledge. I still use it today with my college students. It is based on the saying: *You cannot reason but from what you know.* In plain English, how can anyone do high school algebra without knowing the basic principles of math that we learned in elementary school? Or, how can anyone seriously evaluate the New Testament without the basics of biblical criticism? You cannot reason but from what you know.

My students can see the logic in that assertion. I'm not telling them anything they don't know. But sometimes they fail to grasp its importance. Therefore, at the start of every semester, I introduce them to my devised formula. *(Stay with me on this because I'll be using it throughout this work.)*

Your *IQ*, as most everyone knows, is your *intelligence quotient* (a number indicating—more or less—a person's intellectual capacity). The average IQ ranges from 90 to 110. Most psychologists believe that IQ is primarily determined by genetics (nature, not nurture), and is established in childhood with some environmental assistance. Whatever the case, by the time you reach the age of 18-21 there isn't much you can do to improve your IQ. That's it—you're stuck with whatever you have, although small changes may occur over one's lifetime.

Your KQ represents your *knowledge quotient* (the information you have in your brain about any given subject). The knowledge quotient (KQ), unlike the IQ, can always be changed during one's life. KQ will vary greatly from person to person depending on their upbringing, continued education, and specialized interest. For example, my KQ about cars is very low compared to that of an auto mechanic. But I have a very high KQ about religion compared to most people, and so forth. Hence, everyone has low KQs and high KQs. Sometimes we have to depend on other people's KQ because we can't be up to speed on everything, especially those disciplines that require special education (doctors, lawyers, scientists, clergy, etc.). But let me suggest what you probably already know about KQ. The old cliché that "what you don't know won't hurt you," is only half right; it is also true that what you don't know *can* hurt you. Your KQ plays a significant role in determining not only the quality of your life, but also the accuracy of your observations and opinions, which brings us to the RQ.

Your RQ represents your *reality quotient* (the truth of the matter; your ability to perceive things as they really are, as opposed to a distorted or wrong idea about them). In other words, your RQ reflects how well your mind can perceive the truth, or, at least, the closest approximation of the truth. But this RQ not only depends on how bright you are (your IQ), but more importantly, how knowledgeable you are on any given subject (your acquired KQ). In combination, your *intelligence quotient* (your brain power) plus your *knowledge quotient* (what you have learned) will determine your *reality quotient* (how close you are to the truth, regardless of the subject). Hence the equation, IQ + KQ = RQ. But I repeat, more than any other factor (if one is relatively normal), *it is the KQ that dramatically affects the RQ.* The more you know, the more accurate your perception of reality. Of course, this assumes that the information you're downloading into your brain is not flawed. *Therefore, enhancing the KQ with up to date information is paramount!* In so doing, our KQ and, therefore, our RQ, can evolve properly and rapidly. Today's astronomy, for example, is light years ahead of what we believed only a hundred years ago. Our IQ levels have remained rather constant, but our knowledge of astronomy has increased dramatically. I state the obvious: It is knowledge that pushes us closer and closer toward the heart of the matter. To drive this point home, here is a simple illustration I give my students.

In all fields of thought, new knowledge sharpens our perception of reality. The Hubble Space Telescope, launched in 1990, for example, has revolutionized astronomy by providing unprecedented information about dark matter, dark energy, black holes, and on it goes. To further illustrate this evolving process, consider how the Apollo space program changed some of our beliefs about the moon. "According to Dr. Gerald Wasserburg, Laboratory Director at the California Institute of Technology, the discoveries made by the Apollo mission refuted many highly-regarded beliefs about the moon. '. . . the facts changed everything,' he said. 'Pre-Apollo thinking is absolutely gone. The old moon is dead.'"[1] Reality came into focus (IQ + KQ = RQ).

In like manner, the information issued from biblical criticism has changed everything. On many levels, the "old time religion" is dead for many scholars (even as pre-Apollo beliefs about the moon are now dead for scientists). For most Christians, however, the facts from biblical criticism remain unknown as a result of the Jesusgate influence. The end result is a very low religious KQ that leads to massive religious illiteracy. As I stated in the Introduction, it is possible to have a high KQ about Bible verses, yet still be religiously illiterate (a low KQ about biblical criticism). As a consequence, the religious RQ of the masses remains highly distorted, if not delusional. "You cannot reason but from what you know."

In contrast to the vast majority of Christians, scholars continue to hone their RQ by means of substantial learning. As their KQ continues to soar, their RQ continues to sharpen, as it does in any field of thought. But what do these learned scholars believe, why do they believe it, and why do their beliefs appear so radical to laypersons?

WHAT TO EXPECT NEXT

In this chapter we will view some of the beliefs that mainstream scholars of religion now have about Jesus. In so doing, it will become obvious that the divergence of belief between scholar and layperson could hardly be more striking. We will also explore the dynamics that shaped the convictions of these many scholars. It is crucial that we do so.

A TAD OUTSIDE THE BOX by Ernie Bringas

You Cannot Reason But From What You Know!

Chapter 3

SCHOLAR SHOCK

SCHOLAR: Biblical scholars require a profound understanding of the Jewish, Greek, and Roman cultures (to name a few). This understanding includes the moral, political, ideological, economic, philosophical, theological, and social forces that prevailed during early Christianity. Some of them will have mastered Hebrew, Greek, and Latin. Obviously, the tools of biblical criticism are a necessary must. Additionally, scholars should have an overall grasp of various disciplines (astronomy, psychology, anthropology, and so forth). Thus, their religious and overall KQ will be remarkably high. In short, these are people who know a whole bunch.

(The above description constitutes the "ideal" scholar. But no one can measure up on all counts. Therefore, as in the medical profession, scholars tend to specialize in certain areas and then rely on each other for supportive information. A directory of the 75 scholars utilized herein can be found after the Endnotes section at the end of this work.)

Most of us are familiar with the terms future shock, cultural shock, and sticker shock. I now give you *scholar shock.*

If my assertion about Jesusgate is correct—that the clergy have been unwilling or unable to share the scholar's findings with the laity—then a scholar's view of Jesus should be extremely different from that of a layperson. And is it ever!

To help examine this Jesusgate obstruction of information and the knowledge gap it has created between scholars and laity, I present the following beliefs about Jesus held by three prominent scholars. (Don't be fooled by this small sampling, it is indicative of a much larger pool.) The following comments are drawn from their own publications. I begin this revealing overview with the late Dr. Robert Funk, who was a prominent NT scholar, author, and one of the founders of the Jesus Seminar.[2] (Be advised, these are Christian academic scholars, not detached intellectuals.)

Dr. Funk sees the virgin birth of Jesus as an insult to modern intelligence. He also believes that we should give Jesus a demotion because it is no longer reasonable to think of Jesus as being divine. So, Funk does not believe Jesus to be a supernatural redeemer. "A Jesus who drops down out of heaven, performs some magical act that frees human beings from the power of sin, rises from the dead, and returns to heaven is simply no longer credible. The notion that he will return at the end of time and sit in cosmic judgment is equally incredible." Also, the idea that God killed his own son in order to satisfy his thirst for satisfaction is irrational and unethical. The resurrection of Jesus did not occur; he did not rise from the dead except perhaps in some symbolic sense.[3]

Next, I give you John Shelby Spong, the former Episcopal Bishop of Newark, New Jersey. In 2000 he retired as bishop following twenty-four years of service, after which, he briefly lectured at Harvard University. He is the author of many books, including the national bestsellers, *Rescuing the Bible from Fundamentalism* and *Why Christianity Must Change or Die.*

Bishop Spong believes that the virgin birth, understood as literal biology, makes Christ's divinity, as traditionally understood, impossible. He also believes that the Genesis story of original sin (how humans fell into sin by disobeying God's command not to eat the fruit from the forbidden tree in the middle of the garden) is pre-scientific mythology and post-scientific nonsense. Therefore, he reasons, the view of Jesus as the sacrifice for the sins of the world is a barbaric idea based on primitive concepts of God and must be dismissed. Likewise, the resurrection story cannot be interpreted as a physical resuscitation occurring inside human history.

Bishop Spong (like Funk) has removed Jesus from a supernatural framework. He does not view Jesus as a divine visitor or as a human who possessed supernatural powers. He rejects any teaching about a Jesus that walks on water, stills the storm with a verbal command, raises the dead, feeds 5000 people with five loaves and two fish, and bodily resurrects after crucifixion. The concept of the trinity is also inappropriate and unacceptable.[4]

Finally, I give you Dr. Marcus J. Borg (an unfamiliar last name unless you're a "Star Trek" fan—"resistance is futile"). Dr. Borg was Hundere Distinguished Professor of Religion and Culture at Oregon State University until his retirement in 2007. He has authored several publications, including *Jesus: A New Vision*, and, *Meeting Jesus Again for the First Time*. Here are his thoughts on Jesus.

Professor Borg believes (as do nearly all mainstream scholars) that the birth stories and other Gospel stories about Jesus are not historical accounts. Also, Borg does not believe that Jesus' intention or purpose was to die for the sins of the world, and that his message was not about believing in him. Thus, Borg does not believe that Jesus is God; Jesus is not literally "the Son of God." He believes that all references to the divinity of Jesus are metaphorical; that is, "Just as Jesus is not *literally* "the Lamb of God" (he was not a sheep) . . . so also he is not *literally* "the Son of God" (what would it mean for this to be literally true—biological sonship?). Rather, all involve the metaphorical use of images." Furthermore, he believes Jesus to be a *spirit person*, and draws a comparison to Buddha, as one example.[5]

Having laid out these theological sound bites, some qualifying statements are necessary. First, these former offerings are no more than what I have called them—sound bites. They are skeletal fragments. They do not represent the scholar's overall view of Jesus. For example, I mentioned that Dr. Borg thinks of Jesus as a "spirit person." That's a sound bite. But in his book, *Meeting Jesus for the First Time*, he is very detailed about what he means by spirit person.[6]

Second, it would be unfair to leave you with the impression that these theologians are anti Jesus (they're not), or, that they have walked away from the Jesus event (they haven't). It's quite the opposite. But it is not the purpose of this writing to flesh out their theological reconstruction. The reader is encouraged to pursue their publications.

A third precaution is to keep in mind that, as yet, we have only examined their beliefs. But we need to ponder the educational information that shaped those beliefs (and we will). Until one probes that knowledge, it will appear as though these scholars are nothing more than lettered mavericks. But consider that the Jesusgate mantle that covers one's religious understanding is precisely what might create this premature impression. It will be impossible to appreciate their conclusions until we analyze the facts that these scholars have studied. Let me be clear.

Whether or not you come to agree with their conclusions is not my concern—my concern is that you become acquainted with the information they have gleaned from biblical criticism, and then draw your own conclusions about the validity of that knowledge.

A fourth precaution behooves us to recognize that the above scholars are slanted toward the cutting edge of liberal or progressive theology. They are certainly left of center. Therefore, other prominent scholars would disagree, at least in part, with some of their declarations. Nevertheless, it is safe to say that *most* educators are moving in the same direction as our scholars-three even if they differ with some of their conclusions. This is due to the accuracy and reliability of biblical criticism, the backbone of religious studies.

Returning to our central issue of scholar shock, one can see that our three highlighted scholars (and a host of scholars not mentioned) hold much in common when expressing their views about Jesus. But I doubt that their professional judgments will sit well with lay Christians. Their comments about Jesus are not subtle in nature; they are not in harmony with popular Christianity; they are not in keeping with what we learned at our mother's knee or, from our Sunday school teachers or from the pulpit. It's quite the opposite.

Since almost all Christians have been influenced by the Jesusgate phenomenon, they will consider our above scholars to be far-fetched. Some Christians will call them blasphemous. Some will be dumbfounded. Many will be angry. A few, a very few, will understand why these scholars have made such statements.

It is vital, however, that we all come to comprehend the *why* of it. Why do these professionals revamp their original views about Jesus in ways that are the exact opposite of what Christians believe and what these scholars once believed? After all, these scholars are not outsiders. Most of them came from Christian families and were nurtured in the local church. Take for example Professor Borg as he describes his childhood memories:

> . . . I remember pictures of Jesus with sheep, and
> with children. I knew he liked children; that was a big
> message when we were kids. Clearly, he was important.
> I knew that he was God's son, and that he had been born
> in a miraculous way. Indeed, I knew that he was "born

of the virgin Mary" before I knew what a virgin was. My father's voice reading the birth story from Luke's gospel to my family as we sat around the Christmas tree on Christmas Eve comes back to me still: "And it came to pass in those days that there went out a decree . . . ."

I also knew that Jesus died on a cross and then rose from the dead, and that all of this was very important. Easter mornings ranked second only to Christmas as festive times of the year. I knew you could pray to Jesus and even ask him to be present: "Come, Lord Jesus, be our guest" was our daily table grace. As a preschooler I memorized John 3:16 . . . "For God so loved the world . . . ."[7]

Dr. Borg's experience is similar to those of other scholars and ministers. As a minister, I include myself here. I have vivid memories as a child sitting on my mother's lap and singing: "Away in a manger no crib for a child . . . ." How sweet it was.

In the early years of our faith we voiced with conviction that Jesus was God in the flesh (the Incarnation); that he was a personal savior who died for our sins (atonement—plan of salvation); that someday he would return to raise the dead and pass judgment on us all (the Second Coming). So what happened to those cherished beliefs? In a nutshell, education is what happened; an elevated KQ is what happened. And it happened with unintended consequences.

One can certainly conclude that would-be scholars and ministers did not begin their educational pursuits with the intention of turning their belief system topsy-turvy. I sure didn't. Let's be reasonable. Does anyone believe for one moment that these religious warriors sought to purposely demolish their beliefs with an educational wrecking ball? Can we possibly think that they wanted to pulverize their heart-felt views about a divine Jesus—a Jesus they worshipped? So what is it about education?

FOLLOW THE YELLOW BRICK ROAD

To become qualified ministers and, perhaps, scholars of religion, these hopefuls face a minimum four years of higher education to obtain their B.A. (Bachelor of Arts) degree. An additional three to four years of study at seminary are required to earn their M.Div. (Master of Divinity) degree. Further years of intense study are required if a Ph.D. (Doctor of Philosophy) is to be gained (as was the case with Borg and Funk).[8] By the way, not all scholars go through this exact process. But let's get back to square one of the educational process.

It begins with the playtime and social integration of kindergarten innocence. It is indeed a garden—a garden as colorfully reminiscent of Dorothy's beginning mini-steps on the Yellow Brick Road in Munchkins' land. Surrounded by flowers galore, the blare of trumpets and joyous singing, the journey begins pleasantly enough. But as one travels down this yellow brick road that leads to the Emerald City of greater learning, one encounters a mind-blowing array of knowledge that impacts the mind like a jackhammer.

This of course is true about any discipline. But religious studies carry a special burden because of the deep-seated emotional baggage that one carries into the classroom (in a later chapter, an anecdote about one of my students will help illustrate this point). It is not until cherished beliefs are slowly chiseled away that one begins to comprehend the personal pain of the educational hammer. Over time, one sustains multiple hits that split the hard rock patterns of one's religious indoctrination. Appropriately, beliefs are gradually and painfully reshaped. When that elevated KQ transforms the RQ (shatters what you once thought was the hardcore truth) the experience can be traumatic. As Robert Funk once noted: "Learning the truth about the Christian tradition can be the most agonizing exercise."[9]

The pain is not, however, restricted to the self. It bleeds out to others. Increased knowledge brings separation—separation from family, from peers, and from the general population. Not pleasant. Perhaps that's what the old preacher had in mind when he wrote: "For in much wisdom is much vexation, and he who increases knowledge increases sorrow." (Ecclesiastes 1:18)

Painful or not, there can be no argument that education (increasing one's KQ) makes all the difference. The intake of knowledge is to the mind what the "fountain of youth" would be to the body. Knowledge transforms people. It forces them to be different since they now think differently. It is a natural progression because what the mind can no longer accept, the heart will no longer follow. As Bishop Spong reflects:

> ... I was the first member of my family to attend a
> university. The incredible sweep of knowledge present
> in the university setting, the vastness of the library, the
> open doors into aspects of life that I had no previous
> way of imagining separated me forever from my past.
> The same was true when I embraced the experience of
> graduate school....[10]

The mandate of any good educational institution is to provide the best knowledge available. In this respect, religious studies do not differ from any other academic courses. For the serious Christian, however, religious studies can be unforgettable and life transforming. There is no escape from this educational onslaught unless one chooses to obstinately ignore it or reject it outright. But trying to remain untouched by the discipline of biblical criticism is a bit like trying to dodge raindrops in a pouring rainstorm. ("Resistance is futile.")

Meanwhile, back at the ranch, the folks blame these institutions of higher learning for "ruining" the faith of their sons and daughters. I have often heard these negative remarks from my own family: "You were okay until you went to that seminary; they ruined your faith." This reminds me of an old *Bonanza* episode ("The Savage") in which a somewhat humorous exchange occurs between Ben Cartwright and his son, Adam. Adam says to his father: "What do you have against education?" Ben snaps back: "I don't have anything against education as long as it doesn't interfere with your thinking." (Your beliefs?)

The question that people must consider is not whether the information being taught at the college or seminary level agrees with the preconceived notions of the students or the church from which they come, but whether the information being taught is accurate (or at least the best approximation of the truth). After all, what's the good of an education if all it does is reinforce ignorance and biased opinion, with no regard for the facts at hand? That would be the narrowest form of brainwashing, not education.

Although I can understand my family's misgivings about my educational journey, I believe my beliefs were transformed because I was no longer misinformed. Where knowledge abides, change is inevitable. It will alter one's perception because it is the killer of misconception. It is the killer of gods. But "any god that can be killed, should be killed."[11]

Consider: In the absence of knowledge we'd still be worshipping Sol Invictus (the Roman god of the sun), not to mention scores of other gods that have long since been forgotten or lie buried in the undergrowth of distant jungles.

This is not to suggest that we have a disposable god. We must, however, recognize disposable concepts. Religion, like any other discipline, is progressive in nature; that is, it's in a constant state of evolution. Granted, knowledge does not always lead us to the exact truth. Sometimes it can only help us to understand what is false. But from that vantage point, the truth can be pursued. Therefore, education (or this book, for that matter) should have no better effect, or serve no better purpose, than to override false convictions. The brain that fails to capitalize on the knowledge at hand becomes a dysfunctional wonder. In this regard we might want to add some new verses to the song that the scarecrow sings in the *Wizard of Oz—If I Only Had A Brain*. Sing along:

I could always go to college
And get myself some knowledge
I'd be singing in the rain,
I'd be smarter than a Lincoln
I could really do some thinkin'
With some knowledge in my brain.

I could live in ivory towers
And while away the hours
I'd be singing in the rain,
If I had the information
I could be an inspiration
With some knowledge in my brain.

Of course, we can't know everything about everything, or everything about anything; but when it comes to biblical criticism there is a definite scarcity of understanding in the general population. People need to get up to speed on this academic discipline. Failure to do so impedes not only the evolution of religious thought, but also the welfare of society in general.

So what is actually being taught about religion in educational institutions worldwide? Is it the above conclusions of our scholars three that are being showcased? I teach religious studies at the college level and I can tell you that the material presented is much broader and even-handed. The material is not about the scholars' theological conclusions; it's about the information that brought them to those conclusions. That's an important difference. Depending on the course taken, it is the overwhelming data from emerging scholarship that is being laid out before the student—the very information that Jesusgaters have successfully kept away from their congregants and, therefore, away from the general public.

How do your *knowledge quotient* (KQ), and subsequently your *reality quotient* (RQ), measure up? Hopefully, your religious KQ will continue to be enhanced by this writing, thereby bringing your RQ further into focus. That's the continuing goal of this work because: *You cannot reason but from what you know.*

Intro to Chapter 4

THE CALIFORNIA SOUND

It has been said that imitation is the greatest form of flattery. That certainly is true within the many streams of music. For instance, we can see that Beethoven (from the Romantic era) was greatly influenced by Mozart (from the Classical era); Beethoven's Piano Concerto No. 4 in G major reflects Mozart's Concerto in C major.[1] Anyway, that's what the music experts tell us.

Today, you don't have to be musically astute to recognize a specific musical genre (a category of music characterized by similarities in form and style). Central to early rock 'n' roll in the latter part of the 1950s, for example, would be the drums, guitar, and bass guitar (still popular today). Additionally, in this early rock genre, the saxophone (sax) was also an indispensable part of most recordings. If you're in doubt, listen to some rock classics by Little Richard or the Del Vikings. In 1974, the sax was resurrected in *Jazzman*, performed by Carol King. The sax solos (by Tom Scott) were exhilarating.[2] It's one of my all-time favorites.

Another example of early rock was the extensive use of falsetto (a man singing high-pitched notes above his normal range). One of the best songs that featured this quality was the 1961 smash hit, *The Lion Sleeps Tonight* by the Tokens (out of Brooklyn). The song reappeared in Disney's 1994 movie, *The Lion King*. Anyway, back in the day, falsetto was a key component of rock. That was really fortunate for me because aside from doing an occasional lead vocal, my specialty was singing background vocals, especially falsetto. Bruce Johnston, currently with the Beach Boys, also sang falsetto with our group. In my opinion, he is one of the best.

Although not exclusive to Hollywood, falsetto was an integral part of what came to be known as the *California Sound*. It could invoke a wide range of emotions, but it was mostly an exhilarating sound that was generated by such groups as Jan & Dean, the Beach Boys, the Rip Chords, Ronny and the Daytonas, the Hondels and so on. But the California Sound was only one of several differing sounds.

Who can forget the unique *Motown Sound* that came out of Detroit? It was a cool soul and rhythm and blues class. Front and center were Diana Ross and the Supremes, Smokey Robinson and the Miracles, the Temptations, the Four Tops, Stevie Wonder, Marvin Gay, and Mary Wells, to name a few. Their singing styles and musical arrangements were incredibly captivating.

The *Philadelphia Sound* came out of . . . you guessed it, Philly. There were many other regional sounds as well. Certainly, the country music out of Nashville—with that crying pedal steel guitar signature—has endured into the present.

Musicians in these geographical areas produced a specific breed of music that set them apart. They each nurtured their own winning musical formula and used it over and over again; sticking fast to that old saying, "If it ain't broke, don't fix it." They did, however, tinker with their musical niche in subtle and, sometimes, explicit ways. Even so, the foundational formula always remained, but it was fluid, not fixed. It was also interchangeable.

We can call this ongoing creative process, *Musical syncretism*— a process of musical development in which the sounds, arrangements, instruments, vocal styles, and recording techniques of one group are adopted, adapted, borrowed and tweaked by another group which then gains listeners from the first (that was a mouthful). The end product will be similar to the original and yet simultaneously unique. For example: *Little Deuce Coupe* by the Beach Boys vs. *Hey Little Cobra* by the Rip Chords vs. *The Little Old Lady From Pasadena* by Jan and Dean vs. *Little Honda* by the Hondels, and so on. If you can't catch the similarities here--multiple harmonies, vocal overdubs, driving falsettos—then you're not familiar with 60s rock, or, it's a sure bet that you're tone deaf. But if nothing more, you can at least recognize that the word *little* appears in all of these titles. That's the subconscious side of musical syncretism because I do not believe the songwriters included the word "little" purposely. But it's an obvious part of this genre. Even the hit *G.T.O.* by Ronny and the Daytonas begins with the word, little (*Little G.T.O . . . .*).

But musical syncretism is not unique. In fact, the term *syncretism* is, by definition, considered almost exclusively a phenomenon of religion. Read on.

> From the very beginning his mother knew that he was no ordinary person. Prior to his birth, a heavenly figure appeared to her, announcing that her son would not be a mere mortal but would himself be divine. This prophecy was confirmed by the miraculous character of his birth, a birth accompanied by supernatural signs.
>
> The boy was already recognized as a spiritual authority in his youth; his discussions with recognized experts showed his superior knowledge of all things religious. As an adult he left home to engage in an itinerant preaching ministry. He went from village to town with his message of good news . . . .
>
> He gathered around him a number of disciples who were amazed by his teaching and flawless character. They became convinced that he was no ordinary man but the Son of God.
>
> Their faith received confirmation in the miraculous things that he did. He could reportedly predict the future, heal the sick, cast out demons, and raise the dead. Not everyone proved friendly, however. At the end of his life, his enemies trumped up charges against him, and he was placed on trial before Roman authorities for crimes against the state.
>
> Even after he departed this realm, however, he did not forsake his devoted followers. Some claimed that he had ascended bodily into heaven; others said that he had appeared to them . . . that they had talked with him and touched him and become convinced that he could not be bound by death. A number of his followers spread the good news . . . recounting what they had seen him say and do. Eventually some of these accounts came

to be written down in books that circulated throughout the empire.[3]

The above description is not about Jesus. The man we have been referring to is *Apollonius of Tanya*, a worshipper of the Roman gods. He lived about the same time as Jesus. "What is remarkable is that these were not the only two persons in the Greco-Roman world who were thought to have been supernaturally endowed as teachers and miracle workers. In fact, we know . . . that numerous other persons were also said to have performed miracles, to have calmed the storm and multiplied loaves, to have told the future and healed the sick, to have cast out demons and raised the dead, to have been supernaturally born and taken up into heaven at the end of their life."[4]

From this we can see that someone has borrowed from someone, unless you want to believe that all of these similar stories developed independently of one another. A more rational conclusion would be to acknowledge that all streams of human experience are subject to syncretism. Nothing develops in a vacuum. In most things we are indebted to our predecessors and surrounding influences. Religion is no exception.

WHAT TO EXPECT NEXT

I am approaching Christianity, not as a Christian, but as an historian. As humanly possible, I am trying to see Christianity from an "objective" position; that is, I am trying to apply the same rules of logic and scientific inquiry to Christianity as I do to the other major religions of the world. I believe it is hypocritical—and shortsighted—to apply those rules and standards to all other religions while excluding one's own faith from critical analysis on the basis of presumption and expediency (the Jesusgate approach).

⁓

Although Jesusgate can be seen as having a pervasive influence throughout the past 2000 years, it has had some periodic flare-ups that invite our attention. As we examine the historical record, we will recognize *three* distinct Jesusgate episodes. They stand alone, and deserve our scrutiny. Jesusgate 1 and 2 occurred almost simultaneously between 100 AD and

500 AD. Jesusgate 3 begins around the middle of the sixteenth century (1500s) and continues to the present. All three came about for different reasons. But the underlying and overlapping motivation was to protect biblical authority, Christian doctrine, and the image of Jesus.

This chapter will deal with Jesusgate 1. How and why did Jesusgate begin? To answer that question we will study the origins of Jesusgate as related to the cultural context of the first century. In other words, did the pagan religions of that time influence the development of Christian beliefs? How did Christians react to this real or imagined perception? Was Christianity a copycat religion of sorts? In answering these questions we will encounter some of the information arising from biblical scholarship. This will help put Jesusgate 1 in perspective.

Subsequent chapters will spell out Jesusgate 2 & 3. Thereafter, we will examine even more closely the findings from biblical criticism. "Let's get ready to rumble!"

Chapter 4

JESUSGATE 1: THE BLASTOFF
(ca. 100 – 400 AD)

SYNCRETISM: A process of religious development in which the doctrines, beliefs, rituals, deities and myths of one religion are borrowed, adopted/adapted (tweaked) by another religion (which thus gains followers from the first). The end result is the configuration of a new religious dynamic.

SMOKING GUN: A piece of "indisputable" evidence, almost to a certainty.

GRECO-ROMAN WORLD: A term relating to the overlapping Greek and Roman cultures from ca. 300 BC – 400 AD or later.

Paganism anyone? What's a pagan (or heathen)? In order to understand our first Jesusgate incident, a short historical replay about paganism is necessary.

Pagans conjure up nasty images of violent people. Not always a false read. That's why they picked the actor Jack Palance to play Attila the Hun in the 1954 movie, *Sign of the Pagan*. Palance left me with boyhood movie memories of Attila the Hun sweeping out across the Eastern plains of Europe with devastating brutality. He was a little on the scary side.

By definition, however, a pagan is simply a person who does not believe in—or knows—the God of the Bible or Qur'an; that is, any person who is not a Jew, Christian, or Muslim. Accordingly, pagans are

45

not monotheists, they're usually polytheists. So, the ancient Persians, Mongolians, Babylonians, Syrians, Greeks, Romans, along with the Hittites, Amorites, Amalekites, and the Mosquito Bites, were all pagans. (If you missed the mosquito bites, you're reading too fast.) Okay, let's see what this all has to do with Jesusgate.

During the inception and development of Christianity, pagan religions flourished. The Greek temples of Zeus, Apollo, and Athena were frequented by the multitudes. Their Roman counterparts were equally numerous. The Romans, of course, borrowed and renamed many of the Greek gods. For example, Aphrodite becomes Venus; Poseidon becomes Neptune; Hermes becomes Mercury; Dionysus becomes Bacchus, and so forth.

This pagan religious smorgasbord also included what scholars now call the "mystery religions" (or mystery cults). They are generally defined as having secret initiation rites and coded holy writings, ergo, the mystery religions. The pagan mysteries were quite distinct from other pagan religions. In fact, they were remarkably exceptional in the religious climate of the Greco-Roman world. Unfortunately, information about these groups is scarce (another consequence of Jesusgate as we shall see). Here's what we do know.

Most other pagan religions of that time focused on individual and community needs (health, prosperity, rain, national survival, peace, and so on). They were centered on life in the here and now, not so much on the afterlife. In contrast, although the pagan mysteries were also focused on the individual's well being, their emphasis was on a happy *afterlife* (that's probably one of the reasons they were so popular). Within the mysteries we also find that their followers were generally devoted to one god or goddess (more so than non-mystery pagans). In addition, central to the mystery religions was the belief in the death and resurrection of a god or goddess.[5]

The best known mysteries were the Greek goddess Demeter and her daughter Kore (sometimes called Persephone); the Egyptian goddess Isis and her husband Osiris; the Greek god Dionysus; the god Mithra from Persia (modern day Iran); finally, the goddess Cybele from Asia Minor (modern day Turkey) and her attentive male god, Attis.

Keeping the above facts in mind, we can begin to identify the cultural and religious forces that would help shape Christian belief; to what extent is debated by scholars. We need not be overly concerned about this debate. Shortly, however, I will add some cautionary statements about this dispute so as to avoid oversimplified conclusions. But for the moment, we must understand two truths: (1) the tapestry of pagan belief—for the most part—preceded Christianity and, (2) the early Christians themselves became concerned about a perceived connection between pagan and Christian belief. It is my conviction that this concern became the catalyst that launched Jesusgate 1.

The first hint of trouble, as perceived by early Christians, had to do with the practice of religious syncretism. This syncretistic inclination was evident within the pagan sphere. It seems that pagan religions borrowed heavily from one another. As a consequence, they developed with similar and overlapping religious themes. Notably, this syncretistic tendency was in vogue before, during, and after the inception of Christianity and, evidently, Christians were neither isolated nor immune from this practice. Even a casual inspection—if one knows where to look—will show that Christianity probably adopted some beliefs and rituals from the surrounding pagan religions of the day (even as these religions borrowed from each other). As one example, consider the recurring pagan myth of the *demigod* (someone who is partly divine and partly human).

The demigod was the centerpiece of the mysteries. This so-called man-god was known by different names, by different religions, in different countries. "In Egypt he was Osiris, in Greece Dionysus, in Asia Minor Attis, in Syria Adonis, in Italy Bacchus, in Persia Mithras."[6] *[NOTE: Bacchus was the Roman name for the Greek god Dionysus.]*

Importantly, all of these pagan demigods *predate* Jesus' time. What makes this fact amazingly notable is that many of the qualities we consider exclusive to Jesus, are characteristic of these pre-Jesus demigods. To be clear, *before* there was Christianity, *before* the birth of Jesus, the following mythical themes prevailed in the pagan mystery religions. You will find them to be uncomfortably familiar as we compare them to the later developing Jesus persona.

*MITHRA: Almost 500 years before Jesus, the Persian god Mithra is allegedly born of a virgin (Anahita) in a cave. According to Persian traditions, Mithra was incarnated into human form as a savior on December 25th, and was attended by shepherds. In Roman times, Mithra is known as Mithras (add the s).

*DIONYSUS: was the god of wine in Greek mythology. His chief miracle was turning water into wine (long before Jesus turns water into wine at a wedding feast). In *The Bacchae*, written by Euripides around 405 BC, Dionysus is portrayed as a god in human form born of a virgin whose lover was a god.

*POSEIDON: the Greek god of the sea (as well as of horses, and of earthquakes) is able to ride his chariot across the water (long before Jesus goes one better by walking on the water).

Some of these pagan demigods allegedly experience violent death and resurrection. A few examples follow:

*ATTIS: a youthful consort of the goddess Cybele, of Anatolia (the greater part of Asia Minor, known today as Turkey). He is killed on March 22 and resurrected three days later on March 25th. Some scholars argue that Attis' resurrection account might not precede the Jesus account, but the evidence is inconclusive.

*OSIRIS: an Egyptian god who is cut into pieces by his wife Isis. He dies on the 17th of Asthyr (Egyptian calendar), and is then restored to life on the 19th. (Traditional accounts vary.)

*ADONIS: was a handsome youth in Greek mythology. He was killed by a wild boar or, according to some traditions, by a jealous rival disguised as a boar. One papyrus text reconstructed by scholars indicates that he was resurrected three days later.[7]

Many other comparisons between the Jesus story and paganism could be made. For example, the mystery religions not only promoted the concepts of virgin births and resurrections, but also sacred meals, baptism, and the movement of savior gods between heaven and earth. The evidence indicates that these concepts and rituals were in place *long before the rise of Christianity.*

"Goodness, gracious, great balls of fire!" (We owe that 1950s megahit ditty to Jimmy Swaggart's piano thumping cousin, Jerry Lee Lewis.) This lyric comes to mind and seems appropriate here because this is where some of my students go bonkers when first hearing about these mystery religions. They become very conflicted and they're not alone. When the pagan mysteries first came to light, they created quite a commotion and, they still do. Syncretism may be a natural religious inclination but it can raise serious questions. For example, how much of a role did it play in the development of Christianity? Did Christianity simply absorb the surrounding mythological genre of its day in order to advance its message? Perhaps. But most things in life are not that simple. Therefore, a closer look is warranted.

Upon first hearing of the mystery religions, people generally fall into two categories. First, we have the anti-religion skeptics who relish these facts as "proof" against any claim that Christian theology is legitimate. Second we find those, who, by virtue of blind faith, are unwilling to consider that these pagan religions might have had an impact on Christianity's development. Neither of these positions is defensible. I will explain further.

Let's begin with the skeptics who quickly dismiss Christianity by jumping to conclusions. (Be aware that the following section will be akin to a ping-pong match, with the pro and con arguments bouncing back and forth.)

At the very onset of Christianity it wasn't difficult to make comparisons between Jesus and the surrounding demigods. This certainly was the case with Celsus, a harsh second century critic of Christianity. His sole work, *True Doctrine*, has survived only in quotes and paraphrases found in *Against Celsus*, written by Origen (a prominent third century theologian).[8] Celsus apparently argued that there was very little about Christianity that was original; he complained that it was little more than a copycat version of pagan religion.[9] This line of reasoning has surfaced again in many contemporary writings, including the Internet. But I consider these criticisms to be oversimplified. So let's take a quick look at the other side of this argument.

There are many important distinctions between pagan themes and their parallels in Christianity. In all of the pagan religions the deity dies unwillingly, not by choice. Sometimes the deity dies in bitterness or despair, but never in self-giving love.[10] Also, the characters in these pagan religions were fictitious (albeit unknown to be so at that time), while the central figures in Christianity were, beyond a reasonable doubt, living persons. Furthermore, we must be careful not to blur the distinction between the demigod and Jesus. The demigod by definition is too simplistic. Christians hold fast to a more sophisticated concept known as the doctrine of the Incarnation (to be discussed later).

Additionally, it must be noted that syncretism was, at times, a two-way street. While it can be forcefully argued that certain Christian rituals and beliefs were derived from the mysteries, the argument for a reversed syncretism can also be made, albeit limited in scope. Evidence for this reversed syncretism, as one example, can be found in the cult of Cybele. Although this pagan religion predates Christianity, its ritual of "baptism"—called the Taurobolium—does not. It was not introduced into the rites of Cybele until 160 AD, probably as a means to compete against the ever-growing popularity of Christianity.[11] Based on this fact, we can surmise that Cybele either borrowed this baptismal ritual from Christianity or some other sister religion.

But even if Cybele borrowed this ritual from Christianity—and not vise versa—it cannot be argued that the rite of baptism originated with Christianity. It just didn't. Long before Christianity:

> Baptism was a central rite in the Mysteries. As long ago as the Homeric hymns [ca. 800-700 BC] we hear that ritual purity was the condition of salvation and that people were baptized to wash away all their previous sins . . . . In some Mystery rites baptism was simply symbolized by the sprinkling of holy water.
>
> In others it involved complete immersion . . . .In the Mysteries of [the god] Mithras, initiates underwent repeated baptisms to wash away their sins. Such initiations took place in March or April, at exactly the same time that in later centuries Christians also baptized their new converts . . . .[12] [Brackets mine]

Harking back to resurrection accounts, Celsus reminds us that the world was awash with resurrection stories. Many demigods and persons were said to have resurrected after death. These included Pythagoras in Italy, Zamolix (Pathagoras' servant), Phampsinitus in Egypt, Orpheus among the Odrysians, Protesilaus in Thessaly, Heracles in Greece (renamed Hercules by the Romans), Theseus in Greece,[13] and Zena, Warrior Princess (scratch Zena, I think that was a TV show).

One can see that the concept of resurrection was neither novel to, nor absent from, the ancient mind. As for virgin births, they were even more numerous. It was almost an entry level prerequisite for anyone of reputation.

Again, it must be noted that today's scholars are not agreed as to how extensive this pagan influence was on the development of Christianity. In fact, some scholars believe "... that the Mysteries may not have been as significant a factor in the first century as had been thought, and that the study of the phenomenon is fraught with methodological difficulties."[14]

Nevertheless, it's obvious that Christianity did not originate in a vacuum. It is also clear that the Christianity of today mirrors—in some detail—the mythical beliefs of the Persian, Greek, and Roman worlds. If you disagree with that last point, you may as well argue that the bald eagle is nothing more than a baldheaded chicken. (By the way, the bald eagle is not at all bald; neither are chickens for that matter ... but I almost am.)

Honestly, we must acknowledge that Celsus' allegation about duplication has some merit. The fact that Christianity reflects many of these pagan concepts enhances the probability that early Christians practiced syncretism; that is, they borrowed, absorbed, and tweaked these ideas from the pagan mystery religions of the day. The certainty that most of these pagan themes *predate* the Jesus era, lends credibility to that assertion. Awareness of this timeline can be most unsettling.

Regardless of how one views this matter, it is for the moment, unimportant. What is important is to recognize the effect that this perceived connection between Christianity and the pagan mystery religions had on the early church leaders. The effect was traumatic (boda-bing, boda-bang, boda-boom).

Is it any wonder that the early church fathers, such as Justin Martyr,[15] Irenaeus,[16] and Tertullian,[17] resorted to the desperate claim that the devil had orchestrated the similarities between the mystery religions and Christianity. They advanced the notion that the devil was taking advantage of his foreknowledge; that is, he knew what the future held. Therefore, the devil had purposely leaked the details of the Jesus story through these pagan religions prior to the coming of Jesus so as to obscure his uniqueness. Only the devil could conjure up such a diabolical preemptive strike! (Believe it or not, this theory is still promoted in some evangelical circles.)

As one would expect, "the devil did it" argument failed to convince. A much more drastic solution would be needed.

JESUSGATE 1

Is it possible that some pagan religious themes were adopted and modified by the early Christians? Whatever the truth of the matter, Christians could not shake the appearance of having done so. In order to smother this smoking gun, the "Church" initiated a full-blown offensive. It was the beginning of a cover-up driven by a blatant disregard for other religions that were similar to Christianity. The urgency of this intolerance was driven by fear—the fear of being associated with the pagan themes of the mystery religions, especially those that infringed on the Jesus persona. It was the Jesus persona that had to be protected at all costs (the central concern of all Jesusgates). Although limited in number, handwritten documents regarding mystery beliefs had surfaced throughout the Mediterranean world. They were perceived as a threat to the uniqueness of Christianity. So, they had to be eliminated. Presumption and expediency took the lead.

The first Jesusgate machinery went into high gear. Predictably, Jesusgaters were bent on eradicating the slightest bit of information that brought Christian beliefs into question, especially anything that challenged their one-sided interpretation of Jesus. For that reason, Jesusgaters literally destroyed any pagan religious literature they could find. It was a calculated and well-organized defensive move to obliterate any connection, or perceived connection, between Jesus and pagan belief. These self-appointed protectors of the Christian faith—who we call the early church fathers—were so successful in eliminating these pagan writings, that most of what we know about them today can only be gleaned from the early Christian sources that refer to them (as was the case with the early church father Origen, arguing against the skeptic Celsus). Slim pickings.

This process of eradication was boosted by the increasing popularity of Christianity. In 325 AD, under the Emperor Constantine, Christianity gained approval as the most favored religion of the Roman Empire. In 381 AD, Emperor Theodosius I ("the Great") declared it to be the imperial state religion. By 391, he secured Christianity's ultimate dominance by banning all pagan worship[18] (on punishment of death).

Eventually, the mysteries disappeared from memory. As they faded into the murky past, their contributions were also forgotten—forgotten to the extent that most people reading these pages today are unaware of their probable impact on Christian belief. Jesusgaters—by virtue of presumption and expediency—had successfully slammed the historical door shut on any meaningful dialogue regarding the colorful nature of pagan religion and its overall contribution to Christian development. As time slipped away this created the illusion of a theological slam-dunk; that is, Christian doctrine came to be thought of as a pure, untarnished, direct, and *unique* revelation from God. Swish.

The uncovering of Jesusgate 1, forces one to ask some far-reaching questions: Did certain facets of the Jesus story originate in the pagan soil of the pre-Christian era? Did certain doctrines of faith derive from the pagan mystery religions? If so, what difference does it make? But I leave it to the reader. Next up, Jesusgate 2.

Intro to Chapter 5

THE FICKLE FINGER OF FATE

It was April 24, 1944. Our nation was embroiled in the bloody conflict of World War II. But it wasn't the war that ended the life of my father, Ernie Bringas. No, it wasn't the war; just the insane act of a killer gone mad in the otherwise peaceful city of San Diego, California.

That fateful day had started with my dad's unassuming routine of an "I'm off to work kiss" for my mom, and the wild goodbye squeals of a four-year-old boy and two older sisters who were now six and eight. The heartfelt grief that was yet to unfold that day would be borne primarily by my mother, although the consequences for all of us would be permanent. The final report of the *San Diego Tribune* would read:

> . . . Ernie Bringas died early this morning from cerebral head trauma caused by multiple blows to the head by an unknown assailant . . . police have not found the murder weapon. A fellow employee found Mr. Bringas, the father of three children, lying in a puddle of blood trying to speak on the telephone . . . robbery is suspected as the main motive.[1] [The killer was never apprehended]

Shortly thereafter our family moved to a Los Angeles suburb. We lived with my grandmother on 80th street, an almost middle class neighborhood at that time. During these early years, my mother made sure that we kids made it to church on Sunday mornings. It was a small, conservative, non-denominational church (not that I knew what all that meant).

The half-a-mile walk from our house was much longer by short-legged standards, but it was doable. Spiffy is the word I'd use to describe how my mother put us together those long-ago Sundays. Our family was closer to poor than middle class but my mom always made the best of it. I can still visualize my sisters with their pretty flower print dresses, smart shoes, and colorful ribbons in their hair. As for me, a light blue "manly" suit surrounded my undersized frame. Off we'd go.

When I was eleven we moved to Inglewood (another suburb of LA, about ten miles south of Hollywood). There were other youngsters in the area that would eventually take advantage of Hollywood's proximity. The yet-to-be Beach Boys lived a few miles south of me, while the Turtles were growing up a few miles west. Sonny and Cher, also living in the area, would eventually team up. Examples are prolific. But I digress.

It was during my teenage years that my sisters and I attended the Grace Evangelical United Brethren church (try and tell that to your teenage buddies). It too was conservative, at least in our region (it was part of the Evangelical United Brethren denomination). During these formative years I came to accept Jesus as my Lord and Savior and to understand the basis of Christian faith. I would never trade the nurturing warmth of this experience although, in retrospect, I must admit to its less enlightened side; there were no alternatives to a Bible incapable of error and a one-way plan of salvation.

Beyond the local church, I reveled in the Billy Graham crusades and the newly released cinema spectacles of *The Robe, Demetrius and the Gladiators, The Ten Commandments,* and *Ben Hur.* It was Great theatre. These epics played well against my simplistic understanding of Christianity. It all made perfect sense: Jesus, salvation, miracles, and an unquestionable Bible. Yes, it all jelled together all right; that is, until I started my college education and thereafter my seminary journey (shades of our scholars three I mentioned in Ch. 3). Awaiting my brain was a fount of knowledge the likes of which I could never have imagined, not even in my dreams (or nightmares). For a while, I was bewildered. Eventually, however, education bolstered my KQ by which I was able to override my Jesusgate upbringing.

And so it was that on my way to becoming a United Methodist minister, I discovered a significantly different portrayal of Christianity. It was a Christianity transformed—transformed by the collective knowledge of humankind (both secular and religious), and it was out of sync with what

I had been taught at the local level. In other words, it bore little resemblance to what I had learned from family and church.

I was baffled by this discrepancy. I found it inconceivable that a "parallel" Christianity could have existed without my knowledge. Even worse, it was obvious that most people were (and still are) unaware of this coexistent body. You see, in academic circles, Christianity had morphed (and rightly so). This change was not driven by any disregard for the truth. On the contrary, it was the unveiling of new information that helped scholars to reconstruct a more plausible understanding of Christianity. As we have already seen, this new and refreshing knowledge failed to become fishers of men in the general population. It failed to breach the well-entrenched Jesusgate blockade.

As for me, my childhood indoctrination gave way to a more truthful understanding of Jesus (albeit more disturbing). This is not to imply that my understanding is complete. That's hardly the case since the evolution of our KQ is a lifelong process. However, I am certain that at least on some issues, I have emerged from Plato's Cave. (Google it.)

WHAT TO EXPECT NEXT

As noted earlier, the deliberate suppression of Christianity's syncretistic origins represents only the first of three Jesusgate episodes. We now turn our attention to Jesusgate 2. In the early Christian movement, a great issue of concern revolved around the hotly debated issue of Christology (the nature of Jesus). Various groups defined Jesus in a multiplicity of ways. This made church unity virtually impossible. Eventually, one of these groups emerged victorious and then took action to suppress all other groups to the contrary. Another cover-up ensued. This was the beginning of Jesusgate 2.

Chapter 5

JESUSGATE 2:
THE BOOSTER ROCKETS
(325–451 AD)

CHRISTOLOGY: A theory or doctrine concerning the nature of Christ; the attributes of Christ; the study of Christ.

ORTHODOXY: A generally accepted doctrine or practice; the religious norm.

APOSTLE: Each of the twelve chief disciples of Jesus Christ.

APOSTOLIC: Doctrines or teachings coming from or originating with the Apostles, or any important early Christian teachers such as St. Paul.

CREED: Any statement of faith or belief.

As noted in our previous chapter, the early "church" leaders implemented the first Jesusgate episode. It was an aggressive defense mechanism set against a real *external* threat—the threat of associating the Jesus story with the demigod mythology of the pagan mystery religions. They expediently stamped out pagan literature.

There was yet another threat in these early years, only this time the danger welled up from the inner bowels of the church itself. This *internal* upheaval, which would eventually usher in Jesusgate 2, overlapped somewhat with Jesusgate 1. So, at certain times, the early church found itself battling on two simultaneous fronts.

This second battle swirled around the question of *Christology*. Who was this Jesus, anyway? Was he human? Was he divine? Was he a combination of both? What was his true nature? Equally important, what was his relationship to God? Did God create Jesus or was Jesus God Himself? Or was there another explanation? Although Christians shared the conviction that Jesus was somehow *from* God, they all had different ideas as to what that meant. How these differing beliefs led to Jesusgate 2 will be explained shortly. But first, a brief historical replay on early Christology is needed.

EARLY CHRISTOLOGY

In the early years of the Jesus movement, a core question begged resolution: Who was this Jesus? Was Jesus really the very essence of God (and therefore shared equality with God) or was Jesus, created by God (and thus subordinate to God)? What about his human nature, his overall nature? Christological arguments were inevitable.

In modern times, Christians have assumed that the early church was monolithic (cohesive, uniform, sticking together, theologically united) in its understanding of Jesus. *It wasn't*. It was quite the opposite. We know this for the following reasons.

Since the Enlightenment of the seventeenth century, scholars have sifted through this early Christian era. New discoveries of primary sources over the past few centuries have continued to shed light on this once so-called unified church. By the twentieth century, the idea of early church unity was more than suspect. But the startling discovery of long-lost gospels at the town of Nag Hammadi (Egypt) in 1945, pretty much obliterated the once popular belief that the early church was a tight-knit organization. Scholars could now show that early Christianity was far more conflicted than nearly anyone suspected. In other words, the early church did not foster a simpler, purer, united form of faith. "Among the various congregations scattered throughout the Roman Empire . . . there was no standardized theology, no single pattern of governance, no uniform liturgy, and no commonly accepted scripture."[2] When that ". . . cache of books was discovered in Upper Egypt, the world was suddenly presented with hard evidence of other Christian groups in the ancient world that stood in sharp contrast with any kind of Christianity familiar to us today."[3] (We will examine some of these lost gospels later in this writing.)

But even prior to the discoveries at Nag Hammadi, there was a major study published on the issue of early church unity. It demands recognition. Distinguished scholar Bart D. Ehrman, points out that the German scholar Walter Bauer,[4] in his *1934* controversial and influential work (*Orthodoxy and Heresy in Earliest Christianity*) ". . . argued that the early Christian church did not consist of a single orthodoxy from which emerged a variety of competing heretical minorities." Actually, it was just the other way around; that is, we had a glut of competing *Christianities* before one of these groups eventually won the day; this victorious group came to be known as the orthodox Christianity we embrace today. Ehrman clarifies: "To this extent, 'orthodoxy,' in the sense of a unified group advocating an apostolic doctrine accepted by the majority of Christians everywhere, simply did not exist in the second and third centuries."[5]

To be precise, this truism applies not only to the second and third centuries, but actually applies from the first century all the way through to the first quarter of the fourth century (roughly from Paul's time [45 AD] to the Council of Nicea [325 AD]). Prior to the Council of Nicea (or Nicaea), which we'll get to momentarily, church unity was flimsy, at best. Even after the Nicea milestone, it took another century to homogenize orthodoxy. Be that as it may, kudos to Walter Bauer for his insightful scholarship—eleven years prior to the gospel discoveries at Nag Hammadi—in helping to demonstrate early church discord.

The point is, we now know that the fledgling church was, at best, an alliance at odds with itself. Many divergent groups—none of them dominant—fought to preserve and promote their special brand of Christology (what they believed about Jesus). Which of these many groups would emerge victorious? Before we answer that question, we need to highlight their Christological differences, in order to emphasize the uneven, dragged-out, and up-for-grabs nature of the *Christological battle* that inevitably ensued. This will also serve as a necessary prelude to our understanding of Jesusgate 2. Keep in mind that the following are barebones definitions of the differing Christological beliefs held by these many early groups. Here we go.

1. GNOSTICISM: Gnostic Christians did not accept a literal interpretation of the resurrection.

2. APOLLINARIANISM: These Christians taught that the human, fleshly nature of Christ derived from the virgin birth but he did not become divine until after his resurrection when he had union with the Godhead.

3. DOCETISM: These Christians believed that Jesus only seemed or appeared to be a man but, in reality, he was a pure spirit. Thus, his physical body was an illusion, as was his death by crucifixion.

4. MARCIONISM: Marcion Christians believed that Jesus had not been truly human. If he had a material body, this would nullify his divinity. They were primarily Docetic (see above).

5. EBIONITES: Unlike the Marcionites who saw Jesus as completely divine and not human, the Ebionites saw Jesus as completely human and not divine. Furthermore, they did not believe that Jesus was born of a virgin.

6. ARIANISM: Arian Christians concluded that Jesus was neither God nor man. They saw Jesus as less than God but more than man (Jesus served as a mediator between the two). They believed that Jesus had been created by God. Therefore, Jesus was subordinate to the Father. Jesus was neither coequal nor coeternal with God.

7. ADOPTIONISM: Jesus was born human but, because of his sinless devotion to the will of God, became divine (he was adopted by God; ergo, the Son of God).

8. SABELLIANISM *(also known as Modalism or Monarchianism)*: These Christians fostered a non-Trinitarian belief. They held that God was one being, not a Trinity; Jesus could not be part of the Godhead because there was no Godhead. Rather, God was said to have three faces or masks (3 modes, ergo, modalism), rather than being three distinct persons as it came to be defined in the Trinitarian doctrine.

9. MONTANISM: Similar to Sabellianism but not modalistic. (The Montanists believed that the Trinity consisted of only a single person as opposed to what became the orthodox view (that the Trinity is one

God of three persons.) I will include here the fifth century Christological arguments posed by the Nestorians and Monophysites. Both of these groups still exist today. The Nestorians are found in Lebanon, Syria, Europe, Iran, China, Russia, and even in the USA. Monophysites are primarily in Armenia, Egypt, and Ethiopia.

10. NESTORIANS: They believe that Jesus exists as two distinct persons, rather than as a unified person; that is, Jesus is a man, but he is also the Son of God (or Logos of God). Nestorius, their leading spokesperson "... preached a sermon *against* calling Mary 'the mother of God,' declaring she did not bear a deity, she bore 'a man, the organ of deity.'"[6]

11. MONOPHYSITES: Opposite in belief to the Nestorians, their Christological assertion is that in the person of Jesus Christ there is only one nature, which is divine, rather than two natures (human and divine).

I don't know about anyone else, but I'm a deer caught in the headlights trying to sort out these Christological perspectives. I haven't even listed them all. Regardless, these Christian bodies were/are out of sync with what we now call orthodox Christology.

Christological division was not the only problem in those early centuries. The so-called church was conflicted on other theological matters, as apparent in the teachings of the Donatists, the Pelaginists, and the Manichaeans, to name a few. Arguments swirled around the issues of salvation, baptism, apostasy (forsaking of one's religion), and even how many gods existed. Both the Manichaeans and the Marcions promoted a dualistic version of God; that is, coexisting gods of good and evil. For example, "Marcion argued that the creator God of Genesis was a different and inferior God to the Father of Jesus Christ."[7] (Some scholars believe that this dualistic concept derived from Gnosticism. For further clarification on the various forms and complexities of Gnosticism or, any of these groups, you will definitely need to read beyond this text.) But let's get back to Christology.

Eventually, the questions pertaining to the nature of Jesus would be hammered out on the theological anvil of the *Incarnation* (which assumes the embodiment of God in the person of Jesus). The term "Incarnation" does not appear in the New Testament, but the concept does. It is most clearly stated in John 1:1 & 14: "In the beginning was the Word, and the Word was with God, and the Word was God ... And the Word became flesh and lived among us ...."[8] As we have clearly seen, for the early Christians there was little or no agreement as to what this actually meant. For example, did God and Jesus share equality? Is this what the Incarnation implied, or was such thinking sheer blasphemy. Christological viewpoints were bound to collide. One really couldn't settle the issue of who Jesus was until one could define the nature of Jesus and his relationship to God. Thus, the ensuing debate would incorporate the Trinity (the doctrine that defines the Christian Godhead as one God in three persons: Father, Son, and Holy Spirit).

The Christological arguments grew hotter than a high school romance. Although this hotly contested issue was partly settled at the Council of Nicea in 325 AD, it wouldn't be cooled off until the Council of Chalcedon in 451 AD. During the early centuries of Christian development, ". . . the formulation and reformulation of the dogma were called forth by a doctrinal debate more vigorous [and cutthroat] than the Church had ever experienced."[9] [Brackets mine] It was a real dogfight. Most scholars today would agree with world-renown scholar Jaroslav Pelikan when he writes: "Doctrine often seemed to be the victim—or the product—of church politics and of conflicts of personality."[10]

In our quest to understand early Christology, we must remember three vital points: (1) all of the above groups were vying for theological supremacy because there was no unified, all embracing, orthodox church; (2) all of these groups were more or less in a condition of parity (evenness); no one group had the upper hand although equilibrium between these groups came and went, depending on time and geographical location; (3) orthodoxy, as we know it today, did not solidify its position until the nature of Jesus was somewhat clarified by the Council of Nicea early in the fourth century (325 AD). Up until that time, as we have seen, Christian beliefs were widely varying—a religious kaleidoscope of sorts. But how did the Council of Nicea come together, and what were the results? To answer these two questions we turn our attention, oddly enough, to the Roman Emperor, Constantine.

CONSTANTINE

In 312 AD, Constantine and Licinius became co-emperors of the Roman Empire. However, each ruled different geographical areas:

Constantine controlled the West and Licinius the East. But Constantine was not satisfied with this division of power. His desired end was for *one empire* ruled by a *single monarch* unified under the right worship of the *Summus Deus* ([Latin] supreme god). He was looking for a done deal, a clean sweep, a triple play, winner take all—use your own cliché. Constantine's desire for a single monarch was fulfilled in 324 AD when his armies defeated the forces of Licinius. He became the sole ruler of a once again unified Roman world, and he would claim that Christian divine aid had given him victory over his enemies. This assumption made him grateful to Christianity's God. Based on his belief that God had given him the victory over his enemies, Constantine would elevate Christianity to an unprecedented level of prestige and favor. This was the first important step that eventually led to Christianity becoming the official religion of the Roman Empire under Emperor Theodosius I (AKA: Theodosius the Great) in ca. 381-83 AD. This was not the first time Constantine had given the Christian God credit for battle-victory. But then, it was not unusual for leaders of that time to credit the gods for such outcomes. They were obviously psyched up on religious naiveté. Incidentally, his wife and mother also encouraged this Christian embrace.[11]

But we must remember that the Christological debate was still raging. As I pointed out earlier, a number of Christian groups were jockeying around for ultimate supremacy. Constantine was not pleased with this vibration of Christian discord. He was determined to have harmony. There was now one Empire, one Emperor, and he was determined to have one unified religion. He would have none of this Christological bickering.

To help eliminate this festering predicament, he called for a universal council of the church to be held at Nicea, a suburb of Constantinople--which literally means "the city of Constantine" (modern Istanbul, Turkey). From across the empire, approximately 300 bishops gathered. It's hard to imagine that anyone attending this occasion could have foreseen its theological repercussions.

Constantine convened the proceedings on May 20, 325 AD. Without a doubt, the Council of Nicea was under the strict control of the Emperor as he wielded absolute power. Would he attempt to influence the Christological debate? If so, which version of Jesus would Constantine endorse?

It was during this council that Constantine made his momentous sug-gestion—possibly prompted by his friend, Bishop Hosius—that Jesus, in relationship to the Father, might be expressed by the Greek term, *homo-ousios* (of the same substance).[12] The result was a creed (the Nicene Creed) asserting that the Son was generated out of the Father's substance. For that very reason, Jesus was considered to be part of God (the Godhead); accordingly, Jesus was co-equal and co-eternal with God because he was of the *same* substance (*homoousios*). However, this was not a new concept. It was the early church father, Tertullian (ca. 160-220 AD), who first pro-moted the idea of *homoousios* (same substance). In fact, he gets credit for coining the term *Trinity* (Father, Son, and Holy Ghost).[13]

Nevertheless, prior to Nicea, the term, *homoousios*, was a loaded word and was considered unacceptable. Early on it was condemned by Bishop Dionysius of Alexandria (Egyptian city) in the 260s AD, and again con-demned in 264-68 AD by the Council of Antioch (a city in the southern part of Asia Minor [Turkey]).[14] But at Nicea, no one dared to challenge Constantine's suggestion (at least not in his lifetime). Regardless, the majority of attending bishops were unhappy and embarrassed by its usage.[15] How could Jesus and God be of the same substance? For many, the language seemed blasphemous. Nevertheless, the overwhelming majority accepted it. The Nicene Creed was up and running. In reference to Jesus, the following is a partial read of the Nicene Creed:

> . . . God from God, Light from Light, true God from true God, not created, of the same essence [real-ity] as the Father, through whom all things came into being, both in heaven and in earth; Who for us men and for our salvation came down and was incarnate, becom-ing human.[16] (Brackets are part of the quote.)

Constantine died on May 22, 337 AD, but the idea of Jesus being of the same substance as God, continued to be contentious. There is no doubt that the *homoousios* wording was a theological conundrum. You see their dilemma? If they declare that God and Jesus are of the *same* sub-stance, they risk the charge of blasphemy (How can one say that God and Jesus share equality?). But if they fail to support the concept of *homoosu-ios*, they will not be able to square their belief in Jesus as the Savior of humankind. That is, it wouldn't be enough to say that Jesus was *from*

God (created by God), he had to be *of* God (the essence of God); thereby, sharing that critical power and saving authority reserved only for God. In other words, only God had the power to save. That being the case, how could Jesus save anyone from "sin" if he weren't on a par with God?[17] For this, and other reasons, the Nicene Creed was never overturned in spite of some serious opposition. (Please note that from a Jewish perspective all of this would have been inconceivable; sheer profanity. Very few Jews could have agreed with this doctrine because it undermined hard-core monotheism. That's why the majority of Jews argued with Paul and other early Christian Jews. By Constantine's time, however, the Christian movement was totally Gentile [non-Jewish].)

Although Nicea had defined Jesus and God as being of the same substance, it failed to explain how this was possible. Even if one could adapt to the uneasy feelings created by the concept of *homoosuios*, how could Jesus be both God and man? In what sense was he truly man? In what sense was he truly God? This part of the equation remained unsettled until the Council of Chalcedon in 451 AD. It was here, one hundred and twenty-six years after Nicea that the incarnated nature of Jesus was fully defined. I remember this fact from my second year in seminary because I was astounded to realize that, from the time of Jesus' death, it took the Christian movement about 420 years to finalize the nature(s) of Jesus as understood by most Christians today.

The definition of Chalcedon maintained that the Logos—God's creative and revealing essence—was embodied in the person of Jesus, ergo, the Incarnation. In the NT, however, it is not clear exactly how the *fullness* of God became flesh in the person of Jesus. On the one hand, how would one explain the Lord's Prayer? Was Jesus praying to himself, "Our Father who art in heaven . . ."? Of course he wasn't. Jesus speaks of God as a separate entity: "In my Father's house are many rooms . . . ," and so forth. On the other hand, the Gospel of John identifies Jesus as God's equal (see Ch. 10, pp. 140-45), as Paul also implies (see Ch. 15, pp. 236-43). Thus, can we say with certainty that the *Logos*—that one divine spark of God—that becomes flesh in the person of Jesus is, or is not, God in totality? We'll explore further.

The Creed of Chalcedon now stipulated that Jesus possessed two complete natures—the human and the divine—inexplicably intertwined in one personality, without either nature being diminished.[18] If you didn't catch it, the key word in that last sentence is, *inexplicably*—mysteriously unexplainable. To put it mildly, it sounds a bit complicated. But hey, don't take my word for it. Read this Chalcedonian Creed for your-self. Good luck.

> . . . we unite in teaching all men to confess the one and only Son, our Lord Jesus Christ. This selfsame one is perfect both in deity and also in humanness; this self-same one is also actually God and actually man, with a rational soul and a body. He is of the same reality as God as far as his deity is concerned and of the same reality as we are ourselves as far as his humanness is concerned; thus like us in all respects, sin only excepted . . . [We also teach] that we apprehend this one . . . in two natures [and we do this] without confusing the two natures, without transmuting one nature into the other, with-out dividing them into two separate categories without contrasting them according to area or function. The dis-tinctiveness of each nature is not nullified by the union. Instead, the properties of each nature are conserved and both natures concur in one "person" and in one *hypos-tasis* (the one entire nature of Christ as distinguished from his two natures, human and divine). They are not divided or cut into two persons, but are together the one and only-begotten Logos of God, the Lord Jesus Christ . . . .[19] [Parenthesis mine; brackets are part of the quote]

I mean no disrespect, but these last two paragraphs have given me an Excedrin headache. They sound a bit like those baffling comments made by Alan Greenspan (former chairperson of the Federal Reserve). If you read the above doctrine, you should be as confused as a cow on Astro Turf. Having said this, however, the Chalcedonian Creed should not be dismissed as nonsensical. The following paragraph will clarify.

Starting with the Nicene Creed in 325 AD and finishing off with the Chalcedonian Creed in 451 AD, Christological statements of faith were finally laid to rest, although not everyone followed suit (especially in the Eastern Church). Nevertheless, today the majority of Christians still accept these interpretations, be they ever so metaphysical (abstract, and hard to comprehend). If we can truly be objective, we will admit that these doctrines are puzzling formulations shrouded in mystery, as they should be. One has to appreciate that metaphysical models are not captured by language; that is, language (however well-formed) cannot adequately explain the mystical. In short, we can explain it, but we cannot fully grasp the explanation. (I'm starting to sound like the Chalcedonian Creed.)

In reference to the Trinity, prominent scholar Karen Armstrong puts it this way: "It was not a logical or intellectual formulation but an imaginative paradigm [model] that confounded reason."[20] [Brackets mine] Furthermore, these are statements of faith that, by their enigmatic nature, will remain mystifying. Of course, one has to decide whether these doctrines are little more than convoluted semantics, literal realities, or useful models to partially explain the unexplainable.

However this information plays out in your mind, remember this: It took the Christian movement over four hundred years to "settle" these Christological issues. *The point is, anyone who assumes that early Christians were unified in their understanding of Jesus, knows little about the first five centuries of Christianity.*

Even as our ignorance about the mystery religions and the prevalence of syncretism can be attributed to Jesusgate 1, so it is that today's ignorance about this multi-contentious Christological time period can be attributed to Jesusgate 2 (as we are about to see). It is true, of course, that during Jesusgate 1, all of our assorted Christian groups could rise up as one body against a common foe—suppressing any perceived syncretism of pagan religion by eradicating their literature.

But on the question of Christology, believers were ripped apart by their divergent interpretations. Church unification seemed impossible. Even so, those groups that more or less supported the theological leanings of Nicea and Chalcedon came to dominate the religious landscape. When this occurred, they quickly fell into the Jesusgate mode: *presumption* and *expediency* took the lead. Believing that God had picked them out of the Christological hodgepodge, they aggressively took whatever steps necessary to solidify their base and subdue their opponents.

Their rise to power—the rise of what we have come to call "orthodox" Christianity—started under the reign of the Roman Emperor, Constantine. As we have seen, he was very influential in "settling" the Christological debate and, as a consequence, was the catalyst that ushered in Jesusgate 2. Here's how it happened.

JESUSGATE 2

I have designated the Nicea-Chalcedon time period (325-451 AD) as Jesusgate 2 because of what transpired during these years. It begins with Constantine's assertion that Jesus and God were of the same substance (homoousios). However controversial, it nevertheless became the centerpiece of the Nicene Creed. Those particular Christians who agreed with the Emperor wasted no time solidifying their position. To ensure the creeds acceptance, a rider was attached: *Anyone who was not willing to go along with the Creed of Nicea was threatened with anathema*[21] (to be condemned and excommunicated from the Church, thereby forfeiting eternal life).

Once again we see our two-headed dragon raising its ugly head: presumption and expediency. This time, Jesusgaters were not trying to eradicate pagan religious literature. This time they were bent on eliminating other Christian viewpoints—viewpoints that were not in accord with the Nicene Creed. All other opinions about Jesus—and as we have seen, there were many—would be squelched. All dissenters would now be branded as heretics and excommunicated. This banishment applied to any believer who did not tow the Nicene party line; that is, Nicene Christology.

Few people realize that the Council of Nicea was a *groundbreaking* episode in the development of Christology. Under the direction of Constantine, it was a monumental happening. To help us grasp the impact of Constantine's Nicene input (homoousios), and the resulting Jesusgate onslaught that followed, a modern day "multi-flavored" metaphor is in order.

31 FLAVORS

We might imagine that Constantine created a Baskin Robins 31 flavors ice-cream parlor (Council of Nicea). Each of the 31 flavors represents a specific Christological interpretation about Jesus as claimed by the Arians, the Montanists, the Docetists, and so forth. Naturally, Constantine is the store, owner/manager (Emperor).

All is well, but Constantine has one problem. He is not pleased with the bewilderment generated by the multiplicity of a 31 flavors selection. (We all know what that means.) To achieve his goal for unity and to avoid confusion, one flavor must be chosen for all. But which one should he select? It's a tough choice but he gets by with a little help from his friends. (There's a Beatle song in there somewhere.) He decides to go with raspberry (homoousios/same substance). This raspberry selection (the official way to view Jesus) will not only be the flavor of the month, but the flavor of forever.

Raspberry proponents are jubilant. Hooray for our side! Not unlike the proponents of the other flavors, they too are convinced that their flavor (the way they view Jesus) is the best tasting one (the correct one). This *presumptuous* attitude is immediately followed by *expediency* because those other flavors are straightaway covered with lids and hauled off to some out-of-sight freezer. Consequently, there's only one flavor—one depiction of Jesus—left in the store. As a consequence, anyone who wants a taste of ice cream is now limited to this one flavor (this one portrayal of Jesus). Make no mistake, all other flavors (portrayals) are now deemed to be uneatable (heretical).

Constantine's limited raspberry preference, as compared to the 31 flavors from which it was drawn, became the theological flagship of the Christian movement. What we now call the Roman Catholic Church emerged as, and coalesced into, the dominant Christian body. It did so, of course, by systematically excommunicating those Christians who did not comply with the Nicene Creed's declaration of homoousios (Jesus and God being of the same substance). Fearing banishment and possibly worse, most Christians went along to get along.

Some would argue—and I would agree—that without culling and consolidation, what we now accept as orthodox faith (the majority view in Christianity today) would not exist. But that's the point! If Constantine had selected another flavor (another interpretation of Jesus), it would have automatically become orthodox by virtue of his imperial power. All other flavors, including raspberry (what we presently believe about Jesus), would have been declared heresy and stored away in the freezer with the other rejects—and we would be none the wiser. For example, let us suppose that in our 31 flavors metaphor, chocolate represented Arianism (the view that Jesus *was not* of the same substance as God). If Constantine had hand-picked chocolate rather than raspberry as his flavor of forever, than Arianism would be orthodox today while the raspberry interpretation—Jesus and God being of the same substance—would have long disappeared from Christian consciousness. What all this implies, of course, is that our present Christological doctrine came together by chance, circumstance, and the unquestionable authority of a Roman emperor.

But for most Christians, this somewhat luck of the draw is never considered to be accidental, never a hit-and-miss outcome. On the contrary, they would argue that whatever Christological model emerged victorious at the Council of Nicea (and Chalcedon), was due to the guiding influence of the Holy Spirit (the third person of the Trinity; God's active spirit in the world). That's the standard Jesusgate argument for all historical outcomes. In other words, whatever transpired in shaping Christological doctrine was inevitable because it was God-directed. Elaine Pagels, a stellar professor of religion at Princeton University, nails it this way:

> It is the winners who write history—their way. No wonder, then, that the viewpoint of the successful majority has dominated all traditional accounts of the origin of Christianity. Ecclesiastical Christians [raspberry proponents] first defined the terms (naming themselves "orthodox" and their opponents "heretics"); then they proceeded to demonstrate—at least to their own satisfaction—that their triumph was historically inevitable, or, in religious terms, "guided by the Holy Spirit."[22] [Brackets mine, parenthesis hers]

In this presumptive state of mind, our "raspberry" Christians concluded that God had brought them into the winner's circle at Nicea. In their minds, it proved unquestionably that their Christological conclusions were correct; that is, by virtue of their rise to power—albeit via Constantine—God was obviously on their side. Constantine, if you remember, drew the same conclusion about God's help in his victories over Licinius and others. In short, it was not simply survival of the fittest, but survival of the "goddest." (There's no such word as "goddest," but it sounds right.)

The assumption of being God-favored, led the "raspberry" Christians to intolerance against those with different Christological tastes. In cahoots with the emperor, they pushed hard for doctrinal conformity. Diversity of belief would not be tolerated. Intolerance was the price now being levied as the result of a Roman-favored religion, and a religious faction that claimed itself to be orthodox on the basis that its rise to power had been engineered by, the Holy Spirit.

Of course, we shouldn't blame this presumptive attitude solely on those who emerged victorious at Nicea. Had any one of the other 31 flavors (other Christological views) been chosen, they also would have created a fanfare, and they too would have sought to make everyone else bow in one theological direction—their own!

Regardless, the Nicene Creed became the ultimate benchmark as it set the wheels in motion that helped to define our present understanding of Jesus. But those wheels didn't stop churning with this Creed. The Christological issue would be continuously debated for the next 126 years. It wasn't until the Council of Chalcedon in 451, with its additional "clarification" of the divine and human natures of Jesus, that most parties ratified the Trinitarian doctrine. However, even after the Council of Chalcedon, Christological disputes continued. For example, we have already noted the Nestorians and Monophysites; these outsider groups fought hard to advance their own Christological spin.

Naturally, people who lived during those embryonic years of Christological upheaval were aware that many interpretations of Jesus existed. But these differing descriptions of who Jesus was were suppressed, destroyed, or ignored almost into extinction. With the passing of time, later generations would not even know about the Christological controversy. Similar to our first Jesusgate, where pagan religious influence is stripped away from early Christian development, so it is that the tumultuous and seemingly haphazard journey of Christology is also stripped away.

I say this because, after Chalcedon in 451, this loss of memory was assured by Jesusgaters (the priests),[23] who evidently felt compelled to remain silent on these matters; or, they simply dismissed as unimportant what had been a very messy process of Christological debate. With the passing of time, church leaders failed to give full disclosure—or any disclosure—about what had happened. (Here comes our tandem bicycle again.) As in the spirit of all "gates," their silence was probably triggered by presumption (God made sure that we ended up with the right Christological formula anyway) and expediency (our followers might think otherwise if we present them with the chaotic details). As a result, the Christian faithful were left in the dark (pretty much where they are today).

Eventually, and oddly enough, even the clergy lost touch with this historical record. Not until biblical criticism flushed it out again (an ongoing process over the past three hundred years), did the clergy critically analyze these early meandering church scenarios. And still, aside from a few notable exceptions, the clergy remained mute about their rediscoveries.

The end result of this self-serving silence is that all other portrayals of Jesus have become virtually nonexistent. We are once again left with the problem of misimpression. We are left with the false perception that the Trinitarian doctrine, from the very beginning, had been grounded in one simple, unified understanding of the early church. But it wasn't.

Nevertheless, the portrayal of Jesus Christ as part of a threesome Godhead who possessed two natures, human and divine, emerges as an untarnished, direct, absolute revelation from God (without any balanced explanation about the excruciating process of how this doctrine developed and how orthodox Christianity came to be). Bart D. Ehrman makes a troubling observation about today's Christianity. In his words: "The group that won out [at Nicea] did not represent the teachings of Jesus or his disciples. For example, none of the apostles claimed that Jesus was 'fully God and fully man,' or that he was 'begotten not made, of one substance with the Father,' as the fourth-century Nicene Creed maintained."[24] [Brackets mine]

Very few people are familiar with the information I have divulged thus far. That's because the Jesusgate machinery is still operative, albeit in a different mode. This will become more than obvious in our next chapter as we explore Jesusgate 3. It is Jesusgate 3 that has left us in the illiterate and religious quagmire of our present time.

Intro to Chapter 6

WAS IT SOMETHING I SAID?

Up until the time I entered seminary I had not taken any religion courses. Unlike today, such courses were scarce at the university level. Yes, seminary was an eye-opener. But as I indicated earlier, being subjected to knowledge that runs counter to one's upbringing—no matter when it happens--is no fun for most of us. Breaking loose from indoctrination (one who is taught to accept beliefs uncritically) is quite difficult. During that first year in seminary I stubbornly clung to my "sacred house of cards."

At this very moment I hold in front of me an old notebook on which I took an exam during my first semester in seminary (a little over forty years ago . . . yikes!). Dr. Wayne Barr, our Professor of Old Testament Literature, had placed a couple of questions before us that we were to answer in essay form. One of those questions was in reference to the story of Jonah and the whale (big fish). Specifically: What was the central message or meaning of the Jonah story?

I came to seminary as a fundamentalist. I was itching to set the record straight about the literal interpretation of the Bible that, from my perspective, had been undermined throughout Dr. Barr's course. I answered all the questions fairly well. But when I got to that Jonah question, I decided to stick it to my professor. This was my chance to stand up for my faith. The following excerpt from my long-ago notebook illustrates both the ignorance and dogmatic aspects of my Jesusgate upbringing. Here's what I wrote.

> Dear Dr. Barr, I believe that the Bible is without
> error. Furthermore, I do not believe that the Jonah story,

or any other biblical story, is metaphorical, symbolic, or mythological. I take these stories literally. Furthermore, if the Bible said that Jonah had swallowed the whale, rather than vise versa, I still would believe it. You've got to have faith, brother . . . you've got to have faith. Oh, ye of little faith.

My overall grade for that exam was a solid B. I was surprised because I thought sure I would get docked for those brazen comments. I was also surprised that Dr. Barr made no mention about my sophomoric lunacy. He simply wrote the following in red ink, underneath my statement: "Mr. Bringas, what is the meaning of this story?"

This was his way of helping me to see that the message or intent of the story is what really mattered. Whether or not the story was parabolic, mythical, or literal, was not the main issue (although at that time it was an idea I was still unable to fully embrace). But his mild-mannered approach to my indignation taught me a great deal about how one handles religious dogmatism and fanaticism. I try to apply that same approach with student and non-student alike, not always with success (some of my family members drive me crazy).

After three years of extensive learning, I graduated from seminary. Although I had not been the most attentive student, I was determined to take what I had learned about religious scholarship back into the local church. I was fortunate enough to be affiliated with the United Methodist Church which, compared to most other religious bodies, allowed for theological diversity. Even so, it didn't take long to find out why ministers are reluctant to practice the educational side of their ministry.

Earlier in this writing I listed several reasons why the clergy have failed to educate their congregants on even the most basic findings of biblical criticism. And I will continue to make the case that the clergy are primarily responsible for this knowledge gap. But that's not the whole story. As noted in the Introduction, the laity is also to blame. It seems that laypeople want simple answers to the most complex questions, and they want those answers couched within the womb of certainty. Although there are notable exceptions, the majority of believers push for the simple, cozy, "old time religion." But that's what they want from their ministers because they cannot fathom the alternative. Shades of the

movie, *A Few Good Men*, where Jack Nicholson shouts back at the pros-
ecutor, Tom Cruise: "You can't handle the truth!"

Lay people continue to nurture an erroneous assumption foisted
on them by the Jesusgate network: that which is considered sacred, is
also considered unalterable. Such thinking is misleading. I am reminded
here of that wonderful 1968 song, *The Boxer*, written by Paul Simon (of
Simon and Garfunkel). The lyrics remind us that people hear what they
want to hear and disregard the rest.

And so it is that most religious people are not interested in full disclosure. They are not prone to accept information that contradicts whatever it is they want to hear. Their interest lies solely in nourishing and
protecting the old time religion.

Having come from that mindset myself, I was not totally surprised
at some of the flak I received when trying to bring my parishioners up to
speed. Fortunately, I had some progressively minded people that offset
those negative attacks. But most ministers who try to bridge the knowledge gap find themselves in a heap of trouble. (I'll have more to say about
this in Chapter 13.)

So, what are ministers to do? "Can they drag believers kicking and
screaming into the information age? The difficulty of the situation is
such that relatively few ministers can bridge the two worlds. Usually,
the clergy will water down their personal beliefs in order to preach what
their congregants want to hear. This schizophrenic path of "let's pretend,"
serves only to feed the beast of religious illiteracy. Sadly, these clergy are
forced to maintain the status quo at the expense of truth and integrity. In
so doing, they become part of the Jesusgate camp.

Even the most learned theologians have not escaped this debilitating quandary. Harking back to Chapter 1, the following needs repeating.
Here again is the late scholar, Robert W. Funk, as he reflects on his personal failure to share his educational knowledge with congregants:

> Why had I not thought to share those things . . .
> with people in my church? Instead I do what many
> clergy do and that is dissemble [to hide one's true feel-
> ings or beliefs]. And I dissembled as much by what I
> didn't say as by what I did say.[1]
> [Brackets mine]

WHAT TO EXPECT NEXT

This chapter brings us to Jesusgate 3. We will briefly examine the historical circumstances that propelled this Jesusgate phenomenon into a "permanent" orbit. The evidence for Jesusgate 3 is quite clear. It's a doozey, the mother of all Jesusgates. It suppressed biblical criticism, and brought about the horrendous aftermath of religious illiteracy. (Thereafter, starting with Chapter 7 and continuing throughout, we will bring to light some of the findings from biblical criticism that I claim have been suppressed and ignored by popular Christianity.)

CHAPTER 6

JESUSGATE 3: IN ORBIT

(1500s to the Present)

RENAISSANCE: The great revival of art and learning in Europe during the 1300s, 1400s, and 1500s.

SCIENTIFIC REVOLUTION: The scientific revolution began roughly around 1543, the year that Nicolaus Copernicus published his book, *On the Revolutions of the Heavenly Orbs.* He argued for a heliocentric astronomical model (the sun, not the earth, is at the center of the solar system). This European revolution emphasizes the scientific method and is viewed as the foundation of modern science.

PROTESTANT REFORMATION: This was a movement against the Roman Catholic Church, started by Martin Luther in 1517. The reformers protested against some of the doctrines and practices of the Church. This led to the creation of the Protestant movement.

AGE OF REASON: This movement ran from the 1600s to the late 1700s in which European philosophers emphasized the use of reason as the best method of learning truth.

ENLIGHTENMENT: The European Enlightenment was in play during the 1700s and 1800s. It emphasized rationalism, intellectual freedom, and freedom from prejudice and superstition.

Every episodic Jesusgate has its unique spin, but its overarching purpose is to safeguard the Jesus persona (whatever that might be at any given time). Jesusgate 1 destroyed pagan religious literature in an effort to avoid any appearance of having downloaded some of their rituals and beliefs into the burgeoning Jesus story. Jesusgate 2 sought to crush all opposing Christological views not in tune with the Nicene Creed (Jesus and God are of the same substance). The only reason that laypersons today know little or nothing about Jesusgate 1 and 2 is because of Jesusgate 3. It bears repeating: Jesusgate 3 is also responsible for the nearly complete suppression of biblical analysis over the past few centuries. That is why religious illiteracy abounds.

JESUSGATE 3

We have been flirting with Jesusgate 3 since the very beginning of this work. But a nutshell definition for Jesusgate 3 is as follows: *Since the inception of biblical criticism 300 plus years ago, the clergy have failed to keep their parishioners informed about its many findings. As a result, a horrendous knowledge gap has formed between scholar and layperson, especially when it comes to understanding Jesus, and the many aspects of biblical development.* But why did this happen? The answer is a bit more complicated from what we have discussed thus far.

From a Western perspective, the seed of modern knowledge begins with the scientific revolution (see above definition). But some scholars believe that it was spearheaded as early as the thirteenth century Renaissance. Other scholars, however, trace its origins further back— back to the Muslims (700s AD) and even much further back to the Egyptians and Greeks (Greece was the birthplace of Western civilization about 2500 years ago). Nevertheless, for our purposes, we will accept Copernicus' work as the onset of modern science because, in Europe, it is here that the Scientific Revolution takes permanent root.

Some time after Chalcedon—probably in the 500s AD—until around the time of the Scientific Revolution (1500s), low ranking clergy and all laypersons were in the dark as regards the early development of Christianity. I say this for the following reasons.

First, universities were not well established before 1000, and not in full swing until 1350. Second, up until that time, European education was mainly restricted to monasteries (a religious community of monks or nuns) and cathedral schools such as Notre Dame in Paris, to which many of the clergy—and certainly the laity—had little or no access.

Third, even the religious education of the clergy was spotty and uneven, and mostly restricted to issues of faith and scripture (although they did study the church fathers).[2] Finally, not until the Council of Trent (meeting intermittently from 1545-63), did the Catholic Church order the founding of seminaries for the education of priests. "Up to this time there was no uniform standard, and a priest's theological training was inconsistent . . . The decision to create seminaries was an important and necessary corrective step, but it also enhanced the divide between the clergy and the faithful because priests received academic preparation . . . unavailable to the laity."[3] Protestant reformers had already promoted a well-educated clergy.

However, as I have stated, even today not all of the clergy are knowledgeable. As for those who are, most have failed to share with their congregants the emerging information from biblical criticism. They have done little to raise the religious KQ of their church members and, consequently, the general public. That's why people today are still thinking with a religious mindset that predates the seventeenth century; it is a mindset saturated with ignorance and obsolete concepts promoted by Jesusgaters unwilling or unable to change the status quo. *That's the crux of the problem we face today!*

Nevertheless, it is obvious to see that the continuing evolution for human advancement was jumpstarted by the Scientific Revolution, and the establishment of the university and seminary systems. The emphasis on the scientific method generated interest in natural law and human reason.

During the seventeenth and eighteenth centuries (1600s and 1700s), the continued interest in rational thought blossomed into what came to be known as the *Enlightenment*. It produced great thinkers like Galileo Galilei, René Descartes, John Locke, Isaac Newton, and many others. The Enlightenment, in concert with the Scientific Revolution, became the ghost buster force that radically changed all disciplines of knowledge. From the microscope to the telescope, scientific advancement became the sledgehammer that started pounding ignorance and superstition into submission (a process that continues to this very day). The field of religion was no exception as the discipline of higher criticism was developed. It was a Sputnik moment for all scholars when they accepted the scientific method as the best means for analytical investigation.

Eventually, however, the idea of investigating the sacred did not sit well with church leaders, even though at first they had encouraged the process. They never imagined that their scholars would discover findings contrary to Christian belief. Unlike practitioners in other fields of thought who embraced the liberating affects of the investigative process, the church hierarchy balked. Therefore, in those early days of the scientific method, the scholarly wing of Christianity was persecuted, ridiculed, or ignored. Our tandem bike—presumption and expediency—was on the road again (as always).

Earlier in this writing I spoke of the Inquisition as a tool for suppressing heretics. But a growing awareness of human rights, engendered by the Scientific Revolution and the Enlightenment, led to the abolishment of the Inquisition in the early 1800s. This created a climate of forced restraint. Church leaders could no longer send heretics to the stake. This did not, however, discourage them from striking out at scholars who seemed to be out of step with traditional beliefs. "In 1862, the entire bench of Anglican bishops in England condemned the authors of *Essays and Reviews* for advancing biblical criticism. Similarly, in 1881 the General Assembly of the Free Church of Scotland dismissed its most noted historical critical scholar, W. Robertson Smith, for the same offense."[4]

We have yet to eliminate this shameful practice of theological intolerance. For example, Father Edward Schillebeeckx, an eminent, university scholar was accused of heresy by the Catholic Church in 1979/83. He was charged with questioning the Resurrection and the Virgin Birth. Also, in 1979, the Catholic Church condemned one of its premier theologians, Hans Kung, for raising questions about the Virgin Birth, the inerrancy of scripture, and papal infallibility. Other examples from both sides of the aisle (Catholic and Protestant) could be given.

The point is, church leaders (Jesusgaters) were determined to shield churchgoers, and society as a whole, from any information that might undermine the pillars of faith—faith in the divinity of Jesus, and the infallibility of Bible and Church. Any scholarly findings that might challenge the trustworthiness of these "sacred cows" would not be tolerated. This resistance to modern knowledge applied not only to biblical criticism, but any and all fields of thought that collided with long-held Christian beliefs. Astronomy, as one example, had always been under the religious gun (poor Galileo). But eventually, science, by virtue of demonstrating the successful results of its methodology, could not be trumped by the religious establishment. Much later, for instance, if religionists tried to deny the principles of aerodynamics, their objections would be seen as absurd every time a plane flew overhead. The same would hold true for anyone who tried to deny the effectiveness of vaccines or antibiotics.

Inevitably, the Church was no match for the scientific community. Its loss of power was also hastened when Western society began its march toward the separation of powers—the separation of Church and State. It was this crucial separation, along with the establishment of human rights and civil liberties, not to mention the successive waves of knowledge engendered by the rise of the scientific method, which brought the secular world to center stage. All of this was highly enhanced by the incredible invention of Gutenberg's printing press (ca. 1440) that touched all levels of society. The first book to be printed was a Latin Bible.[5] The printing press is considered by many to be the greatest invention of the second millennium. It might have met its match with the computer. You decide.

Too, the Protestant Reformation (1517) dealt the Catholic Church a one-two punch when it negated the ultimate authority of Pope and Church; for Protestants, the Bible became the sole authority. Oh yes, we must not forget the contribution of King Henry VIII of England, albeit somewhat tainted, as he broke away from papal authority (check your encyclopedia or the Internet for this story, it's a good one). Oops, we also shouldn't forget the life-changing impact of the Industrial Revolution beginning in the late 1700s (the introduction of power-driven machines and the development of factory organization). All this is to say that it was the coming together of several influences during these few remarkable centuries that created a dramatic historical shift in how people came to live and what they came to believe.

Importantly, until these happenings occurred, the Church had almost total say over all aspects of society. But in combination, the above events (and some we haven't mentioned) gassed the presumptuous lungs of church leaders, driving them straight out of what they thought were impregnable castles of unquestionable authority.

Although the Church lost its dominating authority in the secular realm, it still had control over its own affairs. But how would church leaders handle the controversial findings of biblical scholarship that continued to emerge? How could they bring into question (as scholarship was prone to do) that which was considered sacred? Worse yet, the admission of having been wrong about some religious beliefs and assumptions might prove to be the death knell of priestly authority. Furthermore, the issuing of this new knowledge might only serve to nibble away at the very foundations of one's faith. What to do?

The Scientific Revolution and Enlightenment were an educational, scientific, and generally open-minded era of European history. It was during this progressive period that the unwritten policy of Jesusgate 3 emerged. True enough, scholars of religion pursued the quest for knowledge, as was the case for all other disciplines. But as already noted, laypersons were not made privy to the findings of biblical analysis (unlike other disciplines). Thanks in large measure to the clergy, a most damaging KQ gap opened up between scholars of religion and society as a whole. It was the Jesusgate crowd that clogged the pipeline between these two groups. (I acknowledge my redundancy here, but sometimes it's helpful to reemphasize central themes.)

Later, when the entire Church—Catholics, Protestants, and Eastern Orthodox—finally embraced the legitimacy of religious studies, the Jesusgate influence did not abate. The *clergy still failed* in their fiduciary (public trust) responsibility to keep their parishioners abreast of scholarly studies. I have already listed a number of reasons for this default (including presumption and expediency). The failure to educate also smacked of fear, arrogance, and the need to control; it was also prompted by the loss of confidence in the laity's ability to cope with this new knowledge.

Regardless, biblical criticism plowed ahead and became the sole island of sanity that rose high above the murky waters of Jesusgate 3. That is, the findings from this analytical discipline *could not be stymied in the academic community* as they were in the church. Unfortunately, until recently, several problems prevailed at the college level: (1) class selection was limited, (2) qualified instructors were sparse and, (3) signups were usually only by those interested in the various outlets of professional ministry. But today, following the 9/11 attacks in 2001, there is great interest in religion courses, especially World Religions. Furthermore, laypersons can now access many of the findings of biblical studies through libraries and, of course, the Internet. However, religious illiteracy dominates, even on the Internet (be careful here, check your sources). Although the Internet can provide some valuable information, this shark-infested medium is inundated with Jesusgate propaganda. The Internet may appear authoritative and informative and yet be neither.

Without the full weight of clergy cooperation, this paucity of knowledge within the ranks of the laity will continue. The church body must come to grips with its failure to educate its own. Given this failure, it becomes obvious that the most damaging of our three Jesusgates is Jesusgate 3. If the findings from biblical criticism had been allowed to trickle down to the laity over the past three centuries—as it has in other disciplines—everyone today would have a much more realistic understanding of the Jesus tradition and Christianity in general. But trickle down scholarship did not occur. If it had, there would be no Jesusgate 3; no loss of information; no formidable knowledge gap between scholar and layperson; no need for this book, and everything herein would be moot.

Tragically, to this very day, Jesusgate 3 continues virtually unnoticed, and, therefore, unchallenged (with some exceptions already noted). That being the case, we must focus on what Jesusgate 3 has taken away from us; that is, what scholarly findings or information are missing from a layperson's understanding of Jesus and Christianity overall? This question needs to be answered. Therefore, I will no longer explore the religious and social forces that created Jesusgate. Rather, my aim will be to traverse the theological chasm that I claim Jesusgate has created—the knowledge gap between scholar and layperson. *From this point forward, my sole objective will be to showcase the findings from biblical criticism.* Although some of this information has already been disclosed (mystery religions, Christology, the early church, etc.), there is much more to come.

Intro to Chapter 7

QUE SERA, SERA

Over the years I've written many songs. Perhaps you're familiar with *Que Sera, Sera*, sung by Doris Day. Or, maybe you've heard that Christmas classic, *Chestnuts Roasting on an Open Fire*, sung by Nat King Cole. Well, I wrote neither of those songs. Rats. Aside from a couple of Rip Chords' songs I co-wrote, most of my song writing efforts remain largely unknown, although they can be accessed on the Internet (Google: Homestead & Wolfe).

My point here is to highlight what happens to a song from its embryonic inception (humming a tune) to its fully developed end (CD). The transition is amazing: from caterpillar to butterfly (or vise versa). This artistic process, I believe, will serve as a prime example of how something moves from the most simplistic beginning to a highly complex and sophisticated ending (which may or may not be positive).

In the music world, the success of this endeavor rests squarely on the shoulders of the music producer (the equivalent of the movie director in the film industry). The producer will visualize the final product long before anyone enters the recording studio. Even so, the song will go through numerous alterations created not only by the producer (who calls the shots), but also by the arranger, musicians, singers, studio engineers, and so forth. They all bring something unique to the project. Accidental surprises are not uncommon. One way or another, the end product is redefined. In most cases, greatly enhanced. That's because everyone is looking for a way to help make the song stand out. In the industry it's called the "hook." It's not always clear where that hook will surface. Sometimes it's the vocal, a guitar lick, the arrangement, or any one of a number of possibilities in combination that can turn an otherwise mediocre song into a monster hit.

But sometimes, the final cut resonates disappointingly as expressed in Melanie Safka's 1970's hit, *Look What They've Done to My Song, Ma*. The lyrics clearly indicate that the songwriter's musical composition has been turned upside down. Melanie's woeful conclusion is that the finished product fails to reflect what she originally intended. Her anticipation was greater than the realization. Somebody messed up; somebody didn't get it right. It might have been a whole lot of somebodies. Whatever happened, the end result was disappointing.

The overarching lesson to be learned here goes far beyond music. My intent is much broader, especially as we contemplate the origination, development, and transmission of the New Testament. Indeed, how close to the original message of Jesus did we come? Did the New Testament writers (the producers) get it right? Did the scribes (copyists) who came later, get it right? They certainly produced the all-time mega-hit. Even so, would Jesus—assuming he could tell us—utter those frustrating words, "Look what they've done to my song"?

So how does one evaluate the soundness of one's belief—or evaluate anything, for that matter—without the knowledge at hand? How does one improve their religious RQ (Reality Quotient) without raising their KQ (Knowledge Quotient)?

WHAT TO EXPECT NEXT

Upcoming, we will begin to fend off the Jesusgate influence by disclosing some of our most elementary findings—derived from biblical criticism--about the New Testament Gospels (Matthew, Mark, Luke and John). This chapter will also include some general information about the New Testament's formulation, reproduction and transmission. Unless otherwise stated, *the term Jesusgate will hereinafter refer to Jesusgate 3* (the clergy's failure over the past few centuries to share the findings of religious scholarship with congregants).

CHAPTER 7

NEW TESTAMENT POTPOURRI

CANON: The canon is the official list of biblical books proclaimed by the Church to be genuine and inspired (sacred). All religions have their holy writings (their own canon).

CODEX (pl. **codices**): An ancient manuscript volume, especially one of the biblical books.

COPTIC: An ancient Egyptian language that now survives only as the liturgical language of the Coptic Orthodox Church (more than 95 percent of Egypt's Christians belong to this Church).

SCRIBE: A person who copied out documents before the printing press was invented. (In biblical times, also a teacher of the Jewish law.)

Before we proceed, there is yet another term—variant—that needs clarification. As one example, a variant reading is one that differs from the original or standard version. To ensure complete understanding, I will illustrate through a simple nursery rhyme.

STANDARD READING	VARIANT READING
Hickory Dickory Dock, The mouse ran up the clock. The clock struck one, The mouse ran down! Hickory Dickory Dock.	Hickory Dickory Dock, *Three mice* ran up the clock. The clock struck one, *And the other two,* *Escaped with minor injuries.*

In like manner, a literary variant is a later edition or copy of a biblical manuscript that differs from the standard or accepted version because it has been altered or modified in some way. Take heed, you will find this term (variant) throughout our next few chapters.

NEW TESTAMENT POTPOURRI

The NT, as we know it today, contains 27 books (originally written in Greek).

Four of these books—Matthew, Mark, Luke, and John—are called Gospels (good news). Traditionally, the Gospels are thought to reflect the sayings and doings of Jesus. Therefore, they are central to our understanding of Jesus. Before we look at some specifics about their composition (the subject of our next chapter), let's take a look at some accepted overall facts about the New Testament in general.

All of these NT books have journeyed through an incredible, and some would say chancy, process of selection and development. Some of these books circulated independently for 300 years before they were integrated. Traditionally, it is accepted that Athanasius, Bishop of Alexandria (in Egypt), listed the 27 NT books as canon in 367 AD. But how many books were not selected, and why? How does the NT we have in hand measure up to the *autographs* (original manuscripts)? Do we even have the originals? What happened to these writings in transmission? Were they accurately transcribed over the course of multiple centuries? Do they preserve the original meanings intended by their authors? If not, what kind of distortions occurred? What about the unintentional and intentional changes that scribes made during reproduction? What about the old (and revered) King James Version of the Bible (AKA: KJV)—how does it stack up against our newest translations? Indeed, how do our newest translations stack up against each other? Again, what about those non-canonical writings (those gospels that were excluded from the NT)? To help us answer these questions, there are several important points we need to take into consideration.

CONSIDERATION #1 (The Non-Canonical Books)

Scholars now know that at least twenty (not four) original gospels existed in early Christianity. This means that a whole bunch of gospels didn't make the cut when the Church finalized the canon. As we shall see, some of them were unsuited for serious consideration. Ironically, however, a few of these non-canonical gospels, according to some prominent scholars, may contain traditions about Jesus that are earlier than the Gospels of the New Testament.[1]

Prior to the close of 200 AD, the so-called Church (it was not yet a unified body) had only reached a semblance of consensus about which of the many books in circulation should be made official and which doctrinal creeds should be adopted. As noted by scholar Elaine Pagels:

> Before that time [200 AD], as Irenaeus and others attest, numerous gospels circulated among various Christian groups, ranging from those of the New Testament, Matthew, Mark, Luke, and John, to such writings as the *Gospel of Thomas*, the *Gospel of Philip*, and the *Gospel of Truth* [to name a few], as well as many other secret teachings, myths, and poems attributed to Jesus or his disciples . . . Those who identified themselves as Christians entertained many—and radically differing—religious beliefs and practices. And the communities scattered throughout the known world organized themselves in ways that differed widely from one group to another.[2] [Brackets mine]

I highlighted this theological diversity in Chapter 5. Remember our 31 flavors? Aside from ice cream, I also love chocolate. That reminds me of the Forrest Gump movie: "My momma always said, 'Life is like a box of chocolates. You never know what you're gonna get.'"

So imagine if you will a box of assorted chocolates, and liken them to an assortment of Christianities scattered throughout the Mediterranean world. Because of these multi-flavored beliefs, as revealed in the numerous non-canonical gospels and other writings now in our possession, it is obvious that faith convictions (what early Christians believed and what they were writing and reading) were anything but uniform. Many of the early Christians found themselves on opposite sides of a wide range of beliefs. What eventually became orthodox (the accepted norm) was originally up for grabs.

The point is that Christians today are not aware of the many possible Jesus traditions, the many portraits of Jesus, the many Jesus' that might have been. What happened to all those would-be contenders, and the many gospels that never made it into the canon? How different might our Bibles[3] look today and, consequently, Jesus, if the Church had canonized these works at a different point in the historical timeline? In other words, the time and place would dictate different cultural, political, and theological pressures, making the overall process of book selection somewhat contingent on those factors.

I do believe, however, that considerable overlap of our present Jesus configuration would still have surfaced in whichever mix of NT books had been chosen. On the other hand, some of Jesus' acts and teachings would certainly be modified, new, or missing had the NT books been canonized earlier (or later), making the Jesus story somewhat different.[4] For example, the non-canonical *Gospel of Philip* (ca. 275 AD) argues that those who believe Mary (the mother of Jesus) was impregnated by the Holy Spirit "are in error."[5] There goes the Virgin Birth.

(The brackets that follow in the next paragraph are not mine; they indicate a *lacuna* {a gap or empty space} in the ancient manuscript. With imagination, scholars try to fill in the blanks.)

The *Gospel of Philip* implies that Jesus and Mary Magdalene were romantically coupled. It refers to her as his "companion" and suggests that Jesus "[. . . loved] her more than [all] the disciples [and used to] kiss her [often] on her [. . .]."[6] I can see why they left this gospel out of the NT.

That last lacuna is intriguing. Some scholars push the envelope when they insert the word "lips" or "mouth" in that last lacuna. Wisely, most scholars leave it blank. There is no way for them to know if Jesus kissed her on the lips, the forehead, the cheek, or elsewhere. What a place for a lacuna!

There are some other non-canonical gospels that tell very weird stories about Jesus. For instance, The *Infancy Gospel of Thomas* (ca. 175 AD)—not to be confused with the *Gospel of Thomas*, another non-canonical book—portrays a five-year-old Jesus fashioning twelve sparrows out of clay at the waters edge. Unfortunately, Jesus is playing on the Sabbath. That's a no-no because it violates Jewish law. A nearby busybody runs to tell Jesus' father, Joseph, about this transgression. Joseph admonishes Jesus: "Why do you do on the Sabbath what ought not to be done?" In response, Jesus simply claps his hands, brings the birds to life, gives them flight, and sends them away chirping.[7]

As a note of interest, I fortuitously discovered that the Qur'an, Islam's holy book, touches on this incident. It is found in sura (chapter) 5:110 and reads as follows:

> Then will Allah say: "O Jesus the son of Mary . . .
> Behold! I strengthened you with the holy spirit, so that
> you spoke to the people in childhood and in maturity . . .
> you made out of clay, as it were, the figure of a bird . . . and
> you breathed into it, and it became a bird, by My leave.[8]

I find this Qur'anic quote of interest because it tells me that Muhammad—who died in 632 AD and was supposedly illiterate—was reading the *Infancy Gospel of Thomas* in the early 600s AD. It is possible, of course, that someone was reading it to him, or, it was being recited as oral tradition. Although The *Infancy Gospel of Thomas* had not been selected as part of the NT Canon in 367 AD, it appears that it was still in circulation these many centuries later.

Anyway, as this gospel story continues, another boy takes a willow branch and disturbs the water where Jesus is playing. Jesus becomes enraged and says to him: "You insolent, godless dunderhead . . . now you shall wither like a tree . . . and immediately that lad withered up completely." Jesus kills another child simply because the child accidentally bumps into him. Naturally, parents become concerned. They go to Joseph and tell him: "Since you have such a child, you cannot dwell with us in the village; or else teach him to bless and not to curse. For he is slaying our children . . . . And immediately those who had accused him became blind."[9] (These accounts remind me of that TV "Twilight Zone" episode where an entire farming community is terrorized by a child. He can read minds and make people disappear at will. Scary stuff if you can imagine it.) By the way, at the end of this gospel, Jesus has a change of heart; the blind regain their sight, and the dead are brought back to life. Sweet.

As we condescendingly smile at these odd renditions about Jesus, we would do well to remember that if these, or other gospels, had been included in the canon, some of the above stories would be almost as credible and acceptable as those we presently accept in our Holy Scriptures. Conversely, if the NT Gospels we now have had not been selected as part of the canon, their stories about Jesus turning water into wine, walking on the water, and raising Lazarus from the dead, would seem equally peculiar as those we just read from the *Gospel of Philip*; we probably would exhibit that same condescending smile. The difference is that we are so familiar with the NT Gospels in hand that we accept these strange stories as natural and acceptable; that is, we're so used to them that any question about their oddity, has long since faded. Another reason for this carte blanche acceptance, of course, is based on the presumption of unquestionable biblical authority—that is to say, if it's in the Bible it must be true. Be that as it may, scholars believe that these supernatural stories—biblical or non-biblical—are simply different sides of the same mythological pancake, served up to us from the ancient world.

A TAD OUTSIDE THE BOX by Ernie Bringas

Lazurus Goes To Heaven

CONSIDERATION # 2 (The Early Stages of NT Development and Reproduction)

It's the Real Thing. Many of us—certainly coke lovers—will recognize that phrase. It's the 1969-75 Coca-Cola slogan. The jingle rings true as Coca-Cola remains the most popular soda worldwide, although Pepsi isn't far behind.

In 1985, the Coke people supposedly decided to destroy the old safe-locked Coco-Cola formula. Horror of horrors, they were getting rid of the one that "brung them to the dance." Their newly formulated dance partner would be the NEW COKE, thought to be, better tasting. Well, people went crazy...remember? One would have thought the world was coming to an end as Coke lovers rose up in a unified outcry. The story took front page and the media had a field day. As Lucy might say, "Good Grief, Charlie Brown!"

Finally, the Coca-Cola executives yielded to the mounting chorus of dissent. They cancelled their so-called plan to destroy the formula, which, according to them, would have been lost forever. Yeah, right. Anyway, this Humpty Dumpty scenario never came to pass, and we still have *the real thing.*

IN THE ABSENCE OF KINKO'S
(now known as FedEx Office)

Unfortunately, when it comes to the Gospels (or any of the other biblical books in our possession), we cannot say that we have *the real thing*. Except for the very first "Christians," of course, *we have never possessed any of the original NT books.* They were lost or destroyed early on. The copies we do have were made much later. *We don't even possess copies of the first copies of the original copies of the originals.* (You might have to read that last sentence twice.)

Scholars believe that all of the original NT books were handwritten in Greek. In fact, for thirteen centuries thereafter, all the copies of the copies of the originals will also be handwritten—handwritten in the languages of Greek, Latin, Coptic, and so forth. This will make them very susceptible to both intentional and unintentional changes. As we shall see shortly, the texts do not remain virgin. The copies we do possess are certainly not replicas of the originals. Not until Gutenberg's invention of the printing press, ca. 1440, are the problems associated with this method of transcribing eliminated.

Almost all scholars agree that the first NT book to be written was one of Paul's letters, ca. 50 AD (either 1 Thessalonians or Galatians). The earliest, *substantial* copied fragments that we have of those originals date from about 175 AD (although we do have a postcard size fragment of John's Gospel, which is arguably dated ca. 125 AD).

There is also consensus that the first Gospel to be written was Mark, around 70 AD. But the earliest copy of Mark that we possess dates forward to ca. 250 AD. Our earliest complete NT manuscript (all 27 NT books with two additions) is a Greek text known as the Codex Sinaiticus that dates around 350 AD. It includes two additional books called the *Shepherd of Hermas* and the *Epistle of Barnabas*. Those two books were excluded when Athanasius, in 367 AD, listed his NT canon of 27 books, which we have today. Another significant Greek manuscript, although incomplete, is known as the Codex Vaticanus and also dates from about ca. 350 AD; it lacks 1 and 2 Timothy, Titus, Philemon, and Revelation. These two codices (Sinaiticus and Vaticanus) are the most important sources for helping scholars reconstruct the New Testament.

Okay, that's the skeletal framework of the earliest NT copies in our possession, beginning with the substantial fragments from ca. 175 AD. until our more substantial selection in 367 AD. After that time period, more and more copies of all the NT books were made; thousands of more copies would follow, painstakingly handwritten over the centuries by the scribes. Shortly, we will explore their overall journey. That is, their process of reproduction and transmission, up until the time that handwriting was made obsolete by the printing press.

But first, let's stop and think about the NT *originals that we do not possess.* This would include not only the originals, but also the initial copies of those originals. They're long gone. So what can we speculate about what we don't have? Let's see.

Scholars have concluded that even the earliest NT copies that we do possess are highly unlikely to be exact copies of the originals. But the question arises: *How can scholars know that the copies we do possess are flawed if they don't have the originals for a baseline comparison?* The answer to that question comes from analyzing the copy process itself, and the resulting aftermath of that process. That is, scholars recognize what happens to handwritten copies when they are recopied. For example, *by cross-checking any number of manuscripts in our possession* (be they copies of Homer's *Odyssey* or copies of the NT) scholars can clearly see that the process of recopying is not fail-safe; it is anything but error-free. *It's a fact: The hard evidence indicates that handwritten documents become flawed when they are recopied* (more so as the copy process progresses over time). If an exception to this rule of thumb exists, it would have to be the Jewish Torah (check it out).

In any case, one can conclude, almost to a certainty, that the earliest copy of Mark we possess (ca. 250 AD) is not an exact copy of the lost original Gospel of Mark that we don't possess (first written around 70 AD). We don't know what changes occurred between70 and 250 AD, but we surmise that they did. The evidence for this conclusion is very strong. When we compare all of the later NT copies against each other that were made over the centuries, the variance between them becomes greater with each new handwritten reproduction. In other words, with each passing generation of copying, the distortions multiply (we will revisit this issue shortly).

Therefore, it would be ludicrous to believe that anything different happened during the earliest stages of NT reproduction simply because we don't have the originals to compare with the copies that followed. To believe otherwise, one would have to suspend what is most logical and obvious about what happens to documents when they are hand copied over and over again. Too, we must remember that although the early NT books were certainly important, they were not yet considered sacred as a canonized body.

With the overwhelming evidence of copy imperfection, many conservative Christians now admit that the NT copies we possess are not pristine. But they will insist that the original writings were perfect because they were under the supervision and protection of the Holy Spirit (HS) and, therefore, were the absolute Word of God. Of course, we don't have the originals so there is no way to prove or disprove that assertion. Even if that assertion were true, what good would it do us now since we no longer have those exact words? Such a claim makes no sense.

Equally strange, why would the Holy Spirit give up this early supervision of the NT originals and not extend that careful oversight to the copies that followed? It's obvious that any such attentive supervision disappears because the later copies are filled with errors and contradictions relative to each other. If the HS practiced vigilance over the original manuscripts that we no longer have, why did that vigilance come to a screeching halt as evidenced by the later manuscripts we do have? That is to say, why would the HS protect our NT books in the short run, and then abandon them so as to allow literary deterioration over the long run?

As a note of interest, even if we had the real thing (for example, the original Gospels), or even a Kinko's copy of the real thing, we still wouldn't have the exact words or actions of Jesus for the following two reasons. First, mainstream scholars do not believe that the Gospels are eyewitness accounts of what Jesus said and did. If scholars are right about this, many of the words attributed to Jesus, as one example, cannot be verbatim (this issue will be fully examined in the following chapter). Although the essence of Jesus' teachings might be captured by way of the grapevine, one could not persuasively argue that the Gospels contained his exact words. New Testament scholars have proclaimed this for at least three hundred years, but the Jesusgate majority continues to ignore or smother that message.

Second, although Jesus may have been acquainted with Greek—the international language of the day—the Jews in Palestine primarily spoke Aramaic. Therefore, we are fairly certain that Jesus delivered his teachings in Aramaic,[10] his mother tongue. And if Jesus spoke in Aramaic, then his exact words to us are lost forever because the original Gospels were written in Greek. Translating from Aramaic to Greek would not exactly capture the original. So, from the very beginning we had a translation about the real thing, but by virtue of it being a translation, it could not have been the real thing. That would be true of any translation. Of course, reasonable people would conclude that the translation would nevertheless convey a high degree of accuracy.

Even so, scholars must continue to connect these dots in their overall assessment of the New Testament. They neither can ignore the probable distortion of grapevine conveyance (oral tradition), the difficulties of translation, nor the off-centered results of transcribing numerous manuscripts over the centuries.

CONSIDERATION # 3
(The Later Stages of NT Reproduction)

When the Church finalized the NT Canon in 367 AD, many wannabe books were eliminated from biblical consideration. Up until that time, various religious factions argued vehemently for writings they thought should be included as part of the sacred text. Some of these books were held in high esteem while others were rejected outright as heretical, all depending, of course, on the eye of the beholder. However, once the Church settled on the twenty-seven books that would constitute the Holy Text, most everyone fell into line.

After the canonization of the New Testament in 367, the copy process continued on as numerous Greek-language editions of it were prolifically recopied. Although we have thousands of Coptic, Latin, and Syrian copies of the NT in our possession, the Greek-language codices remain our most important sources for cross-checking NT reliability. They came first. Additionally, the writings of the early Church Fathers offer up clues in the search for NT authenticity. For the biblical scholar, it's a balancing act between hardcore evidence, probabilities, and relentless probing of the material.

Today, we have approximately 5,500 of these Greek manuscripts in hand (most of them incomplete). These numerous hand copied manuscripts range in date from the second to the fifteenth century. When these NT documents are analyzed and compared with one another, there is no question or speculation about their variance. Scholars can clearly see that they were changed in many ways as they were recopied over and over. The fact is, none of these manuscripts totally agree with each other. But here's the kicker: *If we compared twenty Greek NT copies of Matthew with each other, we would probably not find one of them identical throughout even a single chapter . . . not one!*[11] New Testament scholar Bart Ehrman puts it this way:

> We don't know how many differences there are among these copies because no one has been able to add them all up. But the total is in the hundreds of thousands. Possibly it is easiest to put the matter in comparative terms: there are more differences in our manuscripts than there are words in the New Testament.[12]

Imagine that for just a moment. Taking the average of various sources, the number of words in the New Testament is about 160,000. That's at least how many differences, contradictions, and errors we have between our numerous New Testament manuscripts. This hardly bodes well for anyone who believes that the Bible is divinely inspired to the point of perfection. (Again, we hear Melanie's joyless and repeated refrains to her mother about the ruination of her creative work. *Look What They've Done to My Song, Ma.*) Can biblical transmission really be that flawed?

On the one hand, we must be careful not to overstate the situation because in most cases, these discrepancies are insignificant (for example, a misspelled word, or words and sentences accidentally overlooked). On the other hand, some of these variant manuscripts can present serious problems. That is why scholars are constantly searching through them, trying to ferret out mistakes and additions that are not reflected in our earliest, most reliable, NT sources. Naturally, restoring the NT as best we can to its original form is important, especially when it pertains to the Gospel sayings and doings of Jesus. But how can this be accomplished if we don't have the original books as a baseline for comparison?

THE ART OF TEXTUAL CRITICISM

At this point it should be very clear to us that any attempt to reconstruct a *perfect* replica of the original NT without the original texts or initial copies, is *impossible.* Even so, the task for scholars is to analyze the thousands of surviving manuscripts so as to reconstitute the most *probable likeness* of the original. That's the best we can hope for and it's not an easy task. (In NT scholarship, this process is known as textual criticism, a subdivision of biblical criticism.)

If I paraded out all the methods used by textual scholars in this process, we'd be mired down in an excess of information far beyond the scope of this work. Therefore, as an example, I will limit myself to one rule of thumb that most textual critics follow in helping them make these difficult determinations. I call it . . .

THE EARLY BIRD GETS THE WORM
(How's that for originality?)

Here's a Rule of thumb for measuring the historical reliability of long ago manuscripts: Almost any document that is closer in time to the event it describes, is *more likely* to be historically reliable than those that come after it. That's because the early sources are less prone to be modified or embellished, as are their later editions. On that account, the early bird gets the nod.

Obviously, you can't remove the human element from the copy process. Therefore, intentionally or unintentionally, exaggeration and theological bias will creep into the handwritten copy process. Alterations are inevitable and lead to the growing of Pinocchio's nose. This literary corruption, between early and later editions, becomes obvious when one compares, for example, a fourth century manuscript (such as the Codex Sinaiticus or Vaticanus), with a seventh century NT manuscript. The content between the two can differ widely.

However, noted conservative scholar, Raymond E. Brown, inserts a word of caution about the "early bird" argument. For example, he argues that a 6th century manuscript could be more reliable than a 4th century manuscript because it may have been copied from a now lost NT manuscript that was even earlier than the 4th-century document we possess.[13] Of course, such a scenario is possible. But how can we know that such a "manuscript" ever existed? This blind alley hypothesis, in my view, does not mitigate (lessen) the overall strength of the early bird rule of thumb. There is overwhelming evidence for early bird reliability as reflected in the study of *all literary genres.* Nevertheless, one must acknowledge that some variables could exist, in addition to the one that Raymond Brown has proposed, that on occasion—be it ever so seldom—could nullify the early bird rule. It's possible, but unlikely. So let's continue with some early bird examples.

As I stated earlier, most variant readings are inconsequential, but not so in other cases. By the comparative analysis of the many NT manuscripts we possess, contradictions between the texts are readily exposed. And it's not always about how these manuscripts might contradict each other. Sometimes it's a question about why certain material is *added* or *excluded* in the later NT manuscripts when compared to our earliest and best manuscripts.

A case in point is the classic story we find in the Gospel of John (8:3-11). To recap, the scribes and the Pharisees bring an adulterous woman before Jesus. They remind Jesus that according to the Law of Moses in the OT, adultery carries the penalty of death by stoning. So what is Jesus to do: condone the killing of this condemned woman, or break the sacred Law of Moses? Jesus finds himself exactly where the Pharisees want him—in a no-win situation. But it is here that Jesus delivers one of his most memorable lines: "He who is without sin, let him cast the first stone." (This wording comes from the King James Version of the Bible which I seldom use because our newer translations are much more accurate. Not so in this case, and the rendering was too pithy to pass up.) If you're not familiar with the story's outcome, the woman is no longer condemned because Jesus left no one with a leg to stand on (so to speak).

Most people will be shocked to discover that this story is not biblical; that is, scholars do not believe that it was ever part of the original Gospel. That is why in most of our modern Bibles you'll find double brackets ([[. . . .]]) at the beginning and ending of the story. The double brackets indicate that the story was not original to the Gospel but was added at a later date. One reason for thinking so is that the story is absent from our earliest and best manuscripts. Another reason for thinking so is that the Greek writing style is significantly different from the rest of the Gospel. Therefore, scholars consider it to be an addition (tacked on) to the original text.[14]

Whether or not Jesus actually uttered those famous lines is unimportant to me. Based on what we can glean from the NT, the story is very characteristic of what Jesus might say under those circumstances. I now see the story as a non-biblical parable about Jesus, not a literal story as many believe. However, I still see it as a beautiful story with a powerful message and I'm glad we still have it (albeit in double brackets).

Another example of the "early bird gets the worm" (that earlier sources are better than later sources) has to do with the Gospel of Mark, the very first Gospel to be written. Although Matthew appears first in the NT, it was written after Mark (as we shall see in the following chapter.) Here's the problem or, should I say, here come the double brackets again.

Our earliest Greek copies of Mark end at 16:8 (the short version) and are therefore thought to reflect the best approximation of the original writing. The longer version verses 9-20 are now in double brackets. In addition to being absent in our earliest manuscripts, this longer ending of Mark also seems to have been unknown by the early Church Fathers.

The short ending—which excludes verses 9-20—is very abrupt inasmuch as the women, who find the empty tomb, simply run away in fear and say nothing to anyone. That's how Mark ends his story. There is nothing said about the resurrection appearances of Jesus, not even appearances to his disciples let alone anyone else. This lack of detailed information about the risen Christ, we surmise, led to additional verses by later writers who were unsettled by this ending (as remedied by the three Gospel writers that followed Mark). Again, in our best NT translations today, all "Markan" verses that follow 16:8 are in double brackets. (If double brackets are not used in your Bible, some notation or footnote should draw your attention. If not, get yourself an updated Bible if you want more accuracy.)

Sometimes one might overlook this bracketed or footnoted material; you might miss it if you're not on the lookout. For example, in Luke's account of Jesus' Passion (the suffering and death of Jesus), we find that verses 43 and 44 in chapter 22 have been bracketed, as in *The New Oxford Annotated Bible*:

> [[Then an angel from heaven appeared to him and gave him strength. In his anguish he prayed more earnestly, and his sweat became like great drops of blood falling down on the ground.]]

Again, these verses do not appear in our earliest and best manuscripts. Furthermore, they're out of sync with Luke's overall presentation of Jesus as calm, cool, and collected. Some scholars believe that a later scribe inserted these verses so as to *harmonize* Luke's Gospel with Mark's Gospel in which Jesus is portrayed as unsettled and very much in anguish. [15]

Textual scholars are quick to notice that this harmonization (the tendency by later scribes to rewrite portions of one book in order to make it coincide with another book) was a common practice. Frankly, scribes were eliminating or reducing discrepancies between the copies they were reading and the copies they were reproducing. Through harmonization they smoothed out what they considered embarrassing contradictions and anomalies between the texts. The purpose for this fiddling and editing was not only to eliminate awkward contradictions, but also to preserve the authoritative concept of divine revelation—revelation that came to be regarded as God-given. Whatever their motivation, by eliminating textual discrepancies, they were sweeping, figuratively speaking, the dirt under the rug. *Please note, however, that it was not a complete sweep. Numerous discrepancies between the texts remained.*

Nevertheless, scribes were able to make some of the later NT copies appear as though they uniformly agreed with each other because copyists were simply reproducing harmonized copies in greater numbers as the years rolled by. This gave later generations the false impression that the NT had always enjoyed smooth sailing almost to the point of being flawless. Even today, people try to make a case for biblical integrity—albeit erroneously—based on the thousands of later manuscripts that do agree with each other without taking into consideration the earliest manuscripts that don't agree with the later copies. They fail to factor in the scribal influence that created this harmonious illusion. But if they take that approach, as most uninformed people do (the Internet is replete with this nonsense), they're missing the point of "the early bird gets the worm" rule of textual criticism; it's not the quantity, it's the quality. Who cares if thousands of these later manuscripts are in agreement with each other if, as it turns out, they're not in agreement with our earliest, most reliable written sources! That's what makes our earliest manuscripts so vital and precious in trying to reconstruct the original NT; by virtue of their earliness, they are more likely to reflect what those missing originals contained and, therefore, they must take precedence over later copies. Textual critics, in our modern translations, have reinstated our earliest renderings that, in many respects, are no longer in sync with the King James Bible.

This reminds me of the 80-year-old monk who had served at the monastery since youth. He had spent a lifetime helping other monks recopy the numerous manuscripts at hand. One day it dawned on him: They were all copying from copies, not from the earliest manuscripts that were locked away in the monastery basement. He reasoned that if some-one had made even a small error along the way, it would be continued in all of the subsequent copies. Following his hunch, the old monk headed for the basement with the latest copy in hand to compare against the earliest manuscripts.

Three days went by and no one had seen the elderly monk. So, the other monks got worried and went to the basement looking for him. They found him wailing and banging his head against the wall. He sobbed uncontrollably as they tried to settle him down. With a choking voice the old monk cried out: "We got it wrong! We got it wrong! We got it wrong! The word was "celebrate," not celibate!

I know I'm repeating myself, but the point is worth stressing: the manuscripts that are closer in time to the events they describe, are much more likely to be historically reliable than those that come after. Therefore, by comparing the later manuscripts with the earliest ones, accumulative deletions, additions, or distortions in the ensuing versions are easy to spot by textual scholars. The word was "celebrate," not celibate!

In pursuit of producing the purest form of the original NT text, schol-ars continue to look for flaws, theological bias, misstatements, and other peculiarities. For example, sometimes scribes would write comments in the margins of some of these manuscripts, only to be inserted into the text proper by subsequent scribes many years later. Since the material was not part of the original document, it therefore needed to be deleted or bracketed in our modern translations.

As we have seen, double brackets (or footnotes) are used to set aside those portions of scripture that are doubtfully genuine to the original. What most Christians don't realize, however, is that sometimes the brackets aren't used, and the words in question are simply deleted from the text. Those words and phrases just disappear from the *newer transla-tions* and no one's the wiser, unless they are well-known verses. For example, check out the Lord's Prayer in Matthew 6:9-13 and you'll discover that the familiar ending most of us grew up with, is missing: *"For yours is the kingdom and the power and the glory forever, amen."* No brackets here, the words have simply been removed from our newest translations because scholars can show that this rendition is the embellishment of later writers and scribes.

Along these same lines, sometimes material is deleted from the text and goes unnoticed as such. For example, you can't dial up Matthew 23:14, Mark 7:16, or Luke 17:36; you will find that those particular verses have been excised from the chapters. They're simply gone and no one seems to notice even though the numbering sequence is interrupted (as in the case of Matthew, the verses jump from 13 to 15, because verse 14 is missing). Most modern translations will footnote the anomaly, and credit the missing line to other ancient authorities. I often think of tex-tual scholars as literary vacuum cleaners: They bracket or delete those portions of scripture that do not occur in our earliest and best NT manu-scripts.

As I mentioned earlier, most alterations found in our medieval man-uscripts are insignificant and are simply the result of misspelled words or the understandable miscue of a sleepy scribe. On the other hand, as we also noted, the early bird versions help textual scholars recognize that within the later (most recent) manuscripts, some significant changes have occurred. Sometimes these ensuing alterations try to support a particular early Church doctrine. In other words, the biblical verse is nuanced or embellished to promote or support a particular theological belief. Take for example the doctrine of the Trinity. (The following infor-mation has been taken—but also rewritten—from one of my previous publications.)[16]

Around 405 AD, a Latin translation of the Bible called the Vulgate was completed by St. Jerome (a biblical scholar, and one of the first theologians to be called a Doctor of the Christian Church). Over the centuries, an estimated 8,000 copies were eventually reproduced. In the *early copies* of the Vulgate, the scriptural passage in question, 1 John 5:7-8 (not to be confused with the Gospel of John) read as follows:

> There are three that bear witness, the spirit and the water and the blood, and the three are one.

In the *later editions* of the Vulgate, the passage was changed to read:

> There are three which bear witness on Earth, the spirit and the water and the blood, and these three are one in Christ Jesus: and there are three who bear witness in heaven, the Father, the Word, and the Spirit, and these three are one.[17]

Here, then, is an expansion of the earlier text that helps to drive the Trinitarian concept from the implicit to the explicit. It became the primary so-called Trinitarian verse in the Bible (two other NT writers use Trinitarian language, although it is not yet a doctrine).[18] Over the past centuries, countless numbers of Christians have used this embellished version as a tidy argument to support the Trinitarian doctrine.

But plainly, this last rendering could not have been part of the original text of 1 John because the Greek manuscripts that *long preceded* the Vulgate do not include it. More than that, even the early copies of the Vulgate don't include it. According to the world-renowned scholar Bruce Metzger (the late Professor of NT Literature and Language at Princeton Theological Seminary), this expanded version was evidently made-up because it did not appear in the Vulgate editions until ca. 800 AD[19] (a good four hundred years after the first Vulgate edition was produced). Since none of the Greek manuscripts and none of the early versions of the Vulgate have this rendition, it is clearly a serious embellishment of the original writing. New Testament scholar, Bart D. Ehrman, goes so far as to call the Trinity a Christian invention, based in part on biblical verses that do not actually appear in the earliest copies of the New Testament.[20]

My personal view is that this rewrite was the work of an over zealous scribe who sought to bring this scripture into line with the newly proclaimed Trinitarian doctrine as formulated by the Council of Nicea (325 AD) and "finalized" at the Council of Chalcedon (451 AD). Whatever the case, most of our newer translations have deleted the excess wording. I can't help but wonder, however, about the many people who once relied on what they thought was unquestionable scripture as solid evidence for the Trinity. In their original format, the verses were not devoid of meaning, but they did not *explicitly* convey Trinitarian support.

Our last example of 1 John (again, not to be confused with the Gospel of John), illustrates the fact that textual critics, using the early bird method (one of several methods), can apply this process to all our existing biblical manuscripts. (Appendix B will provide further information on textual criticism *related to the treatment of women*, especially as it pertains to the writings of Paul.) Check it out it's worth the read. Before moving on, there are four special points I'd like to make about textual criticism and NT reliability.

First, it seems that some people want to make NT reliability (or unreliability) an issue of extremes. That is, diehard, evangelical Christians make claims for the inerrancy of scripture (as totally reliable, totally accurate), while diehard skeptics want to toss it out altogether. The Internet is replete with these extremes but none of them are appropriate.

The accuracy of any text is not simply a matter of truth or untruth; it's a matter of degree. In other words, all NT manuscripts contain truths, half-truths and falsehoods. The question is, how much truth and how much falsehood? For example, through the painstaking efforts of the textual critic, most scholars believe that we can reconstruct a reasonable likeness of the original wording. In this respect, the reconstructed copy would be more accurate, rather than inaccurate, as compared to the original—not perfect mind you, but fairly on target. This is a debatable point, of course, because we don't have the originals or their initial copies to compare with even the earliest copies we do possess. Therefore, we cannot possibly know how many changes of consequence occurred in those intervening years. Nevertheless, most textual scholars are confident that we now have a reasonable reproduction of the original NT in our hands. But even if we had the originals, they could not tell us if the theological content was accurate; that is, was Jesus truly divine, was he really the Son of God, and so forth. Those are metaphysical concepts of faith and belief that are not subject to historical confirmation. That is left to the reader, not the scholar (although scholars, like anyone else, can voice there opinions).

Our evolving KQ about the NT, however, does cast its influence in helping us understand what is most historically plausible. With this knowledge upgrade, we can then make realistic judgments as to how personal matters of faith will be accepted, rejected, or readjusted. (This should be a long life process.) *Importantly, one must recognize that historical accuracy (or lack thereof) is not the sole criterion by which faith in the Jesus story is measured. The power and meaning of all religions go far beyond their historical verifications. But that's another story, which I have not undertaken in this writing.*

My second point about textual criticism and reliability deals with the never-ending need for new translations. We need to understand why newer translations of the Bible are necessary as opposed to the popular belief—consciously or subconsciously—that we have a fixed Bible (a divine revelation from God that needs no help getting straightened out). I'm sure that textual criticism makes it clear that we cannot rest on this misguided assumption of unalterable revelation. Even if we do not find any new undiscovered manuscripts (as we did with the Dead Sea Scrolls and the Nag Hammadi discovery), biblical criticism will continue to enlighten us.

Third, as our understanding of the Greek lexicon (Greek language) increases, so will the need for newer translations. Additionally, the English language is not static. I can remember when "bad," or "gay," had only one meaning. Without a doubt, scholars will continue to persevere in their quest for a more accurate biblical rendering.

Fourth, we must remember that the NT we purchase today, has been pieced together by textual scholars. After sorting and cross analyzing thousands of NT Greek manuscripts and other writings in hand, textual scholars have assembled the NT in accordance with their best judgment. The Bible you have in hand is the finished product of that judgment. It is a compilation of thousands of NT documents, honed down to their most common denominator. This end product is what textual scholars believe to be the most probable NT rendering.

This "final draft," like a football, is also handed off to other scholars for study. The almost unanimous acceptance of this "final draft," creates a uniform baseline for non-textual scholars to further the research of NT content. After all, textual criticism is only one of the many critical disciplines that rest under the umbrella we call biblical criticism. But these other disciplines cannot engage the NT until textual scholars have accomplished their work. Without our textual scholars, all other scholars would be running helter-skelter through the maze of contradicting manuscripts that number into the thousands—an impossible task for the uniform study of the New Testament. A somewhat uniform text is necessary so that everyone is on the same page (if you'll excuse the play on words).

CONSIDERATION # 4
(Why So Many Different Translations?)

One would think that all of our modern Bibles would be the same if, indeed, textual scholars had given everyone a master copy of the New Testament. If they have handed us a finalized rendition of the NT, why aren't all of our modern Bibles identical? Well, since biblical criticism is not an exact science—such as physics—there does exist some wiggle room between textual scholars with differing opinions. In other words, there's more than one "final draft" because textual scholars come from different religious traditions (e.g., Catholic, Protestant, or Eastern Orthodox). Different Christian bodies, different final drafts. But overall, one can say that there is a great deal of agreement between these "final drafts" because all textual scholars are working from the same material. This is my way of saying that all major Christian bodies have the same basic texts (the Old and New Testaments) but with some variations. Using a football as a metaphor, not everyone is agreed as to how much air should be in the pigskin or what kind of lacing it should sport. These and other factors lead to the creation of differing biblical translations. Some of these other factors are as follows.

Our first influencing factor has to do with the time period in which the translation occurred. Take for example the old King James Version (KJV) of the Bible (1611) that is still popular today. When it is compared to our modern Bibles, what a difference! I know that millions of people still cling to the KJV for sentimental reasons and also because they are so accustomed to the poetic flow of seventeenth century English. But really, the KJV has more errors than the ocean has waves. It is highly inferior to our newest translations because at the time the KJV was translated, it was based on the later NT manuscripts (not the earliest). As we have seen, these NT texts (written by medieval scribes between 500 and

1500) have been altered relative to our earlier sources. Sometimes the alterations were intentional. But sometimes they were unintentional (as our 80-year-old monk discovered). Unfortunately, when the KJV was translated, we had not yet discovered many of our best and earliest Greek manuscripts. These discoveries have helped to shed light on the shortcomings of the KJV. (An effort was made in 1980 to bring this version up to speed. It is known as The New King James Version [NKJV].)

A second factor creating discord between our biblical translations has to do with the probable influence of religious/theological bias. There is a difference between an *objective* translation and a *subjective* translation. An objective translation is one in which textual scholars using our best ancient Greek manuscripts attempt to translate them into English almost verbatim. Aside from any minor corrections or additions needed to help smooth out the translation, nothing should be injected into the text that is not original to our earliest and best Greek copies. The end product should be a no frills version that reflects the purest translation possible.

In contrast, a subjective version may spin the translation in directions that favor a personal theological perspective or some other biased concern. The following example leaves little doubt that sometimes less disciplined scholars will alter the scripture (either by an addition or deletion) so as to make the text comply with their personalized theology. Both the New King James Version and The New Oxford Annotated Bible are considered to be modern translations, but see how they differ. Here we find Jesus, according to Matthew 24:36, speaking about the end times.

NEW KING JAMES VERSION	THE NEW OXFORD ANNOTATED
But of that day and hour no one knows, not even the angels of heaven, but My Father only.	But about that day and hour no one knows, neither the angels of heaven, *nor the Son*, but only the Father [Italics mine]

Why did the old KJV of 1611 and the NKJV of 1980 delete, "nor the Son?" Why does the New Oxford Bible include it? The answers, mind you, are not difficult to ascertain. It appears that the scribes in 1611, believing that Jesus was divine, were uncomfortable with the notion that Jesus—the Son of God—would not know when the end time was to come. He had to know. To eliminate this quandary of an all-knowing Jesus not knowing, they simply did away with the thorny wording in the later copies they were reproducing.[21] It seems—as I have shown above with the 1980 NKJV—that some of our modern translators have followed suit to alleviate the same theological discomfort that the earlier KJV translators experienced.

However, it is clear to mainstream scholars that when these translators delete "nor the Son" from the text, they are not being faithful to "the early bird gets the worm" literary rule of thumb. Fortunately, most of our modern translations—such as the New Oxford Annotated Bible—place "nor the Son" back into the text because it is found in our earliest and best NT manuscripts. So once again, the early bird gets the worm (I think the early bird is getting fat).

A third factor that contributes to the discrepancies found within our modern translations has to do with language preference (or taste). Anyone who has ever used a thesaurus—aren't they wonderful—will have little trouble understanding the many—countless, innumerable, numerous, numberless, limitless, endless, umpteen, uncountable, oodles, myriad, multiple, zillions, gazillions—number of alternative word choices they have when writing. It's not only the corresponding words we have that provide great flexibility of expression, but also the manner in which those words are strung together. As a writer I find that quite intriguing. Yet, imagine if you will, trying to translate Greek into English. This task in itself is problematic, but made worse by the number of word choices that scholars have at their disposal.

This leads us to a fourth factor that might cause translational differences: language ambiguity. There are numerous nuances that any one Greek word or phrase can take. Language ambiguity can lead to variant translations. Sometimes, the Greek text, or whatever text the scholar is reading (Coptic, Syrian, Latin, and so forth), can offer up wording that is not clearly understood by modern translators or perhaps originally was not written clearly. In other words, sometimes there is a language barrier, and sometimes the language is simply ambiguous—open to more than one interpretation. As time goes by, scholars become more skilled at deciphering the subtle nuanced wording of these languages. It's an ongoing process. Still, they can't do much about words that are truly ambiguous or have more than one meaning. At times, scholars must make an educated guess. They do not all arrive at the same conclusions. Thus, there will be some circles of disagreement that will lead to differing translations. Consider, for example, the differing renditions of I Corinthians 7:1, where Paul is trying to address the thorny issues of sex.

(a) "It is well for a man not to touch a woman." (New Revised Standard Version, Oxford edition, 2001)

(b) "It is a good thing for a man to have nothing to do with women." (New English Bible, 1961)

(c) "It is good for a man not to marry." (The New International Version, 1984)

(d) "Is it a good thing to have sexual relations?" (The Message, 2002)

(e) "Yes, it is good to live a celibate life." (New Living Translation, 2004)

It's not difficult to see how semantics might be a problem here because all of these renderings have differing shades of meaning. In case you're wondering, it's letter "a" that conforms the closest to our earliest Greek sources. By the way, Paul's admonition not to touch a woman may have been based on his belief that the return of Jesus was imminent, so why bother? (Sometimes I wonder about Paul.)

A fifth factor that promotes disagreement between our modern translations, is caused by a dispute about the number of books that should be included as part of the Christian canon. For example, aside from the Old and New Testament books, Catholic and Eastern Orthodox Christians include fourteen books or portions of books known as the Apocrypha, which they consider to be sacred scripture. (They are sometimes known as "intertestamental" books because they were written roughly in the time period between the Old and New Testaments.) The Apocrypha is not part of the Jewish or Protestant Bibles. Therefore, these additional books—Tobit, Maccabees, Sirach, and so forth—are generally unfamiliar to non-Catholics.[22]

Not only do Catholics and Protestants (which make up the majority of the Western church) disagree on what constitutes the whole of the canon, but the Greek, Russian, Armenian, Coptic, Ethiopian, and Syrian groups (which make up the Eastern church) also disagree on this issue. In fact, hardly any of these groups agree with one another on what should comprise the canon as a whole. Moreover, the Ethiopian Orthodox Church also includes in its canon 1 Enoch and Jubilees, writings considered as unworthy by other religious groups.[23]

The point is, we have several Christian groups with different Bibles, and each group claims to possess the one true revelation. This should lead thinking people to ponder an obvious question: Which canon is the right canon? Whatever Bible we subscribe to, or don't subscribe to, will not tell us to which Bible we should subscribe. We generally accept the Bible of our tradition and then view it as an unquestionable authority, not caring, or perhaps not realizing, that one Christian's sacred text is not necessarily the same as another Christian's sacred text.

In all fairness, however, we must not exaggerate the situation. I don't know of any Christian body that does not accept as part of its canon the very heart and soul of the New Testament (from Matthew to Revelation) as suggested in 367 AD. It does not, however, eliminate the problem for those who have additional books, especially if they insist that there can only be one true canon, their own, of course. Nor does it eliminate the disagreements that inevitably occur because of translational discrepancies between the textual scholars who come from different Christian perspectives (e.g., Catholic, Protestant, Eastern Orthodox). But even in this case, there is a great deal of general consensus about NT content since most scholars are following the early bird rule of thumb, along with other investigative techniques.

A sixth and final reason for variant modern translations is that not even our earliest and best manuscripts have uniform wording or agreement. As we have already noted, discrepancies between manuscripts are evident from the very beginning. Therefore, textual scholars can pick and choose which rendering they prefer, say, for example, between the Codex Sinaiticus and the Codex Vaticanus (both are fourth century manuscripts), and then make the alternative reading a footnote in the translation.

—

I remind the reader that we have explored only one of several techniques employed by textual scholars. Noticeably missing, for example, are the investigative techniques of *multiple attesting, contextual credibility, and the criterion of dissimilarity.* (Different scholars may apply different terms to these techniques.) If interested, one can upgrade their KQ on these matters through independent research. One will also discover that the field of textual criticism is much more complex than what I present here. Also, consider that I am presenting the general consensus of mainstream scholarship; that doesn't mean that alternative views are not in the offing. Okay, enough already.

Intro to Chapter 8

"I'M DROPPING THIS CLASS"

"... and you call yourself a minister? You're a disgrace to your profession ... I'm dropping this class!" These are the words from one of my college students who, in the middle of one of my lectures, could no longer endure the findings from New Testament scholarship. I was not totally surprised by his emotional outburst. After all, almost everything I was teaching ran counter to almost everything he had been taught in his upbringing. I opened the door and sincerely wished him well as he stomped out of the classroom. I actually empathized with him because he reminded me of me in my younger day (shades of my seminary experience, although I never stormed out of a class).

One of the problems we educators face—at least in NT studies—is that students arrive on our doorstep with preconceived notions about the Bible and Jesus. Their religious KQ is almost nonexistent when it comes to biblical criticism. This makes their religious RQ very much off target. They have been raised and nurtured within the insulated world of Jesusgate and are therefore oblivious to what is about to unfold. The experience is traumatic. At the onset I give my students plenty of warning of what to expect. But like a chickenpox vaccination, it doesn't always take. They walk into the classroom with emotional baggage strapped to their psyche, and they are easily perplexed even though I try to ease them into the learning curve.

You'll be interested to know that my pained and discombobulated student apologized for his outburst and asked to be reinstated. I told him no. Just kidding. Of course, I reinstated him. He finished with a B, a higher KQ, and a better RQ (I hope).

WHAT TO EXPECT NEXT

This chapter continues with a look at the questions of Gospel author-ship (Matthew, Mark Luke and John), New Testament chronology, and the historical development of the four Gospels. How was the Jesus per-sona developed? Are the sayings and doings of Jesus historical realities? Reliability is the question. What do the findings of biblical analysis indi-cate? What do the scholars think?

Chapter 8

WHO WROTE THE BOOK OF LOVE?
(Part One)

HELLENISM: the ancient Greek culture (its ideals, spirit, gods, language, customs, and so forth). Hellenism denotes the spread of this Greek culture by Alexander the Great (356 – 323 BC) after he conquered the Mediterranean world. Hellenism derives from the word Hellas (the Greek name for Greece).

GRECO-ROMAN: After the Greeks, the Romans came to rule the Mediterranean world. But Greek culture (Hellenism) was so pervasive and entrenched, that historians call this period the Greco-Roman era (ca. 300 BC – 400 AD or later).

APOSTLE/DISCIPLE: these two words are used interchangeably in the literature. The term *Apostle,* however, generally refers to one of the 12 followers of Jesus during his lifetime, or a very early Christian leader such as Paul. The term *disciple* can also refer to one of Jesus' followers (which is my preference), but also to a follower or student of any teacher, leader, or philosopher.

GOSPELS: The first four books of the New Testament - - Matthew, Mark, Luke and John. Therein is the sole record of the sayings and actions of Jesus. (Gospel means "good news.")

WHO WROTE THE BOOK OF LOVE?

The above heading was taken from a classic rock & roll song (if you're old enough to remember) sung by the Monotones. It peaked at #5 on the Billboard Hot 100 in 1958. According to Wikipedia, the Monotones came together in 1955 with seven original singers. The group launched their career by winning first prize in a 1956 appearance on Ted Mack's *Amateur Hour* television program.

Book of Love—as it is sometimes called—is an obvious love song about the many games that lovers play and the rules that govern that game. More importantly, the lover wants to know who wrote those rules in the first place. He's got to know the answer; was it someone from above? Indeed, *Who Wrote the Book of Love?*

Spun metaphorically, the title poses the perfect question about the Bible, especially the New Testament (NT). Who did write the book of love? Was it heaven sent? What do the scholars know? Our focus will be on the Gospels, although other NT books will briefly be discussed.

The majority of Christians assume that the Bible reflects God-given direction. Therefore, it has become an unquestionable authority. But no one, *I mean no one, should assume that their religious text is the ultimate guiding truth*—be it the Muslim Qur'an, the Judeo-Christian Bible, the Buddhist Pali Canon, the Hindu Vedas, or whatever. (A lesson not only lost on those talking Simians in the sci-fi blockbuster, *Planet of the Apes*, who worshipped the writings of their great Law Giver, but also a lesson lost on human primates living on today's planet Earth.)

The habitual assumption that the Bible represented unquestionable authority was accepted up until the sixteenth century. We didn't know any better. When Europe's version of the scientific revolution took off, everything changed. From Nicolas Copernicus' heliocentric model in 1543 (Sun is at the center of our solar system),[1] to the roaring ignition of space shuttle engines, our intellectual journey continues unabated in all disciplines. As a result, our grasp of the literary composition and development of ancient texts has also greatly advanced, and it is now virtually impossible for scholars to accept biblical authority without qualification. As we saw in our last chapter, textual criticism is only one of the many subdivisions of biblical criticism that has elevated the scholar's religious KQ. This chapter, and those that follow, will continue to highlight some of the most basic underpinnings of NT scholarship.

Who wrote the Gospels? How reliable (historically accurate) are they? These are a few of the questions we need to consider because our understanding of Jesus is based squarely on this body of literature. To begin with, we will flesh out a couple of misconceptions about the NT that must be addressed.

NT CHRONOLOGY

A common misconception about the NT has to do with chronology. When you open up the NT you'll find 27 books beginning with Matthew and ending with Revelation. The majority of these books are not in chronological order; that is, they are not all arranged in the order in which they were written. For example, Matthew was not the first NT book to be written, and Revelation wasn't the last. As another example, the first four books in the NT—known as the Gospels of Matthew, Mark, Luke, and John—were all written long after Paul's Epistles (letters).[2] His letters were written ca. 50-63 AD, but the Gospels were composed ca. 70-100 AD. And yet, the four Gospels appear at the very front of the NT—and they themselves are not in proper sequence; Mark, not Matthew was the first Gospel to be written. Shortly, the importance of knowing all this will become evident. *[NOTE: Since Mark was the first of the four Gospels to be written, I will henceforth list the Gospels in their chronological order—Mark, Matthew, Luke, and John (the only four Gospels we have in the NT.)]*

Before moving on, we must mention a side issue of great importance (oops, I think that's an oxymoron). Anyway, I indicated above that the Gospel of Mark was the first of the four Gospels to be written. In order to get a handle on NT scholarship, one needs to accept this fundamental premise of *Markan priority*. The supporting evidence for this proposition is extensive, but I'll keep it short.

When one compares the material in the first three Gospels of Mark, Matthew, and Luke, it becomes obvious that somebody is copying somebody. That's because some of the verses that appear in all three of these gospels are identical (or nearly so). The odds of this duplication being accidental are beyond astronomical. But who is copying whom? Scholars have concluded that Matthew and Luke are duplicating Mark. But why do they come to this conclusion? As we proceed through the coming chapters, the signposts for Markan priority will be pointed out. But for the moment, I'll offer up one telltale sign for that premise.

Consider, as one example, *Mark's writing style*. Although we don't have his original composition, the early copies that have come down to us indicate that he was not well versed in the Greek language. His Greek writing is not fluent or polished. It's rather rough. Of course, one wouldn't know this by reading the English versions because translators have smoothed out the difficulties. But the early Greek manuscripts tell us a different story. Whereas Mark's language in a given passage is ambiguous or clumsy, the same verses that appear in Matthew and Luke are clear and smooth. Matthew and Luke's Greek is nicely written.[3] It's easy to see why Matthew and Luke would correct Mark's deficiencies, but it's difficult to explain why Mark would take their well-crafted work and turn it into a rough draft. That doesn't make any sense. Therefore, Mark must precede Matthew and Luke. (Other indications of Markan priority will surface throughout this text.)

As already noted, Mark was the first Gospel to be written, but it was not the first NT book to be written. There is absolutely no doubt that the first NT writings come from Paul. His first letter, scholars would agree, is either 1 Thessalonians or Galatians (ca. 50 AD). Presently, the *exact* date for any NT book cannot be ascertained. But scholars can apply investigative techniques (find clues) that give them a ballpark time slot for a particular composition. The following sequential list (give or take a few years) is the most widely accepted. It will illustrate our Bible's traditional sequencing of NT books as compared with their true chronological order. I will highlight the Gospels in both columns. (Keep in mind that Jesus is crucified, ca. 30-33 AD.)

NEW TESTAMENT ORDER	CHRONOLOGICAL ORDER
Matthew (Mt)	1 Thessalonians ca. 50 AD (from Paul)
Mark (Mk)	Galatians ca. 51 AD (from Paul)
Luke (Lk)	1 Corinthians ca. 55 AD (from Paul)
John (Jn)	2 Corinthians ca. 55 AD (from Paul)

Acts of the Apostles (Acts)	Romans ca. 57 AD (from Paul)
Romans (Rom)	Philippians ca. 60-64 AD (from Paul)
1 Corinthians (1 Cor)	Philemon ca. 62 AD (from Paul). [Note: Paul dies ca. 67 AD.]
2 Corinthians (2 Cor)	**Mark** ca. 70 AD
Galatians (Gal)	**Matthew** ca. 80 AD
Ephesians (Eph)	**Luke** ca. 85-90 AD
Philippians (Phil)	Hebrews ca. 70-90 AD
Colossians (Col)	Acts ca. 90 AD
1 Thessalonians (1 Thess)	Ephesians ca. 90-95 AD
2 Thessalonians (2 Thess)	Colossians ca. 90-95 AD
1 Timothy (1 Tim)	1 Peter ca. 63-95 AD
2 Timothy (2 Tim)	**John** ca. 90-100 AD
Titus (Titus)	Revelation ca. 95-100 AD
Philemon (Philem)	1 John ca. 100-105 AD
Hebrews (Heb)	2 John ca. 100-105 AD
James (Jas)	3 John ca. 100-105 AD
1 Peter (1 Pet)	James ca. 80-105 AD
2 Peter (2 Pet)	2 Thessalonians ca. 110 AD
1 John (1 Jn)	Jude ca. 100-125 AD
2 John (2 Jn)	1Timothy ca. 95-135 AD
3 John (3 Jn)	2 Timothy ca. 95-135 AD
Jude (Jude)	Titus ca. 95-135 AD
Revelation (Rev)	2 Peter ca. 140-150 AD

The above dating system should not be taken as certain. Although no two mainstream scholars would be in total agreement with this timetable, they generally concur with the above dates. Aside from this general consensus, some scholars have challenged its accuracy. Take for example, John A. T. Robinson (1919-83). He was a NT scholar, author, and former Anglican bishop of Woolwich, England. Although Bishop Robinson was firmly within the liberal camp, on this issue of dating, he broke ranks in his 1976 publication, *Redating the New Testament*. In this work he concludes that the NT was written before 64 AD, partly because it said very little about the Jewish Temple's destruction in ca. 70 AD. He surmised that because the destruction of the Temple was so momentous, any NT book written after that time would certainly make reference to it. But mainstream scholars have not bought into this argument. On the contrary, the evidence continues to mount for the more widely accepted above dates.

The dating and chronological order of the New Testament documents may seem inconsequential. Not so. As we shall see, the above chronology will serve as a reference point for what follows.

HISTORICAL AUTHENTICITY (Historicity)

A serious misconception about the NT—especially the four Gospels—has to do with historicity. Are the Gospels historically genuine (accurate); that is, are they based on fact? The overwhelming majority of Christians assume that they are. That is a *partial* misconception.

Scholars have shown, almost to a certainty, that Mark, Matthew, Luke, and certainly John, are not historical narratives of what Jesus said and did. According to one group of liberal scholars, of the 1500 Gospel sayings attributed to Jesus, only about 18 percent (270 sayings, more or less) were actually spoken by him. To make matters worse, these prominent scholars also reject the historical accuracy of all but 16 percent of what the Gospels claim Jesus did.[4]

Although moderate New Testament scholars might wince over these numbers, there is consensus on what they imply—the Gospels are not primarily historical accounts about Jesus' life. *This is not to say that the Gospels are devoid of historicity.* It simply means that whatever NT historicity about Jesus does exist, it is flanked on all sides by Jesus stories that have been embellished, or even fabricated.

At first glance, this declaration may appear to be a devastating blow against one's belief about Jesus. If the Gospels are historically unreliable, how can they be truthful? After all, one could argue that in the absence of history, there is an absence of truth. However, this is not necessarily the case. Professor Bart D. Ehrman explains it this way:

> On one level, even modern people consider "moral truth" to be more important than historical fact. That is, they will occasionally concede that something can be true even if it didn't happen. Consider, for example, a story that every second grader in the country has heard, the story of George Washington and the cherry tree. As a young lad, George takes the axe to the tree in his father's front yard. When his father comes home and asks, "Who cut down my cherry tree?" George confesses, "I cannot tell a lie. I did it."
>
> Historians know that this never happened. In fact, the Christian minister who proposed this story (known as "Parson Weems") later admitted to having made it up. Why then do we tell the story? . . . We use the story to teach children that our country is rooted in integrity . . . George Washington . . . was the father of our nation. What kind of man was he? He was an honest man, a man of integrity . . . The point of the story? This country is founded on honesty. . . .
>
> The account of George Washington and the cherry tree is told for at least one other reason . . . personal ethics . . . We tell this story to children because we want them to know that they should not lie under any circumstances . . . So we tell the story, not because it really happened, but because in some sense we think it is true [conveys truth].
>
> The stories about Jesus in the early church may have been similar. To be sure, many of them are accounts of things that really did happen . . . others are historical reminiscences that have been changed, sometimes a little sometimes a lot, in the retelling. Others were made up by Christians . . . But they all are meant to convey the truth, as the storyteller saw it about Jesus.[5] [Brackets mine]

Of course, I do not wish to pretend that the George Washington analogy somehow resolves all the questions raised by accepting the Gospels as mostly unhistorical. We can easily see how ethics, morality, and other teachings ascribed to Jesus might play out through storytelling. But how does one reconcile the theological heavyweights of sin, salvation, resurrection, and Son of God considerations that we find alluded to not only in the Gospels, but also throughout the New Testament? Some possible explanations to this quandary will surface soon enough. For the moment, in order to avoid derailment, we will continue to unveil the findings of biblical criticism as regards NT reliability.

What other reasons might scholars have for bringing the historicity of the NT into question? Would this have anything to do with the Gospel writers?

WHO WROTE THE GOSPELS?

Another serious misconception about the NT centers on the question of Gospel authorship: Who wrote the four Gospels? Could any of the disciples have written one or more of these Gospels, as most people believe? If so, who? Well, I won't keep you in suspense. Scholars have concluded—almost unanimously—*that the Gospels were not penned by any of the disciples.* There are numerous ways that scholars justify this premise, as we shall see in our upcoming chapter. Until then here's two lightweight teasers.

First, scholars know that 85 percent to 90 percent of the people living in the first century were illiterate. So what are the chances that a company of fisherman could actually read and write?

Second, if the dating of these Gospels is anywhere within reason, as most scholars believe (Mark, 70 AD; Matthew, 80 AD; Luke, 85-90 AD; John, 95-100 AD), they must then conclude the following. If any of these Gospels had been written by a disciple, he would have been bald or very gray at the time of composition—about 70 years old in Mark's case, 80 in Matthew's case, 85 to 90 in Luke's case, and 95 to 100 in John's case (assuming they were contemporaries of Jesus). Writing these documents at such an advanced age is not impossible, but highly unlikely in a world where the average life expectancy was 45 years of age. (The Beatles composing in the first century: "Will you still need me, will you still feed me, when I'm 45?")

This is not to imply that some people of that time couldn't live to a ripe old age. Statistics can be misleading. What it really means is that many people of that time, compared with today, didn't reach old age. And if they did, they would still be in jeopardy of many debilitating maladies.

So, if the disciples did not write the Gospels, who did? Can the Gospel accounts be eyewitness accounts, written perhaps by another contemporary of Jesus? Obviously, any eyewitness account (disciple or otherwise) would be preferred. This would increase the probability of historical credibility. But again, scholars will nix the idea of an eyewitness account. Aside from the aging problem we just explored, there are many other known factors that bring the eyewitness proposition into serious doubt (disciple or otherwise). Again, we will discuss some of these issues in the following chapter. In the meantime, suffice it to say that the general consensus of scholarship about the four Gospels is that neither the disciples nor any other eyewitnesses wrote them.

If the Gospels were not written by the disciples, or by any other eyewitnesses, then who are these writers we call Mark, Matthew, Luke, and John? Truth is, we really don't know. So how did we come by those names? Scholars agree that originally the Gospels circulated anonymously. It was only decades later that these books were assigned their prominent names, in order to provide them with status and authority. But how did scholars come to these conclusions?

This aspect of authorship is somewhat complex. The information would be somewhat tedious for many readers. So as not to impede the flow of this work, I have transferred a good part of this information to Appendix C. This is not to say that the info is not valuable, it's just a little more involved. It will be of interest to the reader who wishes to dig a little deeper.

Nonetheless, next up, we will delve further into Gospel composition. How can we be so sure that the Gospels were neither written by any disciple of Jesus, nor by any other eyewitness? If that's the case, where did the Gospel writers—whoever they were—get their information about Jesus?

As we explore these issues, we will find that the assurance for a historically accurate record of the sayings and doings of Jesus is somewhat questionable. For sure, this uncertainty is not based solely on what has been presented thus far. Not even close.

Intro to Chapter 9

(IN {or out of} KEY)

When I look back on my recording extravaganza at Columbia Records, I am amazed at what we were able to accomplish. Basically, our group consisted of four voices (see: www.ripchords.info). More often than not, we recorded in blitzkrieg mode, especially when we did the album cuts. We would walk into the studio at 8 pm, for example, and knock out tunes for hours on end. Many of these songs were unrehearsed and unheard by some of us until the very night (or day) we recorded them. Of course, our producer, Terry Melcher, had a musical blueprint ready to go when we arrived. Even so, we often recorded on the fly. It was magical and exciting.

One evening, during a late recording session at Columbia, Terry ordered some take-out food brought into the studio for us. When it arrived, I noticed a few sandwiches, some vodka, and a bottle of orange juice. Everyone knew I didn't drink liquor so I assumed that the orange juice was for me. "How thoughtful," I thought to myself as I drank the OJ. But the OJ had been ordered as a mixer for the vodka (called a screwdriver, as I learned later). Anyway, I was definitely out of sync with the matters at hand. Needless to say, they weren't too happy with me.

—

Any successful group (duet or otherwise) depends on tight harmonization. The tighter the harmony, the better the results. In a group situation, it's not just the quality of the voice that's important. An ear for harmony is essential. Studio work can always be corrected, but one needs to adapt quickly because studio costs can become astronomical. It's not a free ride. (Of course, if the record company is legitimate, one never pays out of pocket; it comes out of one's royalties. If your record fails to generate enough revenue, the company eats the loss.)

Harmony has always been a big part of music. Looking way back, I marvel at such groups as the Andrew Sisters, the Ink Spots and, later, the Platters, the Temptations or Smokey Robinson and the Miracles. Talk about harmony, they were great. Every now and then, however, a singer would go off key. If you have an ear for music, it's not hard to know when a singer is in (or out) of key. Take for example an old Jan and Dean hit called *Surf City*. At the very ending of the song, when it modulates for the last time ("two girls for every boy"), you can hear the falsetto go slightly flat on the word "boy" (he doesn't hit the note straight on but sort of slides into it). I'm not picking on these guys because the same thing happened to me, albeit not on a national hit. My vocal slip came on an album cut Phil and I wrote called *Ding Dong Baby*. It's on the *Hey Little Cobra* album. I went flat on the falsetto right in the middle of the chorus. I cringe every time I hear it. I'm not sure why we didn't fix it (maybe we didn't catch it right then). But once the album was released, we couldn't go back and do it over. Anyway, whether you're playing an instrument or you're singing, it's paramount that you stay on key, stay in sync.

WHAT TO EXPECT NEXT

In this upcoming chapter we will delve further into eyewitness and reliability issues. We will continue to explore Gospel composition. What sources did the Gospel writers use to compose their works? What are scholars talking about when they speak of the Q source, and the synoptic problem?

Accordingly, we will explore the issue of harmony (or lack thereof) between the four Gospels. We know that historical reliability comes into question when the Gospel accounts conflict with one another. We also know that there is a great deal more harmony (agreement) within the Gospel material than disagreement. One would naturally assume that this bodes well for NT reliability; but does it really? The following will sound counterintuitive to what we have already discussed about harmony and pitch. Unlike music, though, one may be surprised to discover that too much harmony (verbal agreement) between the four Gospels is not necessarily a good thing, as most people assume. How can this be?

Chapter 9

WHO WROTE THE BOOK OF LOVE?
(Part Two)

In our previous chapter we noted a few reasons as to why scholars no longer consider the Gospels to have been written by any disciple or other eyewitness to Jesus' ministry. Additionally, they also believe that these Gospels are to be viewed as statements of faith rather than historical facts about Jesus. There are several considerations that will help reinforce these conclusions.

To begin with, the style of Gospel composition (the way they are written) speaks volumes. Indeed, a casual reading shows that they are not written in a manner indicative of an eyewitness observer; they do not reflect the personal involvement of a participant, or bystander. For example, there are no first person references of "I," "we," or "us." In other words, they are not written with the flare of one who has lived through the experience. The following is a more serious telltale sign that the Gospels were not written by any disciple or other eyewitness.

With the exception of the birth narrative and resurrection appearances, scholars note that the Gospel of Matthew is basically a reproduction of Mark. *In fact, Matthew copies 90 percent of Mark's Gospel as a foundation for his own.* Additionally, scholars overwhelmingly agree that *Mark was neither a disciple nor an eyewitness* (see Appendix C). Therefore, scholars reason, if Matthew were truly an eyewitness to Jesus' ministry, why would he borrow 90 percent of Mark's Gospel as the foundation for his own Gospel. That doesn't make any sense. After all, if the author of Matthew had been on site, he would have written his Gospel in his own words. He certainly wouldn't have relied so heavily on someone else's version—someone who wasn't even there.

As for Luke, he borrows about 70 percent of Mark's Gospel.[1] Between Matthew and Luke, they incorporate 637 of Mark's 661 verses.[2] If you do the math, that's 96 percent of Mark's Gospel being redeployed throughout Matthew and Luke. Although Matthew and Luke edit and rearrange some of Mark's material to suit their own theology and social setting, it is obvious that these writings from Matthew and Luke are not independent eyewitness accounts of Jesus' ministry. Scholars believe that after Mark composed his Gospel (primarily from oral tradition, fragments of songs, poems, and other sources), Matthew and Luke followed suit and used his Gospel as a primary source to construct their own Gospels (sometimes word for word).

Before we continue much further, we need to understand a fundamental premise that involves Matthew and Luke. It is this: *Scholars have strong reason to believe that Luke was unaware of Matthew's Gospel* (I will forgo their explanation). *As for Matthew, he wrote his Gospel about ten years before Luke's. Obviously, he wasn't copying anything from Luke's Gospel because it didn't exist.* And yet, both of these Gospels share "identical" material *not found in Mark*, sometimes *line for line*. How can this be since Mark's Gospel doesn't have this material, and neither Matthew nor Luke is copying from the other? Scholars conclude that Matthew and Luke must be copying the same material from some other independent source. Here's the way I explain it to my students.

Suppose that a professor requires all of her college students to write a term paper on the meaning of the Declaration of Independence. One student copies 90 percent of the document in her term paper, the other, 70 percent, and they both make additional comments about its meaning (somewhat similar to what Matthew and Luke did with Mark's Gospel). Upon reading these papers, the professor will expect to see overlapping material (duplication) because they are copying from the same Constitutional language; that is, "We hold these truths to be self-evident," and so forth. No problem.

However, upon reading the papers, and the personal comments made by the students therein, the professor notices that the two papers have one complete, identical paragraph that's not from the Declaration. How can this be? *This material should not be identical since it's not from the Declaration.* These are supposed to be their personal evaluations of the Declaration. This draws the attention of the professor because the odds against this duplication being accidental are out of the question. Some personal ideas may be similar, but compound sentences within one paragraph from two different writers cannot be so closely worded by coincidence. You'd have a much better chance of winning the lotto. One of these students has copied from the other.

She confronts her students with this irregularity, but both students swear up and down that neither copied from the other. They don't even know each other but for the time they share in class. Based on the good reputation of the students, the professor accepts their statements as truthful; neither one copied from the other (even as Luke didn't copy Matthew, and as Matthew couldn't have borrowed from Luke because of the timeline). This leaves the professor with only one alternative answer. She concludes that they had each unknowingly copied this exact paragraph from a mutual source (CliffsNotes, Internet, book, magazine article), and failed to footnote the source. They might have gotten away with this piracy but for the fact that neither one of them reworded the paragraph in question. They copied their common source verbatim. The word for word duplication was a critical oversight, a dead giveaway. It was obvious to the professor that an *outside source* had been tapped since the students had not copied the material from each other. They had not plagiarized each other, but they had plagiarized.

ENTER THE Q SOURCE

Matthew and Luke present us with the same puzzle and with the same obvious conclusion. Both of them contain substantial material, almost identical material, that is *not found in Mark* and which neither copied from the other. This leads scholars to conclude that both of these writers (Matthew and Luke) obtained this corresponding material from a common source other than Mark. They call it "Q" (the Q stands for the German word "Quelle" which means source).

The Q document is strictly hypothetical because we don't have it. But we extrapolate the probability of Q's existence based on the same logic we used with our students and the analogy of the term papers. Examples of Q material—material not found in Mark—would be The Beatitudes (Matthew 5:3-12; Luke 6:20-23) and the Lord's Prayer (Matthew 6:9-13; Luke 11:2-4). An even more striking example for the likely existence of Q is apparent when one compares the following. *I will underline only those words that are exactly the same in both Gospels, and italicize the ones that are not.* (The scene describes John the Baptist baptizing people in the Jordan River.)

MATTHEW 3-7-10	LUKE 3-7-9
But when he saw many Pharisees and Sadducees coming for baptism, he said to them, "You brood of vipers! Who warned you to flee from the wrath to come? Bear *fruit* worthy of repentance. Do not *presume* to say to yourselves, 'We have Abraham as our ancestor': for I tell you, God is able from these stones to raise up children to Abraham. Even now the ax is lying at the root of the trees: every tree therefore that does not bear good fruit is cut down and thrown into the fire.	*John said to the crowds that came out to be baptized by him,* "You brood of vipers! Who warned you to flee from the wrath to come? Bear *fruits* worthy of repentance. Do not *begin* to say to yourselves, 'We have Abraham as our ancestor': for I tell you, God is able from these stones to raise up children to Abraham. Even now the ax is lying at the root of the trees: every tree therefore that does not bear good fruit is cut down and thrown into the fire.

We can clearly see that in the above comparison ... "verbal agreement is 99 percent: only in the choice of one verb and whether or not one noun is singular or plural do they differ, except for the transitional remarks in v.7 in both gospels."[3] Since this material does not appear in Mark, and because it is practically identical, it is clear that Matthew and Luke have pulled this material from a mutual source unknown to us, the source that scholars call Q.[4] We should note that not all NT scholars agree with the Q hypothesis, and some arguments have been made against the idea of Q. However, most scholars adhere to it because, at least for the present, they see it as the most cogent (convincing) explanation for how the Gospels came to be written. I agree.

Aside from the Q material shared by Matthew and Luke, each of these writers also has material that is found only in their Gospels. In Matthew this unique material is called the "M" source (material found only in the Gospel of Matthew; ergo, M). For example, when Jesus is on trial for his life, it is only in Matthew (27:24) that Pontius Pilate takes some water and washes his hands before the crowd, saying, "I am innocent of this man's blood; see to it yourselves." That is M material.

In Luke this unique material is called the "L" source (material found only in the Gospel of Luke; ergo, L). For example, in the Gospel of Luke (10:29-37) we have the parable of the Good Samaritan. It is unique to Luke; this is an L source.

As we can see, Matthew and Luke do present some new and important material not found in Mark (Q, M, and L). But, as we have also seen, Matthew and Luke relied heavily on Mark; that is, *most of the material used to compose their Gospels came from Mark.*

THE SYNOPTIC GOSPELS

Here's the result of all this cascading literary dependency: a considerable amount of harmony is reflected between Mark, Matthew, and Luke. Based on this interlocking harmony, scholars have categorized these three Gospels as *Synoptic Gospels* (Gospels with a similar point of view about Jesus); that is, the sayings and doings of Jesus found in these Gospels are very much alike. The Gospel of John, on the other hand, reflects a much different view of Jesus. The Gospel of John, therefore, is not considered to be a Synoptic Gospel and we'll get to it shortly. As for Mark, Matthew, and Luke, they are indeed—as the old song goes—"Three Coins in the Fountain."

This tri-Gospel[5] harmony between Mark, Matthew, and Luke, is what drives people to conclude that the Gospels must be historically sound because there is so much agreement between them. Yet how can there not be literary agreement if Matthew and Luke are tracing—sometimes word for word—over Mark's literary page? Again, that's why we call them the Synoptic Gospels—they tend to reflect a very similar picture of Jesus. Consider the following chart.

MARK 2:16-17	MATTHEW 9:11-13	LUKE 5:30-32
When the scribes of the Pharisees saw that he was eating with sinners and tax collectors, they said to his disciples, "Why does he eat with tax collectors and sinners?" When Jesus heard this, he said to them, "Those who are well have no need of a physician, but those who are sick; I have come to call not the righteous but sinners."	When the Pharisees saw this, they said to his disciples, "Why does your teacher eat with tax collectors and sinners?" But when he heard this he said, "Those who are well have no need of a physician, but those who are sick . . . For I have come to call not the righteous but sinners."	The Pharisees and their scribes were complaining to his disciples, saying, "Why do you eat with and drink with tax collectors and sinners?" Jesus answered, "Those who are well have no need of a physician, but those who are sick; I have come to call not the righteous but sinners to repentance."

If these Gospels were truly eyewitness reports, that is, not relying on other sources as a foundation for their testimony, then this Gospel trilogy would be a terrific historical source. But the Synoptic Gospels are not written as if three people are writing about three separate and unique experiences of the same event. These three Gospels were written between 40 and 55 years after the events they describe. So how could they describe some of these happenings word for word without some recording device? It's quite obvious that Matthew and Luke are copying Mark. Moreover, it's also quite clear that they are copying from another source, Q.

As for the M and L material, it is sparse relative to their entire Gospels. However, Luke's *Good Samaritan* story is a good example of the fact that this material is not simply garnish (Luke 10:25-37).

THE SYNOPTIC PROBLEM

Ironically, although the Synoptic Gospels are quite harmonious (owing to the duplication tendencies we have pointed out), they sometimes reveal chronological disparity (the order in which events are presented). If Matthew and Luke are copying Mark, why do they rearrange his story line? This is part of what scholars refer to as the Synoptic Problem (or puzzle). For example, in Mark, (1:29-34), the healing of Peter's mother-in-law (and a crowd of people) is followed by the healing of a leper (Mark 1:40-42); the order of these three events is reversed by Matthew (8:1-4; 14-17).

Similarly, In Mark, (4:1-34; 35-41), the teaching of parables by Jesus takes place just before the crossing of the lake and the stilling of the storm. But in Matthew, (8:23-27), the crossing of the lake and subsequent storm occur long before the teaching of parables.[6] Numerous other examples of chronological discrepancy could be demonstrated. But it's not just the chronological order of events that is thought provoking. It's also about the conflicting details between these Gospels. Some of these inconsistencies are more serious than others. *This brings us to the core of the Synoptic Problem.*

We know why these Gospels are *so similar*; it's a consequence of Matthew and Luke copying Mark's Gospel and the Q source, sometimes line for line. On the other hand, why is it then that these Gospels can be *so different?* In other words, although the corresponding stories in these three Gospels are alike, some of the *details* in these accounts have been significantly changed—changed to the extent that they sometimes affect the entire meaning of the story.[7]

To help shed light on these self-contradictions, a few comparative examples between Mark and Matthew will suffice. These examples derive from *redaction criticism* that is another subdivision of biblical criticism. The word redaction means to edit, revise, or rewrite. Redaction analysis reveals how and why the Gospel writers modified, or redacted (edited or rewrote) their sources.[8] Matthew, for example, was not simply duplicating what he borrowed from Mark; he also modified it by rewriting or excluding some of the material. His editorial and theological imprints are obvious.

We know that Matthew copied over 90 percent of Mark. Keep in mind that Matthew's Gospel (ca. 80 AD) is being written about 10 years *after* Mark's. Also keep in mind that Christology (the image and nature of Jesus) is on a trajectory of enhancement that will continue to escalate over the next 400 years (divinity; Incarnation; Trinity, and so forth). From this perspective, consider how Matthew rewrites some of Mark's comments so as to reflect his own evolving Christological interests and concerns. Most conspicuous is Matthew's desire to make Jesus look "Presidential;" apparent is his editorial eagerness to remove any negative stigma about Jesus that he perceives in Mark's writing. Let's begin with a very simple example.

MARK 6:3A	MATTHEW 13:55A
Is not this the carpenter, the son of Mary . . .	Is not this the carpenter's son? Is not his mother called Mary?

It is obvious that Matthew removes Mark's reference about Jesus being a carpenter. In Matthew, Jesus is now the *son* of a carpenter. Why would Matthew edit Mark's wording to make this point? For scholars the answer is clear because they know that being a carpenter in first century Palestine was anything but a compliment. Today, it's a fine career and can also be quite lucrative. Back then, however, being a carpenter, or any artisan, was considered unworthy for anyone of importance. Matthew partially eliminates this embarrassment by disassociating Jesus from what people of his time considered to be an unimpressive occupation.

Elsewhere in his Gospel, Matthew portrays Jesus as perfect goodness and divine power, and edits out or modifies any verses from Mark that might detract from this image. To that end, Matthew *excluded* Mark's references to Jesus' harshness toward the leper (Mark 1:43); to Jesus' anger against the Pharisees (Mark 3:5); to his indignation against his disciples (Mark 10:14); to Jesus' recognition by evil spirits and demons, probably on the grounds he was accused of being in league with the Devil (Mark 1:24 and 3:22); to the charge of insanity against Jesus (Mark 3:21); and to Jesus' effort to walk past his disciples who were distressed on the sea of Galilee (Mark 6:48).[9] Matthew is copying much of Mark's Gospel, but he's deleting all of Mark's negatives about Jesus.

Strangely enough, this purification process reminds me of Walt Disney's 1928 Mickey Mouse cartoon, *Steamboat Willie*. It's a good analogy for how Matthew edits Mark. One of the striking features about *Steamboat Willie* is how violent and cruel Mickey is to animals. Not the Mickey we know today. Mickey's character was softened when Disney moved toward family oriented film. They had to recast Mickey in a much more flattering light. To preserve Mickey's current reputation of goodness and kindness, *Steamboat Willie* is seldom shown in its entirety. "A full thirty seconds of scenes have been deleted from the original cartoon. A few of the cut scenes include Mickey pulling a cat's tail and then swinging the cat by the tail above his head, picking up a nursing [female pig] and "playing" its babies like an accordion keyboard, and using a goose as bagpipes."[10] Let's get back to Matthew.

Looking at our former examples, one can deduce that Matthew is cleaning up Mark's portrayal of Jesus; he's knocking off the rough edges. Matthew wants Jesus to look more Messianic. (The Messiah would be the anointed warrior of God, slated to liberate the Jewish nation from her enemies as foretold in the Hebrew Bible. However, Christianity will put a different spin on Messianic ideas.)

Let's take a closer look to see how Matthew softens Mark's portrayal of Jesus as he encounters his disciples on the Sea of Galilee *(see example on the next page)*. I have underlined those sections that would draw the attention of redaction scholars.

Scholars recognize that Matthew has eliminated Mark's comment, "He [Jesus] intended to pass them [the disciples] by." Scholars must then ask themselves, "Why this deletion?" A probable answer is that Matthew saw Mark's version as a negative portrayal of Jesus; too many character flaws. For example, it didn't sound like something Jesus would do, or should do (try to pass by his disciples when they're in distress).

MARK 6:47-52	MATTHEW 14:22-33
. . . boat was on the sea . . . <u>He intended to pass them by</u> . . . when they saw him walking on the sea, they thought it was a ghost . . . and were terrified . . . he spoke to them . . . "Take heart, it is I; do not be afraid" . . . And they were utterly astounded, <u>for they did not understand about the loaves, but their hearts were hardened.</u>	. . . He came walking towards them on the sea. But when the disciples saw him walking toward them on the sea, they were terrified saying, "It's a ghost!" . . . Jesus spoke to them and said, "Take heart, it is I; do not be afraid." <u>And those in the boat worshipped him saying, "Truly you are the son of God."</u>

Also, as we consider the ending of this story, Matthew again spins Mark's version into a much more positive outcome. In Mark's version, the story is capped off by making the disciples look mean spirited ("But their hearts were hardened"). But in Matthew's ending we have a positive triple whammy. First, the disciples are no longer portrayed as lacking understanding about the miracle of the loaves because Matthew has deleted it. Second, there is no negative stigma placed on the disciples because again, Matthew deletes any mention of "hardened hearts." Third, and here's the twist that Matthew *injects into the text*—the disciples worship Jesus and proclaim him to be the "Son of God," whereas in Mark no such proclamation is made. It is not difficult for the redaction critic to see that Matthew has redacted (edited) the negative aspects from Mark into a win-win situation for both Jesus and the disciples. It is clear that Matthew's motivation is to raise the Christological bar, and also to present Jesus' disciples in a much more favorable light.[11]

The story about the woman with the hemorrhage is another clear example of Matthew's editing inclination to add more Christological punch to Mark's Jesus. Notice at what point the woman is made well in each of these Gospel stories.

MARK 5:25-34	MATTHEW 9:20-22
Now there was a woman who had been suffering from hemorrhages for twelve years . . . she . . . came up behind him in the crowd, and touched his cloak, for she said, "If I touch his clothes, I will be made well." Immediately, her hemorrhage stopped . . . she was healed of her disease . . . He [Jesus] looked around to see who had done it . . . He said to her, "Daughter, your faith has made you well; go in peace, and be healed of your disease."	Then suddenly a woman who had been suffering from hemorrhages for twelve years came up behind him and touched the fringe of his cloak, for she said to herself, "If I only touch his cloak, I will be made well." Jesus turned, and seeing her he said, "Take heart, daughter; your faith has made you well. And instantly the woman was made well.

Matthew's redaction here indicates his concern about associating Jesus with the *magical* aspects of Mark's story. Mark tells us that the woman was healed immediately after she touched Jesus' garment. But Matthew changes the story to have the actual healing occur, not upon her touch of his garment, but upon the power of his spoken word. As the German scholar E. Kasemann observes:

> The idea that the garments of the miracle worker communicate divine power, which leaps forth and is capable of healing, is a vulgar Hellenistic [Greek] notion that appears in exactly this way in the account of Peter's healing shadow and Paul's miraculous handkerchief

(Acts 5:15; and 19:12) . . . Matthew corrects this crudely magical view . . . .[12] [Brackets mine]

(For clarity, the above scriptures appear below.)

ACTS 5:15—Peter's Healing Shadow:
". . . so that they even carried out the sick into the streets, and laid them on cots and mats, in order that Peter's shadow might fall on some of them as he came by."

ACTS 19:11-12—Paul's Miraculous Handkerchiefs:
"God did extraordinary miracles through Paul, so that when the handkerchiefs or aprons that had touched his skin were brought to the sick, their diseases left them, and the evil spirits came out of them."

(Keep in mind that Acts was written ca. 90 AD by the same author that wrote Luke (ca. 85 AD). Thus, the above healing stories about Peter and Paul, who died around 67 AD, are being written from hearsay twenty-five years thereafter. Objectively speaking, these magical [superstitious?] stories are doubtful.)

Okay, for the moment, enough said about our Synoptic three coins in the fountain. Let's turn our attention to the coin of a different mint altogether, the Gospel of John.

Intro to Chapter 10

ABRAHAM WHO?

As I mentioned earlier, my childhood upbringing was quite conservative when it came to religion. Looking back I would classify myself as having been a fundamentalist. I did mellow out a bit owing to my university experience, but I remained hardcore to the right.

After graduating from California State University, Long Beach, I made my way east to United Theological Seminar in Dayton, Ohio, where I would spend the next three years increasing my religious KQ. I had a lot of work to do for two reasons. First, my college career had not been a stellar one to say the least. I had too many outside activities that sapped my time and energy, one of which was trying to land a recording contract. Second, I had majored in Psychology and never took a course in religious studies. Actually, at that time there were not many religion courses being offered. That was a bummer. Anyway, I arrived at the seminary dorm with all the baggage of a Jesusgate expert. I was in need of what that Hank Williams' song called an *Attitude Adjustment*.

It didn't take long to get intellectually and emotionally disoriented because I felt like a Neanderthal who had just been thrown into the 20th century. I ran smack dab into the rigors of biblical criticism. My first year was a theological mind-bender. Aside from the studies at hand, I remember an incident that was especially helpful in adjusting my religious attitude. It all started when I heard from one of my peers that the seminary faculty had invited Dr. Abraham Heschel to speak to our student body. My first reaction was: Abraham who?

Unbeknownst to me, although I was quickly informed, Abraham Heschel was an eminent Jewish scholar, one of the leading Jewish theologians of the 20th century. But I struggled to understand why in good conscience our faculty would invite a Jew to speak to a group of young theologs who were studying for the Christian ministry. It didn't make any sense. I had known since childhood that Jews were headed for hell because they had never accepted Jesus as their Savior. The Gospel of John (14:6) made it very clear where Jesus says: "I am the way, and the truth, and the life. No one comes to the Father except through me." Therein was the standard argument for what happened to people who stood outside of the Christian faith. (This is not to imply that all Christians hold this narrow view.)

I remember sitting in the basement of our dorm, along with other students, faculty, and community leaders awaiting the great Abraham Heschel to arrive. I was, at the very least, curious to hear what this lost soul had to say. At last, he entered the room. What happened next came as an utter surprise, or should I say shock. The following may sound eerie, but I'll try to explain it as best I can.

The minute Dr. Heschel walked into the room everything went quiet. It was as though we were instantly mesmerized. Even as I think back on it today, I get goose bumps. It's almost impossible to explain. I can't speak for everyone who was there that day, but for me it was an electrical jolt. It felt as if a divine presence had entered the room. The way he looked with his white beard, the way he moved; his overall essence captured my immediate attention. Even before he uttered a single word I detected a gentleness and a power about this man I had never encountered elsewhere. He slowly came to the podium and then proceeded to give one of the most eloquent opening prayers that my ears had ever heard. His voice and the chosen words of his morning message had the flow of divine poetry. It was the coming together of both intellectualism and spiritualism the likes of which were indescribably delicious.

Upon his departure I was left with an unsettling realization: If this guy was going to hell, what kind of chance did I have? I was left pondering the words of Jesus as found *only* in the Gospel of John: "No one comes to the Father except through me." Something was terribly wrong.

WHAT TO EXPECT NEXT

The Gospel of John is considered to be the least reliable and, therefore, the least historical of all the four Gospels. Our next chapter reveals the numerous and compelling reasons why scholars have arrived at this conclusion. This will continue to shore up the argument against any claim for eyewitness composition of the Gospels, be they disciples or bystanders.

[NOTE: Although I have already defined Hellenism in Chapter 8, I will give it again here because of its importance to this chapter.]

Chapter 10

HEEEEERE'S JOHNNY!

HELLENISM: the ancient Greek culture (its ideals, spirit, gods, language, customs, and so forth). Hellenism denotes the spread of this Greek culture by Alexander the Great (356-323 BC) after he conquered the Mediterranean world. Hellenism derives from the word Hellas (the Greek name for Greece).

MESSIAH: This is a term derived from Hebrew that means, "the anointed one." In a Jewish context, Messiah refers to the leader and liberator of the Jewish nation promised by the prophets of the Hebrew Bible (Old Testament). [This definition will be repeated and expanded from a Christian perspective in Chapter 11.]

Of all the four Gospels, scholars have determined that John is inherently the least historical. The Gospel of John is certainly not an eyewitness account, and, for the most part, probably not the words of Jesus. Mainstream scholars have echoed this sentiment for a few centuries. Today, even conservative scholars concur, as in the case of noted New Testament scholar James Dunn: "For John clearly felt free to attribute to Jesus words and sentiments that Jesus himself probably never uttered while on earth."[1] These conclusions have come about primarily for two reasons: (1) John's account is out of sync with the other three Gospels and, (2) the lateness of its arrival. In dissecting these two points we begin with the latter.

BETTER LATE THAN NEVER

The old axiom, "better late than never," usually rings true. Still, sometimes it brings with it some obvious drawbacks. This would be the case when trying to discern historical authenticity in documents that surface long after the event in question. Remember the early bird? As we have already noted, the general rule of thumb is that the earliest sources carry the most weight (reliability). That's one reason why scholars believe that the Gospel of Mark (ca.70 AD) is somewhat historically more accurate than the other three Gospels, especially the last Gospel—John—written about twenty-five years later (ca. 90-100 AD). It is considered by scholars to be the least reliable in its presentation of Jesus. This is not to say that John lacks historicity. But again, in literary matters, the earlier Gospels of Mark, Matthew, and Luke are considered to be more trustworthy because the Jesus stories that formulated these earlier Gospels had less time to be corrupted through modification or embellishment as they passed from one generation to the next. This dovetails into our next point.

In contrast to our Synoptic "three coins in the fountain" (Mark, Matthew, and Luke), John's Gospel gives us a different depiction of Jesus—*very different*. Although some overlapping between John and the other three Gospels does occur, it is not considered a Synoptic Gospel because it does not share the same view of Jesus. The Gospel of John is not only a coin of a different mint, it's in a different fountain altogether. It literally moves Jesus from Clark Kent to Superman! This last point requires serious attention.

POLES APART

For openers, in the Gospel of John, it is quite obvious that Jesus comes across as theologically polished and out of sync with the Synoptic Jesus. Consider the following contrasting images of Jesus in the Synoptic Gospels and John.[2]

SYNOPTIC GOSPELS	JOHN'S GOSPELS
1. Jesus speaks in parables and short proverbial sentences.	1. Jesus speaks in long, involved discourses.

2. Jesus is a sage (a profoundly wise man.)	2. Jesus is more of a mystic (more spiritual, otherworldly, supernatural.)
3. The theme of Jesus' teaching is the Kingdom of God.	3. Jesus himself is the theme of his own teaching.
4. Jesus has little to say about himself.	4. Jesus reflects extensively on his own mission and person.
5. Jesus speaks on behalf of the poor and oppressed.	5. Jesus has almost nothing to say about the poor and oppressed.

The point is, in the Gospel of John, historicity fades even further into the background while theological formulation takes the forefront. Although none of the Gospels are considered by scholars to be historically weighted biographies of Jesus' words and actions, scholars believe John's Gospel to be even less credible (historically speaking, that is). They see it more as a theological expression of faith, the highpoint of Gospel Christology. Nowhere in the NT, for example, is the miracle working power of Jesus more highly emphasized. Exclusively, it is here that Jesus turns water into wine (2:1-11), and raises Lazarus from the dead (11:1-45). For this reason, sometimes the Gospel of John is called the *Signs Gospel*. "Narrowly defined, these *signs* are mighty works, miracles, that have the power to reveal God in Jesus."[3] This Gospel highlights the divinity of Jesus far beyond its three predecessors. The following will help shore up this viewpoint.

In John's Gospel, Jesus speaks of himself, uncharacteristically, in the first person. Jesus uses the emphatic phrase, I am: "I am the bread of life;" "I am the light of the world;" "Before Abraham was, I am;" "I am the gate," "I am the good shepherd;" "I am the way, the truth, and the life;" "I am the true vine." There are several factors that NT scholars would have us consider regarding these "I am" declarations.

They would have us remember that *these "I am" statements come very late in the Gospel tradition* (90-100 AD). They are not found anywhere in the earliest literature that precedes John; that would include most of the NT, including all of the other Gospels and also the writings of Paul (see NT dating in Ch. 8, pp. 117–18). This makes the "I Am" statements of Jesus highly questionable because earlier writers would not have ignored these important proclamations.[4]

Also, by the time these "I am" statements in the Gospel of John were written, Christianity had escaped its Jewish homeland (Palestine)—thanks to Paul's earlier missionary work—and was now exploding across the Greco-Roman territories (such as Greece, Asia Minor [modern Turkey], Syria, Egypt, and so forth). The *Gentiles* (non-Jews) were the primary inhabitants of these territories, although many Jews also lived there. Ironically, there were more Jews living in these Greco-Roman lands than in Palestine; the ratio was about 6 to 1 (1.5 million in Palestine, 5 to 6 million outside of Palestine).[5] With the possible exception of the Jewish homeland, Hellenism (Greek culture) was a permeating influence throughout. Therefore, most of the people in these Greco-Roman territories—Gentile or Jew—spoke the Greek language. In any case, there was a growing need to further the meaning of Jesus within the Hellenistic world following Paul's demise around 67 AD. But there was a problem.

For the Jews, Hellenistic religion presented a theological nightmare. Jewish thinking and Greek thinking were incompatible on a couple of major points. The Jewish mind was monotheistic; the Greek mind embraced polytheism (belief in many gods). Also, the Jewish mind did not accept the concept of the demigod (one who is partly human and partly divine); the Greek mind promoted it. (Do you remember our mystery religions from Chapter 3?) It was a clash of worldviews.

However, the theological divide between Jew and Gentile soon became moot owing to Paul's overwhelming, successful ministry among the Gentiles. As an unforeseen consequence, the Gentiles quickly came to dominate the Christian movement (originally started by Jews). One may say with some degree of assurance that Christianity morphed away from Jewish theology toward Hellenistic theology. There is little doubt that Gentile Christians, with their Hellenistic mythology (the mobility of gods in human form between heaven and earth), took center stage. According to the late Norman Perrin[6] this is clearly reflected in Paul's letters and other NT writings which depict Jesus as a Redeemer who, via a miraculous birth, descends to earth from a higher sphere, fulfills his assigned mission and then ascends to be with God (Phil 2:6-11; Col 1:15-20; 1 Pet 3:18-19, 22; 1 Tim 3:16; Eph 2:14-16; Heb 1:3). Perrin also believed that "The understanding of Jesus as a descending-ascending redeemer is one of Gentile Christianity's most significant contributions to Christological development."[7] We'll look at some of Paul's writings later in this work. Remember, Paul dies around 67 AD. John's Gospel surfaces around 90-100 AD, well into the Gentile takeover of Christianity.

As one might expect, the scriptural evidence indicates that John is targeting the Gentiles because he plays to their theological mindset. Aside from the "I am" sayings of Jesus, the Gospel's prologue is laser hot with its searing pinpoint interpretation of Jesus as the *Logos* (a Greek term, roughly translated: the eternal reasoning and creative *Word* of God). John writes: "In the beginning was the Word and the Word was with God, and the Word was God . . . And the Word became flesh and lived among us . . . ." (John 1:1, 14) It is here that the author of John feeds the growing need to share Jesus in terms most suitable to the Hellenistic mind. It is here that the scriptural promotion of Jesus as a divine Son of God reached its pinnacle.

John's approach to his Gentile audience was nearly perfect. After all, the Gentiles didn't know or care anything about a Jewish Messiah who might advance the welfare and good fortune of the Jewish nation. But Jesus as the Logos (the Word), that was a concept with which they were well acquainted and it fit nicely into their mythological worldview. (As we noted earlier, John's rhetoric will help to solidify the doctrines of the Incarnation and Trinity hundreds of years later at the Council of Nicea in 325 AD.)

Although Jews were familiar with the term Logos, they could not have accepted this non-monotheistic trajectory. Thus, it appears that John attempted to interpret the meaning of Jesus in a manner that would have the greatest influence in Gentile circles.[8] As further support for this premise consider once again the "I am" statements that John places on the lips of Jesus.

Scholars would have us note that the expression, *I am (Greek: ego eimi), ". . . was widely used in the Greco-Roman world, and would have been recognized by John's Gentile readers as an established formula in speech attributed to one of the gods."*[9] Whether or not John's interpretation of Jesus moves far beyond the original intentions of Christianity, has long been debated. But whatever one chooses to believe, there are several conclusions agreed upon by scholars as regards John and the three Synoptic Gospels that preceded it.

First, that the Gospel of John is even less historical than the Synoptic Gospels. That is, whatever little history can be gleaned from Mark, Matthew, and Luke, is further reduced in John.

Second, although some similarities are apparent between all four Gospels, there is no way to reconcile the Synoptic portrait of Jesus with John's portrait of Jesus. Even the chronological order of events, differ widely between John's Gospel and the Synoptic Gospels.

Third, the writer of John's Gospel is writing with language intended to reach the Gentile mind. The "I am" sayings and the "Logos" concept, is clearly taking aim at this demographic.

Fourth, the Gospel of John reflects what early Christians came to believe about Jesus toward the end of the first century—a divine Jesus—rather than trying to give a strict biographical presentation of Jesus himself. John's Gospel explicitly identifies Jesus as being divine. Although Jesus was called the "Son of God" in the other Gospels, the term did not imply divinity. The phrase simply meant that a person had a close relationship with God and would, as a mortal, do God's will on Earth. In other words, the ancient Jew did not equate a Son of God as being God. John, however, presents Jesus as the Logos come to Earth. That expression made Jesus more than human.

Fifth, in the evolution of Gospel development, beginning with Mark (ca. 70 AD) and culminating with John (ca. 90-100 AD), there is sufficient evidence to indicate that the divinity of Jesus takes a quantum leap in John's Gospel. In effect, Jesus was elevated to Godhead status, a proclamation that would be argued for centuries in terms of its definition. On this last point of Christological evolution, it would be misleading to leave you with the impression that the idea of a divine Jesus was nonexistent prior to the Gospels. That is not the case, as we'll see when we get to Paul's writings. (Paul's letters predate the Gospels; see Chapter 8, pp. 117–18.)

Finally, scholars would have us remember that regardless of the obvious contrast between the Synoptic Gospels and John's Gospel, they classify *all* of these Gospels as mainly proclamations of faith (belief), not documents of history. But they will also say that the Gospels are tied to the thread of history; that is, Jesus did live and proclaim a message of

alternative wisdom against the dominating systems of religious hypoc-
risy, religious conformity and political oppression, which finally led to
his execution (of these events we can be fairly certain). What else can we
know about the historical Jesus?

THE LOST JESUS

The dramatic difference between the Synoptic Gospels and John's
Gospel is only part of the problem when trying to nail down factual story
lines about Jesus. The three Synoptic Gospels themselves present us with
wide-ranging contradictions. When you add in the out-of-sync Gospel
of John, the idea that these books are accurate accounts of Jesus' sayings
and doings becomes highly questionable. Certainly, to suggest that the
Biblical Jesus is without contradiction is way out of bounds.

As we have noted in these past three chapters, there are *many reasons*
why scholars do not ascribe eyewitness authorship to the Gospels. One
of those reasons is NT discrepancy. Most lay people know that contradictions exist in the NT, even though they may not know exactly where.
Nevertheless, they continue to insist that some of the Gospels were
penned by, eyewitnesses. These holdouts would argue that the scriptural
inconsistencies we have pointed out—and those yet to be mentioned—
are part and parcel of all eyewitness accounts; disparity between eyewitnesses is a natural phenomenon. They would use the example of four
witnesses (presumably symbolic of the four Gospel writers) who see the
same car accident yet come away with differing details as to what actually happened. Which car ran the red light, or was it yellow, or was it
green, or what? Therefore, people might differ as to what they saw and
heard, but that doesn't mean they weren't eyewitnesses. Accordingly,
some Christians would conclude that one should not dismiss the eyewitness consideration on the basis of conflicting testimony. (I first heard and
accepted this argument as a teenager.)

These holdouts have a point. Some inconsistencies will occur between
eyewitnesses. However, you would not expect (or accept) easily discern-
able facts to be grossly contradictory between so-called eyewitnesses.
There is a crucial difference between a two-car collision and a five-car
collision; a notable difference as to whether it happened on Hollywood
Blvd or Sunset Blvd; a notable difference as to whether it happened at
night or in broad daylight; a notable difference as to whether the accident

happened in Phoenix or Los Angeles. Although eyewitness accounts may vary, a red flag should go up if these accounts drift beyond rational limits (facts that any normal bystander could not exaggerate beyond credibility if actually at the scene). Consider the following examples when we compare the Gospel of John with the three Synoptic Gospels (Synoptics).

1. In John's Gospel Jesus cleanses the Temple at the beginning of his ministry; in the other three Gospels the event takes place during the last week of Jesus' life.

2. 'The Synoptics show Jesus working mainly in Galilee and coming south to Judea only during his last days. In contrast, John has Jesus traveling back and forth between Galilee and Jerusalem [between north and south] throughout the duration of his ministry. [Brackets mine]

3. The Synoptics agree that Jesus began his ministry after John the Baptist's imprisonment, but John states that their missions overlapped (3:23-4:3).

4. The earlier Gospels mention only one Passover and imply that Jesus' career lasted only about a year; John refers to three Passovers (2:13; 6:4; 11:55), thus giving the ministry of Jesus about a three-year duration.

5. Unlike the Synoptics, which present the Last Supper as a Passover celebration, John states that Jesus' final meal with the disciples occurred the evening before Passover . . . .'[10]

The Synoptic Gospels and John also differ as to the day Jesus was crucified. Many other contradictions and differences have already been noted, including the monumental issue of divinity. There are other problems that should be considered. The following discrepancies are not simply between John and the Synoptic Gospels, but between all four Gospels.

Biblical scholars find that the contradictions in the resurrection story are even more disjointed. For example, "In Mark, Luke, and John, the women find the tomb open. Matthew, however, states that when the women reached the tomb it was closed and an angel appeared and opened it. In Mark and Matthew only one angel appeared; in Luke and John, two angels appeared. In each of these Gospels the angels (sometimes described as men in dazzling white garments) make different statements and perform different acts, and the women's actions also differ. In Matthew, Jesus does not confront Mary Magdalene at the tomb. But in John's account, Jesus appears to her outside the tomb. Also, in Matthew, Mary is frightened by the Resurrection phenomenon and says nothing to anyone. In John, she runs to tell the disciples."[11]

Whoever wrote these Gospels must have been drawing their information from conflicting sources (oral and written). Take for example what they say about the early beginnings of Jesus' life. In the birth narrative of Matthew, Jesus is born in a house; in Luke, Jesus is born in a manger. In Matthew, after the birth of Jesus, Joseph takes the family and flees to Egypt in order to escape Herod's diabolical plan to kill the infant Jesus; in Luke, following the birth of Jesus, the holy family returns almost immediately to their hometown of Nazareth in Galilee.

Anyone versed in the history of biblical criticism will know that scriptural inconsistencies are hardly new to scholars. Biblical analysis tracks back to Richard Simon's controversial 1678 and 1689 publications. It continued with the German philosopher Herman Samuel Reimarus in 1750 and scholar Gotthold Ephraim Lessing in 1777 (see footnote 11). New Testament scholar D.F. Strauss, in his 1835 publication *The Life of Jesus Critically Examined*, showed that the Gospel narratives contained unhistorical elements that he called mythology. In 1910 (the English version), Albert Schweitzer blew everybody away with his publication of *The Quest of the Historical Jesus*. That was a corker. The entire question about the historical Jesus (will the real Jesus please stand up) seemed to coalesce around this publication and still reverberates today. This issue has been seriously debated (and continues to be debated). Can we know the *historical Jesus*? That is, can we know what Jesus actually said and did? The four Gospels are the only real sources that make the attempt. As for Paul, he hardly gives any information along these lines. Therefore, the question is: Can we backtrack from the belated Gospel writings to Jesus himself?

According to many scholars, the historical Jesus cannot be known. We can only know what his second or third generation of followers thought about him, but we cannot know Jesus himself. In other words, as the NT developed, we can see what subsequent generations came to believe about Jesus, but we can't know how close that biblical portrayal squares with the real sayings and doings of Jesus. Accordingly, the historical Jesus—as many theologians will argue—is scantly visible within the four Gospels; that is, from a strictly historical perspective, the real Jesus has been lost.

In this regard, there is a growing consensus that the Gospel stories are primarily the reflection of evolving faith about Jesus rather than history remembered. It was an evolving faith that eventually declared a resurrected Jesus. This is what scholars refer to as the "Christ of faith" as opposed to the "Jesus of history." This Christ of faith reflects post-resurrection belief--belief in the *saving* power of Jesus as the resurrected Son of God.

This concept of salvation from sin via the Messiah's death and resurrection did not exist in Judaism. Therefore, it is unlikely that this belief came from Jesus or from those who surrounded Jesus, but from those who wrote much later about Jesus. In short, later Christians developed these religious convictions based primarily on the retroactive writings of St. Paul and the Gospel writers.

Regarding the lost Jesus, the above scenario is not comprehensive in scope. We have merely waded into the breaking waves of the ocean, as compared to its deep underwater currents. Even so, one thing is clear: We can easily see that these matters are much more complex than what the Jesusgate crowd would have us believe.

IN SUMMARY

Scholars have concluded that the historical content of the Gospels is quite thin, more so in John's Gospel than its three predecessors. They have also deduced that overall the Gospels are not so much biographical accounts of Jesus' life, as they are statements of faith (what Christians came to believe about Jesus based on their view that he had been resurrected). Furthermore, most scholars have reasoned that we may know Jesus to some degree by way of the Gospels (more so in Mark). Even so, they believe that much of the historical Jesus remains out of reach. As we have seen, these judgments are not simply based on a few pieces of evidence. Rather, it is the overwhelming compilation of many facts and indications (some of which we've examined here) that push scholars in this direction. It is the continued bolstering of their religious KQ that leads them to an ever-increasing RQ—a more realistic view of these matters. This is not to say that all of the information issued from biblical criticism is flawless, or that all scholars are on the same page. Many of these issues—certainly the historical Jesus—are hotly debated. Like any other discipline, biblical scholarship is on a journey of discovery. In the search for truth, it must travel the same bumpy road to enlightenment as all other disciplines. *It has, it does, and it will.*

My point here is that we must grasp the importance of holistic thinking that biblical criticism affords us (seeing the big picture). But until we neutralize the Jesusgate factor, most people will remain unaware of the scholar's world and, therefore, be unable to visualize the wider theological (or, perhaps non-theological) possibilities that are before us. The old axiom continues to haunt: "You cannot reason but from what you know."

MOVING ON

There is much more to cover about the Jesus tradition. As the Carpenters put it in their beautiful song (with Karen singing), *"We've Only Just Begun."*

I remind the reader that we are in the process of divulging information generally held back by Jesusgate leaders and institutions. In so doing, we will help close the knowledge gap between scholar and layperson.

In our next two chapters we will turn our attention to the topic of prophecy, especially as it pertains to Jesus. This analysis of prophecy will continue to raise questions regarding the authority and historical reliability of biblical writing as *traditionally embraced.* Unless I miss my guess, you will find these chapters to be quite interesting.

Intro to Chapter 11

HIGH NOON
(Do not forsake me, oh my darling)

I was around eight years old when I first fell in love with music (late 1940s). We didn't have TV but I was glued to the radio. My insatiable appetite for music was spurred on when my mom brought home a new RCA record player (about the size of a car battery). It was revolutionary in that it could play the new 45-rpm records.

Like most kids, I'd sing along with the Hit Parade's top hits. It didn't take long to recognize that I had at least a smattering of musical ability. I could sing along with the best of them and add harmonies to boot. My favorite singer was Frankie Laine, even though I didn't sound anything like him. But I liked his songs. I found myself singing, *Mule Train*, *Jezebel*, and, *That Lucky Old Sun*. Laine had 36 hits that included title songs for western movies such as *High Noon (Do Not Forsake Me Oh My Darling)*, *Gunfight At The OK Corral*, *3:10 To Yuma*, and, much later, Mel Brooks' *Blazing Saddles*, to name a few.

Early on, music became an obsession for me. As a kid, I came to envision myself as a recording star, just like Frankie Laine. I held that dream through my high school years. I remember watching Dick Clark's American Bandstand and thinking to myself: "Someday I'm going to be on that TV show; someday I'll be a recording star; someday I'll be on the charts." Of course, any kid with half a voice—and some without—will imagine the same brass ring. Few will be able to grab it.

As for me, I can relate to the World Book Dictionary's definition of *self-fulfilling prophecy:* "becoming fulfilled, or realized, by the very fact that it is predicted or believed inevitable." My dream and prophetic vision came to pass during my college and seminary years. I was lucky. (I'll touch on this again in Chapter 14.) For the moment, I'll only say that I was sky high upon hearing the news from Columbia Records that we (my partner Phil and I) would be signing a contract with the biggest recording company in the world! What a day! I was so excited that I hastily grabbed the tube of Brylcreem on my bathroom counter—true story—then proceeded to vigorously brush my teeth—for about two seconds—after which came the ick, ugh, yuck!

Say, do you remember that tuneful Brylcreem commercial? It was basically a promise. All you had to do was rub a little in your hair to look really debonair; a little dab would do you and the gals would all pursue you. (By the way, I did rub a little in my hair. But the gals never did pursue me.)

I don't consider myself a prophet, but I will admit to some uncanny predictions I have made in my lifetime that have come to pass. Recording was one of them. And hey, the Rip Chords did make it to American Bandstand (although I was not able to appear because of my seminary studies). No regrets. However, recording aside, I have made numerous predictions that have come to pass. I won't bore you with the details but here is one prophecy I presently own. *I predict, without a doubt, that this book will be published.* Of course, if it doesn't get published, you'll never know about my failed prediction. No egg on my face.

Here is something I could never have predicted or envisioned in my childhood imagination. For me this was totally mind-boggling. At Columbia Records, in 1963, the Rip Chords (Phil and I) were asked to do the backup vocals for none other than, yep, Frankie Laine. What are the odds? We were on the flip side of a 45 but I can't remember the name of the song. That means it probably didn't make the charts. Even so, that's a memorable hoot, and Walt Disney was right: "It's a small world After all."

WHAT TO EXPECT NEXT

One of the most misunderstood features of biblical writing is that of prophecy. Christians believe that the Old Testament predicts (gives clues) about the coming of the Messiah (God's anointed one, promised by the Jewish prophets), and what he will experience. It is then believed that the New Testament portrays Jesus as fulfilling those predictions.

The scholar's view of prophecy is quite different. This chapter looks beyond the Jesusgate wall to see what the scholar has discovered about this genre we call prophecy. It is one of the most misunderstood topics of religion. I trust that the following information will bring some clarity to this complex issue.

Chapter 11

PROPHECY AND JESUS
(Part One)

MESSIAH: This is a term derived from Hebrew that means, "the anointed one." In a Jewish context, Messiah refers to the expected leader and liberator of the Jewish nation promised by the prophets of the Hebrew Bible (Old Testament).

In a Christian context, Messiah refers to Jesus of Nazareth who is identified as the *Christ* (a Greek word that is synonymous with the Hebrew word Messiah, meaning: "the anointed one"); ergo, for Christians, Jesus is the Messiah (the Christ). But since Jesus was executed and did not fulfill the Jewish expectations of a warrior king, early Christians redefined the Messiah's mission; he was no longer seen as a conquering hero who would liberate the Jews from their enemies, but was now heralded as a sacrificing savior for the sins of humanity.

HEBREW BIBLE: The sacred writings of Judaism, but known to Christians as the Old Testament (abbr. OT). [*NOTE: Hebrews, Israelites, and Jews tend to be interchangeable terms. These differing designations are sometimes indicative of the time period in question, e.g., early Jews are referred to as the Hebrew people.*]

A two-hour TV special—*Uncovering the Truth About Jesus*—first aired on the PAX channel, Nov. 14, 1999. The introduction centered on Jesus as the fulfillment of Old Testament (OT) prophecy. According to this presentation, there were four hundred fifty six OT prophecies fulfilled in the New Testament by one man—Jesus. Twenty-four of these OT verses were paraded out as examples of these fulfilled prophecies.

They are as follows: seed of a woman (Gen. 3), born in Bethlehem (Micah 5), time of his birth (Daniel 9), to be born of a virgin (Isaiah 7), slaughter of the innocents (Jeremiah 31), his ascension to God's right hand (Psalm 68), flight to Egypt (Hosea 11), declared the Son of God (Psalm 2), Galilean ministry (Isaiah 9), a prophet (Deut. 18), to heal the broken hearted (Isaiah 61), rejected by his own people (Isaiah 53), triumphal entry (Zechariah 9), betrayed by a friend (Psalm 41), sold for thirty pieces of silver (Zechariah 11), accused by false witness (Psalm 35), silent to accusations (Isaiah 5), hated without reason (Zechariah 11), vicarious sacrifice (Isaiah 53), crucified with malefactors (Isaiah 53), pierced through hands and feet (Zechariah 12), scorned and mocked (Psalm 22), given vinegar and gall (Psalm 22), prays for his enemies (Psalm 109).

What all this means, in case you missed the point of this formidable list is that Jesus had to be the Messiah. What else could you conclude if indeed Jesus fulfilled these prophecies? In support of this premise, the program's narrator offers the following explanation:

> The science of probability has some interesting things to say about the OT prophecies regarding the Messiah. Professor Emeritus of Science, Peter Stoner of Westmont College,[1] with the help of 600 college students, calculated the probability of one man fulfilling just eight of the Messianic prophecies in the OT . . . .
>
> According to the science of probability, the chance of one man fulfilling all eight prophecies is one in ten to the seventeenth power. How big a number is ten to the seventeenth power? If you covered the entire state of Texas to a depth of two feet with silver dollars and then dropped in a single marked dollar and mixed them all up, your chance of finding that marked dollar on your first try wearing a blindfold, would be one in ten to the seventeenth power.
>
> Another moderator concludes: Statistical science, then, suggests a high degree of probability that Jesus was the Messiah predicted by the prophets of the Old Testament.

If the above OT prophecies with the ensuing argument for Jesus as the fulfillment of those prophecies ring true for you, then you are a casualty of Jesusgate. By no means are you alone. It is what most Christians believe. They accept this *connective sequence between Old and New Testaments* as obvious because that is what they (we) were taught from day one. Assuredly, we were told that the OT predicts (gives clues) as to how and what the coming Messiah will experience, while the NT portrays the life of Jesus as having fulfilled those predictions; therefore, Jesus must be the Messiah.

Of course, early Christian Jews took the Messianic concept and redefined it so as to fit their fallen Messiah. They said that Jesus was divine, had the power to forgive sin, and eventually declared him to be part of the Godhead (Trinity). This was a whole new Messianic trajectory. They had to search out the Old Testament in order to support this new interpretation. We will momentarily analyze the legitimacy of their efforts. In any case, such interpretations were blasphemous for the Jewish community as it violated their strict adherence to monotheism. That is one reason why the early Christian Jews were unable to convince their brethren to join the new movement.

Let's get back to the silver dollar analogy. It leads one to the conclusion that Jesus was the Messiah by demonstrating the impossibility of having so many of these prophecies satisfied by one person unless, of course, that person truly was the Messiah. It may not be obvious, but this type of reasoning cries out for qualification and outright criticism.

Scholars would consider this assumed prophetic hookup between Old and New Testaments as too simplistic and, in many respects, misleading. They would view it as another casualty of religious illiteracy. The scholar's concern here is not whether the silver dollar analogy is statistically accurate (we'll leave that to the mathematicians); rather, their concern is with the two basic underlying assumptions that float this analogy.

First, is the assumption that all of those OT verses were in fact prophecies about Jesus; second, that Jesus actually fulfilled them. While laypeople take these assumptions for granted, a scholar's overall grasp of biblical criticism will not allow for such a convenient explanation. In fact, the scholar's view is quite different. With these preliminary comments in mind, it's time to look over the Jesusgate wall to see what the scholar has discovered about this genre we call prophecy.

In order to shed light on this confusing issue, I have identified four main types of OT prophecy applied to Jesus. I categorize them as follows:

LAUNDERED PROPHECY
FISH OUT OF WATER PROPHECY
FRAMEWORK PROPHECY
STEALTH PROPHECY

These four categories highlight OT verses that Jesus supposedly fulfills in the New Testament Gospels. Although these four prophecies contain overlapping similarities, they each carry unique qualities that merit separate consideration. Our first two categories (laundered prophecy and fish out of water prophecy) will fill out the remainder of this chapter. Our other two prophetic models will be covered in the following chapter along with a fifth category I call "hindsight prophecy." I did not list it with the above four categories because it's in a different class altogether (as I will demonstrate shortly).

LAUNDERED PROPHECY

There's a gem of truth in that old classic 1935 song, *It Ain't Necessarily So,* written by George and Ira Gershwin for their opera, *Porgy and Bess.* The lyric challenges the accuracy of scripture by unequivocally stating that reading something in the Bible doesn't make it necessarily so. Ironically, it is a drug dealer in this opera who expressed doubt about certain statements in the Bible. Biblical scholars found nothing new in this declaration. They had sounded that clarion call centuries ago. But the clergy failed to echo that clarion call, and the insight regarding biblical discrepancy was lost to the laity. I believe laundered prophecy is the poster child for that loss of insight.

What is laundered prophecy? To answer this question we must first define the word "laundered." Used figuratively, it means to make anything that is tainted appear to look innocent, legitimate, or acceptable. The phrase "laundered prophecy" is used here to expose the practice of some NT writers passing off OT scripture as prophecy about Jesus when, in reality, it was *not prophecy at all.* Used in this way, the term "prophecy" is a misnomer. In other words, laundered prophecy refers to OT verses that are not prophetic in any way, but are nevertheless passed off as prophecy by the NT writer.

We need go no further than the Gospel of Matthew to recognize these laundered prophecies. When these non-prophetic OT verses surface in Matthew's Gospel, they sure look like prophecies because that's the way he presents them.

Now the Jews had a high regard for OT prophecy. Matthew seeks to capitalize on this interest by claiming—ten times in all[2]—that Jesus is the fulfillment of OT prophecy (sometimes called "formula quotations," "fulfillment quotations," or "reflection citations").[3] Matthew's literary hook is as follows: "This was to fulfill what had been spoken through the prophet . . . ." Prophecy is uppermost in Matthew's mind. He is constantly trying to connect Jesus to OT Scripture. But he goes over the top.

Scholars have revealed a writing technique of Matthew that is both interesting and disturbing (what I call laundered prophecy). In his exuberance to highlight Jesus as the fulfillment of OT prophecy, he interprets OT scripture as prophecy where no prophecies are intended. He fudges. He fabricates prophecies where none exist. He doesn't make up these OT verses he just invents an entirely new meaning for them, and then transplants (launders) them into his own writing. The "flight to Egypt" story is a great example.

According to Matthew's birth narrative, King Herod—who was sponsored by the Romans as the client king of Judea—was tipped-off by the wise men about the potential kinship of Jesus. Consequently, Herod saw Jesus as a future threat and ordered all the children in and around Bethlehem—two years old or under—executed. As Matthew tells it (2:13-15), Joseph takes Mary and the infant Jesus and high-tails it to Egypt in order to escape the paranoid Herod who is out to kill the little one.

After Herod's death, according to Matthew, the family leaves Egypt and returns to Judea (Palestine). Matthew then claims:

> This was to fulfill what had been spoken by the Lord [God] through the prophet, "Out of Egypt I called my son." [Brackets mine]

This so-called prophecy (fulfillment) that Matthew quotes, was taken from Hosea 11:1. It actually reads as follows: (I have included 11:2 for clarity.)

> When Israel was a child I loved him, and *out of Egypt I called my son.*
>
> The more I called them, the more they went from me; they kept sacrificing to the Baals and burning incense to idols. [Italics mine]

The prophet here, Hosea, is simply describing the Exodus event and its aftermath; how God delivered the Hebrews (Israelites; Jews) from the bondage of the Egyptian pharaoh, and the subsequent unfaithfulness of those Hebrews as they worshipped other gods. Originally, then, this OT passage was never intended to be a Messianic prediction, and it certainly couldn't have anything to do with Jesus (or any other Messiah figure). Clearly, Matthew has conveniently seized this one-liner—*out of Egypt I called my son*—and has called it something it isn't—a foretelling incident about Jesus. By transferring this one-liner out of the OT into the NT, Matthew makes it appear as if we have a genuine prophecy when in reality, we don't. This is laundered prophecy. Clever. If you think that this contrived rendering by Matthew is the exception to the rule, you'd be wrong. In fact, all ten of these fulfillment quotations are problematic.[4]

Another example of Matthew's laundered prophecy occurs as part of our last story (Matt. 2:17). As we noted, Herod (in his search for baby Jesus) orders all the male children in Bethlehem killed who are two years old and under. Matthew proclaims that this incident fulfills the prophecy as spoken by the OT prophet, Jeremiah.

> A voice is heard in Ramah, lamentation and bitter weeping.
>
> Rachel is weeping for her children; she refuses to be comforted for her children, because they are no more.

But again, this verse from Jeremiah (31:15) that Matthew quotes, is neither prophecy nor about Jesus. It simply describes the historical setting in which the Babylonians had won a great victory over the Hebrews in 586 BC. The captured people of Jerusalem are led away on a long march to Babylon.[5] Jeremiah's words describe the mood of the captives as they are taken away from their homeland. As they move toward an alien land, they pass the city of Ramah,[6] the place where Rachel[7] lays buried. Jeremiah, with poetic imagination, portrays Rachel as weeping, even in the tomb, over the fate that had befallen her people. It is obvious that Matthew is serving his own ends by taking this unrelated OT text and applying it to Jesus as a prophecy fulfilled where no prophecy was ever intended by the OT writer.

It is important to realize that the problem with all of this is not simply that a Gospel writer took liberties with OT verse. This wide-open approach to the OT not only dilutes the concept of Messianic prophecy itself, but also brings into question the historicity of the NT narrative. In Matthew's story, for example, did Joseph's family's flight to Egypt ever happen? Did Herod actually have children murdered? Is this truly history or something else?

Now the story that Matthew tells is not unrealistic. The idea that Herod would kill children, if it served his purpose, is well within his personality makeup. From non-biblical sources we know that he could be brutal. He did, after all, slaughter three hundred court officers; murder his wife Mariamme, his mother Alexandra, his eldest son Antipater, and two other sons, Alexander and Aristobulus.[8] Need I say more?

But the "flight to Egypt" story remains in question because Herod is exactly the kind of villain that Matthew would choose to fill the bill of his creative imagination. Furthermore, the Gospel of Luke gives us a completely different version of what happens to Jesus after his birth; however, I'll leave that for later. Bottom line: It is difficult to know whether Matthew has laundered an OT verse so as to compliment what actually happened (flight to Egypt), or, whether he has laundered in an OT verse so as to compliment a fictional story he has created. *Either way, the claim that these verses represent Messianic prophecy, is invalid.*

FISH OUT OF WATER PROPHECY

What is a fish out of water prophecy? Unlike our former category (laundered prophecy), a fish out of water prophecy is, indeed, a genuine prophecy. That is, the OT verse being used by the NT writer is an honest-to-goodness prediction. But, and this is a BIG BUT, the OT verse being used was never intended to be a Messianic prediction; *a prophecy, yes, a Messianic prophecy, no;* it was a prophecy about something altogether different. So, although the OT verse is prophetic, its application to Jesus is totally pretentious. It is therefore a misfired, misdirected, and/or misrepresented prophecy. It is a prophecy removed from its intended purpose and incorrectly applied. In effect, the NT writer has yanked a legitimate OT prophecy out of its original context and misapplied it to Jesus; ergo, a fish out of water prophecy.

Note of clarification: Both laundered and fish out of water prophecies, are OT verses taken out of context. The difference between the two is that the component of prophecy is nonexistent in the laundered verses, but present in the fish out of water verses (albeit misapplied prophecy to Jesus).

The following is an excellent example of a fish out of water prophecy. In this instance, Matthew is trying to convince us that Jesus had a miraculous birth as predicted in Isaiah 7:14. The following information will help us to understand a "fish out of water" prophecy. Matthew declares and quotes:

> All this took place to fulfill what had been spoken by the Lord [God] through the prophet: "Look, the virgin shall conceive and bear a son, and they shall name him Emmanuel," which means, "God is with us." (Matt. 1:22-23;
> (Brackets mine)

Although Matthew has latched onto a real prophecy—an improvement over his laundered "prophecies"—there are several problems with his interpretation and application.

For openers, we know that Matthew misquotes Isaiah because Isaiah doesn't use the term virgin. There is no miraculous birth in Isaiah's original, prophetic story. Look it up yourself and you'll see that Isaiah writes: "Look, a young woman is with child...." [If your Bible doesn't have the Hebrew rendering of Isaiah 7:14 ("young woman"), you might be looking at a Catholic Bible or, a modified reading outside of mainstream Protestant scholarship.]

Recently, however, the Catholic hierarchy aligned itself with Protestant scholars. After almost 20 years of study by nearly one hundred Catholic scholars, linguistic experts, theologians, and bishops, the need for this change became obvious. In 2011, America's Catholic bishops authorized an updated edition of their official English-language Bible, the *New American Bible, Revised Edition* (NABRE). The new text will replace the word "virgin" with "young woman."[9] Finally, after 400 years! (The first printed Bible was the KJV in 1611.)

Today, the general consensus by scholars is that Matthew's NT rendition (using the word "virgin") doesn't square with Isaiah's original OT wording, "young woman." So, how did Matthew get this wrong? Could he have done this purposely?

Biblical scholars believe that this verbal mix-up derives from the probability that Matthew *is not* translating directly from the Hebrew Bible (OT). His wording appears to be coming from a Greek translation of the Hebrew Bible called the *Septuagint.* Thus, Matthew is drawing his verses from a secondary source. Unfortunately, this secondary source (the Septuagint) uses the Greek word "parthenos" (virgin), in place of the original Hebrew Bible wording "almah" (young woman). Therefore, the term "virgin" (not young woman) shows up in Matthew's Gospel because he is translating from the Septuagint, not the original Hebrew Bible. You can see the problem. This dilemma, along with other complexities surrounding this issue, will be discussed in conjunction with the virgin birth doctrine in Chapter 13.

For the moment, we're trying to see whether Isaiah's prophecy has anything to do with Jesus. Scholars do not believe it does, *regardless* of whether you employ the terms "virgin" or "young woman." That's because there is a much more serious problem than the translational glitch we've just revealed. *The obvious problem is that Isaiah's prophecy has nothing to do with Jesus, as Matthew claims.* This OT verse that Matthew transplants into his NT book, is totally out of context; ergo, it's a fish out of water prophecy. A quick overview of Isaiah's original setting will help us understand this prophecy's actual meaning. In so doing, we will come to see how Matthew reinterprets the text, and why we should now classify it as a fish out of water prophecy. Judge for yourself.

Isaiah is writing around the early part of the eighth century BC (700s). At this time, the Hebrews (eventually called Jews), are divided into two sovereign states: Israel (northern Palestine), and Judah (southern Palestine). A third country in Isaiah's scenario is Syria, which sits immediately north east of Israel. Isaiah's story revolves around King Ahaz, the King of Judah. The following is a simplified version of what transpired.

As the story goes, the kings of Syria and Israel are threatening King Ahaz. Poor King Ahaz outnumbered by his enemies two to one. Enter the prophet, Isaiah.

Isaiah assures king Ahaz that the alliance between Syria and Israel will come to naught. God will protect him. So he is not to worry. Isaiah's prophecy to Ahaz is that God will provide a sign as proof of the matter. The foretelling sign will be that a young woman, who is with child, will bear a son, and shall call his name Emmanuel (which means, God is with us). Furthermore, Isaiah predicts that before that child is old enough to tell the difference between good and evil, Syria and Israel will have been destroyed. In Isaiah's words:

> Therefore the Lord himself will give you a sign. Look, the young woman *is with child* and shall bear a son, and shall name him Immanuel ....
>
> For before the child knows how to refuse the evil and choose the good, the land before whose two kings you are in dread will be deserted. (Isa 7:14, 16) (Italics mine)

Sure enough, about the time the child is reaching maturity, the kings of Syria and Israel have been eliminated as promised by Isaiah's prediction. King Ahaz is saved.

Actually, if you read the text carefully, it shows that the young woman is already present and pregnant ("the young woman is with child"). Matthew's NT rendition not only incorrectly describes the young woman as a virgin, but also incorrectly describes the pregnancy as a future event ("Look, the virgin shall conceive," in place of, "Look, the young woman is with child").

The highly respected *New Interpreter's Bible* (NIB) puts it this way:

> In its original context, Isa 7:14 refers to the promise that Judah would be delivered from the Syro-Ephraimitic War before the child of a young woman who was already pregnant would reach the age of moral discernment .... In Isaiah 8:8, "Immanuel" [the child] is addressed as already present. It is thus clear from both the context and the meaning of the word translated "young woman" (alma) [or almah] that the Isaiah passage neither referred to a virginal conception nor predicted an event in the long-range future, but was directed to Isaiah's own time.[10] [Brackets mine]

What we need to keep in mind—and this is most important—is that Isaiah's intent is to provide Ahaz with a visible sign for deliverance from his enemies (Syria and Israel), and to set a time frame for their destruction. His symbolic, but visible sign of salvation, can be seen by the presence of a pregnant young woman whose natural (not virginal) birth of a child is at hand. The child will be called Emmanuel, which conveys the assurance of God's presence throughout King Ahaz's ordeal. *Even if one insists on calling this young woman a virgin, this story is not about the foretelling of an event 700 plus years into the future.* It is also important to recognize that the child in this prophecy is not portrayed as the conquering hero, the deliverer, or for any other importance beyond his arrival as a good omen for King Ahaz.[11] The end.

Obviously, Matthew does not attend to the context and original intent of Isaiah's words. He may have done this intentionally. After all, from the previous examples we have considered, we can see that Matthew takes great liberty with his use of the Old Testament. As noted earlier, none of his ten "fulfillment quotations" can be applied to Jesus without some tortuous mental gymnastics. Accordingly, perhaps what we have here in this "virgin" declaration is nothing more than Matthew's creative license; turning OT verse into an assumed Messianic prophecy as claimed in his Gospel. For the unsuspecting reader of the NT, however, this creates the powerful illusion of prophecy fulfilled!

There are some NT scholars who are not bothered by Matthew's overreaching tactics. The *New Interpreter's Bible* (NIB) chimes in on this one. If I paraphrase them correctly they are saying that Matthew interprets the OT (as a whole and in all its parts) to be prophecy. He "can illustrate and augment the Jesus story with affirmations from the OT, irrespective of their original meaning." As a consequence, there isn't any part of the OT that isn't prophetic free game for Matthew. Therefore, he can cite Isaiah (or any OT verse) as "what had been spoken by the prophet."[12] With tacit approval the NIB states that ". . . Matthew interpreted scripture in a way appropriate for his time." The NIB also says that we "may take seriously . . . Matthew's theology, without being bound to adopt Matthew's interpretative methods as our own."[13]

What? Generally I'm in agreement with the NIB. Here, however, I must conclude that they have been out in the sun too long. I accept their view that Matthew should be given a pass on his indiscriminate use of OT scripture since it was an acceptable practice in his day. But by our standards today, pulling something out of its historical context would be considered deceptive and unethical (although some politicians, lawyers, and theologians are quite adept at this slight of hand). Nevertheless, we cannot hold Matthew to our modern standards. So I do not disagree with the NIB that Matthew was writing in accordance with the accepted practices of his time.

My dissatisfaction with the NIB centers on how they gloss over the serious ramifications of what Matthew's indiscriminate use of scripture means for us today, not whether his writing technique was right or wrong for his day. In my opinion the NIB is a bit schizophrenic on this issue. On the one hand they are asking us to embrace Matthew's theology (Jesus as the Messiah), but not necessarily the interpretive method by which Matthew sought to validate that theology. We can see that Matthew is trying to prove a point with methodology that, by its very nature, is flawed; therefore, it proves nothing (except to highlight Matthew's passion and conviction).

Where does that leave us in terms of how we might view Jesus? Does this weaken our Messianic view of Jesus? The NIB tells us we should embrace the theology and ignore the methodology. How can that be? The ends cannot be verified by the means if the means themselves are flawed. In other words, simply because Matthew's convictions were genuine, or his contrived writing techniques were appropriate for his time, that doesn't obligate us to accept his theological proposals—proposals based on tactics that by today's ethical standards would not be tolerated and would prove nothing.

For Jesusgaters the issue is moot. They will declare that Matthew's stretched interpretation of OT verse must be accurate because the NT is now considered sacred. God's Word cannot be wrong! Armed with this *presumption* they can *expediently* dismiss any consideration to the contrary. With this mindset, they can indeed imagine that God really intends a double-barreled prophecy: one for Ahaz, and one for Jesus. Honestly, these theological assumptions ring hollow and appear to be arguments of convenience rather than substance.

Matthew was not alone in rummaging through the OT as though it were a garage sale. The authors of Mark, Luke, and John, also made freewheeling use of OT verse. Far and away though, Matthew was the most prolific opportunist.

Our next chapter will continue to shed light on the issue of prophecy. "We've only just begun."

DEAR KAREN

A-well my baby's name is Karen she's the
Girl that I adore, and everyday I love my little
Karen even more;
Whenever she's around me I'm always satisfied,
Well I could never love another woman if I tried,
She's fine, so fine,
Someday I'm gonna make sweet Karen mine!

(The above lyrics come from a simple ditty that my Rips Chords partner (Phil Stewart) and I wrote. This song actually made it to the flip side of our first Columbia hit record called *Here I Stand* [released in the Spring of 1963]. *Karen* also made its way onto numerous CD reissues of our albums, including the 2006 CD release, *Summer U.S.A.! The Best of the Rip Chords* [Sundazed Music].)

The pain in my right knee flares up on occasion. Is it arthritis? I'm not sure.

More years ago then I care to remember, I double dated with a high school buddy as we took two girls from our church out to Disneyland. My friend was going steady with his girl but it was the first time out of the gate with mine. Karen was anything but shy; she had no reservations about telegraphing her intentions. I tried to be cool, but as our one-hour drive to Disneyland progressed, she became more and more demonstrative.

The year was 1958 and I was a teenager driving a 1950 Plymouth. In those days our cars didn't have bucket seats or dividing consoles to slow down any unwanted advances. Of course, in most cases, the advance was from left to right, not right to left. But if the girl wanted to move across, she could. This one wanted to. I remember being thankful for the limited security provided by the steering wheel. But in the end it proved to be as effective as an ice cream cone in a microwave.

I know what the guys are thinking as they read all this: "Is he crazy? I'd kill for that kind of a problem!"

Ordinarily, so would I. In my case, such happenings are as rare as a hairy-nosed wombat. But her touchy-feely moves, for whatever reason, were a turn-off. It was a long night at Disneyland but there were enough attractions to keep us occupied.

In spite of her unwanted attention, the drive back from Disneyland provided some psychological relief since I knew the evening was coming to an end. But my optimism was short-lived. When we pulled up to her parent's home I discovered, much to my chagrin, she was not about to fade off into the night gracefully. Karen had other plans. My buddy and his girlfriend took her prearranged cue and proceeded to excuse themselves for a so-called quick stroll around the block. Karen and I were left alone in the car. It was entrapment, pure and simple.

I politely hinted that it was late and I needed to be on my way. She understood. But first, she boldly requested a goodnight kiss (this girl was ahead of her time). Feeling pressured, I simply told her "no." After all, I wanted to be the "chaser," not the "chasee" (actually, there's no such word as "chasee").

I told her it was up to me as to whether I would kiss her. That's when I discovered her stubborn streak. We argued hopelessly. It was time to walk her to the door. I started to turn so as to exit the car. At that moment she shamelessly threw her arms around me in a crushing bear hug. There I was, pinned against my car door!

I didn't have much wiggle room, and I couldn't get enough leverage to break her grip. Karen was incredibly strong (or maybe I was incredibly weak). I struggled as best I could. That's when I smashed my right knee into the steering column—"ouch!" ("Ouch" is not exactly the word I used.) The battle raged on. The old car was rocking back and forth as I spotted my supposed buddy and his girlfriend walking by. I signaled in desperation. They looked at me and smiled, then quickly moved away. I would learn later that they mistook our jostling around for something else.

On the promise that she would release me, I finally puckered up and planted one. But after our lips met, she insisted on another. That did it! I was determined to escape. I gave up an arm and was lucky to find the door handle behind me. Thrusting my full weight against the door, I yanked the handle and immediately fell out onto the street. A passing car nearly ran me over! I'll never forget that night.

The irony of it all is that we ended up going steady. I'm not sure how that happened, but it did. That first kiss must have worked its magic. Equally important, I think our mutual interest in Christianity was helpful. We were both very much involved with our church. I remember a very special night when we went to a Billy Graham crusade at the Los Angeles Memorial Coliseum. For a couple of years we were very tight and came close to getting married. But eventually we broke up. We were just too young and foolish (she was young and I was foolish).

Fast-forward to 2011. It's Karen on the line. We have maintained our friendship over these many decades and she is calling to say "hello." Usually our conversations are funny, light, and breezy—but not today. Somehow the conversation turns toward religion; a subject that can be a real spoiler if one's not careful. She knows my belief system has changed, but she's not sure about the "why" and the "how." She wants an answer. "What do you think about Jesus?" she politely demands. "Do you still accept him as your personal Savior?"

I hesitate to answer. She continues on with her own understanding of Jesus, supported with the assurance that he indeed is the promised Messiah as foretold by the prophets of the Old Testament. "Don't you believe in prophecy?" she asks.

(Where's that "don't ask, don't tell" policy when you need it?)

Her queries jar my psyche; they feel alien and drive me back to long-ago memories. It's a time warp of sorts. I hear the dogmatic whispers of my Jesusgate upbringing and I *feel* the theological distance between us. We have chosen different paths and the answers to her inquiries are way beyond a phone conversation. I resort to humor and we manage to chit-chat our way out of an awkward situation. For the moment our friendship is intact.

I would never insist that Karen think as I do, but I want her to understand why her questions are no longer relevant for me. And I don't want her to fret over what she would consider to be the loss of my "salvation."

When I hang up, I feel the pain . . . but this time it's more than my right knee.

P.S.—My girlfriend's name was not really "Karen." The above name is fictitious. But the story is true.

WHAT TO EXPECT NEXT

This chapter will continue to wrestle with the traditional assumptions that surround prophecy. We will explore what I call Stealth Prophecy and Framework Prophecy. We will then conclude with what I call Hindsight Prophecy; those prophecies placed on the lips of Jesus by the Gospel writers.

Chapter 12

PROPHECY AND JESUS
(Part Two)

CHRIST: The New Testament was written in Greek. The Hebrew word *Messiah* translated into Greek is *Christ*; the terms are synonymous. But the Gentiles could neither comprehend nor identify with the original notion of a Jewish Messiah. Therefore, the statement of hope within the title Messiah (Jesus *the* Messiah) was lost. Jesus the Christ became Jesus Christ (a proper name).

This chapter picks up where the last chapter left off: NT writers Cherry-picking the Old Testament to beef up a biographical portrait of Jesus that included a Messianic résumé. The idea that any part of the OT could be used (interpreted) as Messianic prophecy was a prevalent concept of early Jewish Christianity (nearly all of the first Christians were Jewish). When people came to believe that Jesus was the Christ (the Messiah), it was quite natural for them to assume that the OT would lend support to that belief. It was precisely this assumption that led to the wide-open hermeneutical (interpretive) lens through which the OT was now seen. Of course, with an "everything goes" mentality, the entire OT was considered fair game; that is, *any OT verses could be construed as prophecy.* Any and all OT verses could be used as evidence for Messianic fulfillment. Enter, if you will, the Gospel writers of Mark, Matthew, Luke, and John.

RAIDERS OF THE OLD TESTAMENT

Many eminent scholars are prone to believe that the details of Jesus' life, as depicted in the Gospels, have been padded for lack of information about what actually happened. Furthermore, they believe that these created stories about Jesus were developed in such a way so as to dovetail with OT verse. That is to say, the OT supplied the feeder line for creating part of the Jesus story. As a consequence, scholars would argue that it was not so much that Jesus literally fulfilled OT scripture, as it was about making Jesus look as if he had. Significantly, this puts an entirely new twist on the subject. Is this prophecy or the illusion of prophecy?

If the scholars are right, the illusion of prophecy fulfilled is not unlike the old farmer, Jeb, who fired his six-gun standing three feet away from the side of his barn. He then stepped forward and drew the target circles around the nicely clustered bullet holes. After moving 50 yards back from the so-called target, he reloaded and awaited the prearranged meeting with his smart aleck, young neighbor. When the old farmer saw that the approaching lad was in earshot, he hurriedly fired his handgun six more times, taking care to direct his aim just over the barn.

"Hey Jeb," the youth said mockingly. "What you aiming at? You know you couldn't hit the broadside of a barn!"

"I've been practicing," replied Jeb. "What I aim at is what I hit, and what I hit is what I aim at."

The young boy laughed. "Ha, only in your dreams, you old codger. But I'll humor you. Let's go see if you even hit the target."

Upon reaching the barn, the youth could hardly believe his eyes. He was looking at six bull's-eyes!

"Six in a row!" the youth shouted. "What are the odds? That's no coincidence!"

—

As Professor John Dominic Crossan[1] explains it, scholars agree that the NT narratives have an historical core; Jesus lived, taught, was arrested, and crucified. This is what Crossan calls *History remembered*. (That's Jeb's barn.) Scholars also argue that the details of those narratives (what Jesus literally said and did and how the events unfolded) are fictionalized in a manner to make Jesus appear as if he lived and died in accordance with

OT prophecy. This is what Crossan calls, *prophecy historicized*.[2] (That's the neatly clustered bullet holes.)

I reemphasize for the reader that although there is an historical core to the Gospels, almost all scholars agree that these books do not record firsthand remembrances about Jesus. The most likely scenario is that these early Gospel writers had a skeletal history about Jesus and it was left up to them to flesh out the story. In view of the fact that they lacked detailed knowledge of what had actually occurred, the Gospel writers methodically combed the OT for material they could use to fill in the blanks (in a manner of speaking). Some of these blanks may have also been filled in through oral tradition—oral tradition about Jesus that had evolved over more than three decades. Whatever the case, these NT writers—long after Jesus had disappeared from the scene—believed that he was the Messiah. Believing that Jesus was the Messiah gave them license to become raiders of the Old Testament. This writing was, after all, God's revelation, and that's why they believed that the OT was more than the sum of its parts.

For that reason, they reached back and grabbed OT verse, then wrapped it around Jesus in order to present him in the most impressive manner; bingo, prophecy fulfilled. Obviously, these OT verses were not prophecies fulfilled. They were verses borrowed from the OT and weaved into the NT so as to give the impression of fulfillment in Jesus (as we saw in Matthew's Gospel). This impression of prophetic fulfillment is akin to Jeb's so-called miraculous bull's-eye cluster. ("Six in a row!" the youth shouted. "What are the odds? That's no coincidence!")

Of course, this is the practical conclusion of scholars based on the principles of biblical criticism, the likes of which do not include supernatural presumptions.

We have already examined laundered and fish out of water prophecies, which indicate biographical padding to bolster the Jesus persona. Aside from these two examples, there is yet more evidence that highlights this type of embellishment.

STEALTH PROPHECY

Our former examples of laundered and fish out of water prophecies, pictured Jesus as having fulfilled OT verse. These so-called prophecies were either made up or misapplied. They did, however, help to fill out the Jesus story.

Stealth prophecy is equally functional, but it's not as transparent. That is, the Gospel writers—all of them—are borrowing OT narrative to help beef up the Jesus story but they don't always identify it as prophecy. The words, "prophecy fulfilled," or "scripture fulfilled," or "to fulfill what the Lord had spoken through the prophet," do not appear in the text. Therefore, similar to a stealth bomber, stealth prophecy does not appear on the radar. It remains invisible unless one recognizes the verses in question as coming from the Old Testament. (Of course, today's Bible will automatically footnote that connection for us.) When these Gospels were first written, however, it was left to the reader (or listener, since most people couldn't read) to identify OT verses scattered about in the Gospels. Many Jews could have spotted the connection, but anyone outside of Judaism would have been oblivious to these OT verses now appearing in these Gospels, unless tipped off by a knowledgeable rabbi.

The crucifixion narrative, found in all four Gospels, is a perfect example of stealth prophecy. You'll find a slew of verses from various OT books (e.g., Psalms, Exodus, Zechariah, Amos, Zephaniah) that form the basis for what happens to Jesus on the cross (see Mk 15:21-39; Mt 27:32-54; Lk 23:26-48; Jn 19:17-37). These verses served a dual purpose. For Jews who were interested, these OT verses that appeared in the crucifixion narrative, tied Jesus to so-called Messianic prophecy; for non-Jews, these verses made for good reading as they filled out the ending account of Jesus' life.

As a case in point, consider what all the Gospel writers borrow from Psalm 22. Although I'm only using Matthew as an example, some of these Psalms verses are found in all four Gospels.

> **Ps 22:18:** they divide my clothes among themselves, and for my clothing they cast lots.

> **Mt 27:35a:** And when they had crucified him, they divided his clothes among themselves by casting lots.

~

> **Ps 22:16:** For dogs are all around me; a company of evildoers encircle me.

Mt 27:38: Then two bandits were crucified with him, one on his right and one on his left.

—

Ps 22:7: All who see me mock at me, they shake their heads.

Matt 27:39: And those who passed by derided him, shaking their heads . . . .

—

Ps 22:8: Commit your cause to the Lord; let him deliver—let him rescue the one in whom he delights!

Matt 27: 43a: He trusts in God; let God deliver him now, if he wants to;

—

Ps 22: 1: "My God, my God, why have you forsaken me?"

Mt. 27:46: And about three o'clock Jesus cried out with a loud voice . . ."My God, my God, why have you forsaken me?"

As noted earlier, when reading the crucifixion story you will notice that the Gospel writers—*with the exception of John*—do not give any indication that they are drawing verses from the Book of Psalms, or that these verses are prophetic in any way. That's why I call them stealth prophecies.

Today, however, most everyone recognizes them as coming from the OT because our Bibles provide identifying notations. Also, Christians have been informed every Easter about these Old and New Testament connections. What were once stealth verses are now quite visible. That is why today these verses are used as a powerful argument for prophecy fulfilled. But is this genuine prophecy, or six more clustered bull's-eyes? Personally, I choose the latter, and here's why.

I would subset these OT stealth verses attributed to Jesus as "laundered" or "fish out of water" prophecies. I say this because all of the Gospel writers have taken them out of context in one way or another. The Psalms, for example, ". . . speak of a righteous man who suffers at the hands of God's enemies and who comes to be vindicated by God. Originally, these *'Psalms of Lament'* may have been written by Jews who were undergoing particularly difficult times of oppression, and who found relief in airing their complaints against the evil persons who attacked them and expressing their hopes that God would intervene on their behalf (e.g., see Psalms 22, 35, and 69)."[3] However, regardless of their original meaning, the Gospel writers transplanted these heart-rending verses into their writings in order to fill out the crucifixion story of Jesus, and to create the illusion of prophecy fulfilled for those who were familiar with Old Testament verse.

As I have indicated, John is not totally stealthy. Unlike the Synoptic Gospels, John uses variations of the phrase "in order to fulfill scripture," throughout his crucifixion scene. In this context, scripture fulfilled means prophecy fulfilled. Nevertheless, whatever claims he makes for the fulfillment of OT verse cannot be justified. These verses must fall under the laundered or fish out of water categories since he too has transplanted them and used them in a manner contrary to their original intention. But let us not forget that this technique of reinterpreting the "sacred" words of the past, so as to lend new meaning to a current situation, was perfectly acceptable to the Jewish Christian mind of the first century.

My point, however, harkens back to the scholar's point: The Gospel accounts are not so much history remembered, as they are OT scripture being historicized. I reiterate: In the absence of knowing the actual details about what happened to Jesus on all counts, it appears that the authors of the Gospels siphoned off OT verses so as to put flesh on the skeletal Jesus story they had received from previous generations. In other words, it was the indiscriminate transfer of OT verses into the Gospels that created the illusion of prophecy fulfilled by Jesus. Two thousand years later we have people walking up to the side of that barn and saying: "Six in a row! What are the odds? That's no coincidence!"

What other evidence do we have that indicates this biographical padding?

FRAMEWORK PROPHECY

What I choose to call *framework prophecy* is in a league of its own and stealthier than stealth prophecy. I never would have spotted it myself had I not had the advantage of the scholar's lead. In this case, I am indebted to John Dominic Crossan for his revealing insights in his book, *Who Killed Jesus*. The following will illustrate once again how the Gospel writers used the OT to fill out the Jesus story line. Unlike our former prophetic examples, however, framework prophecy is much more *extensive* and *comprehensive*. Here's what I mean by extensive and comprehensive.

One will notice that our previous NT examples of "prophecy," as taken from the OT, are generally restricted to *one sentence* excerpts (for example, "Out of Egypt I have called my son" or, "My God, my God, why have you forsaken me?"). In contrast, framework prophecy is extensive and comprehensive in that it uses a running sequence of an entire OT story, not just random isolated verses. In other words, the NT story follows, in sequential order, the framing plot of an OT story (yes, it is similar to the Psalms 22 run, but it's still a different genre because it is story oriented).

Visualize framework prophecy as an old house with new owners that replace the old furniture with new furniture--same framing structure, new content. Dr. Crossan uses aspects of the Passion story about Jesus (story of the sufferings and death of Jesus) to illustrate the OT framing structure and its *reuse in the New Testament*. That is, Jesus prays; Peter pays allegiance to Jesus even unto death; Judas betrays Jesus; Judas is remorseful and hangs himself. This same sequence of events—with different characters in play—can be found in the ancient OT story of King David and his son, Absalom (specifically in 2 Samuel, chapters 15-17). As the ancient story goes, Absalom conspires against his father, starts a rebellion, and declares himself, king. But the uprising comes to naught and Absalom is killed. The whole sordid affair is a heartbreaking incident for King David. The point is: part of what happens to David in the OT story now happens to Jesus in the New Testament. Before we draw the actual comparison, a few preliminaries are necessary.

We begin by noting King David's importance to the Jewish mind. As a young lad he had defeated the Philistine giant, Goliath, in battle. Later, David became the greatest king in the history of Israel. As a warrior king, he was without equal as he championed the nation of Israel through its glory days.

A TAD OUTSIDE THE BOX

by Ernie Bringas

A Mother's Advice Goes UnHeeded

David did, however, run afoul of God's law; that is, he slept with Bathsheba who was married to Uriah the Hittite. David got her pregnant, got Uriah killed by putting him in the front lines of his army, and then took Bathsheba as his wife. Nice guy. (I don't think most people would want somebody like that in their family tree.) Nevertheless, King David made amends and, over time, came to be revered. Long after his death, the nation suffered hard times. But they never forgot their all-time hero. Eventually he became the prototype for the coming Messiah, their liberator (the anointed one of God; the prime example of power and hope for a beleaguered people).

That is why Matthew and Luke—oddly enough using different genealogies—trace Jesus back to the Davidic line at the outset of their Gospels. Once the early Jewish Christians had concluded that Jesus was indeed the Messiah, how could it be otherwise? *The link to David was crucial; it solidified the status of Jesus as Messianic; the long-awaited promise was now fulfilled.*

We will now compare the OT story of David with the NT story of Jesus. By tying Jesus to this old Davidic story, the Gospel writers are not simply borrowing at random an OT storyline, but are also illustrating their belief in Jesus as the culmination of Messianic prophecy. They otherwise would never have connected the two (David and Jesus) by moving Jesus into the same OT framework story occupied by David.

It appears that Mark (the first Gospel to be written), took the historical sequence of what happened to David, and filtered Jesus into the same story. The other Gospel writers followed suit. I will list some of the parallels that Dr. Crossan gives us to consider. Please note: I have paraphrased—and eliminated—some of the information in Crossan's presentation; but the insight remains his. Let's proceed.

First, there is a traitor in each case. King David has a close friend and counselor named Ahithophel (good luck with the pronunciation). He conspires against King David by joining forces with Absalom, David's renegade son. Ahithophel betrays David as Judas betrays Jesus.

> **2 Samuel 15:12, 31a:** While Absalom was offering the sacrifices, he sent for Ahithophel . . . David's counselor . . . David was told that Ahithophel was among the conspirators with Absalom.

> **Mark 14:10:** Then Judas Iscariot, who was one of the twelve, went to the chief priests in order to betray Jesus to them.

Second, both David and Jesus make their way to the Mount of Olives. (The Mount of Olives is about one-half mile east of Jerusalem. It is also called Mount Olivet. A garden area, half way between the Mount of Olives and Jerusalem, is called Gethsemane.)

> **2 Samuel 15:23, 30a:** . . . the king crossed the Wadi Kidron [Valley], and all the people moved on toward the wilderness . . . But David went up the ascent of the Mount of Olives.

> **Mark 14:26:** When they had sung the hymn, they [Jesus and his disciples] went out to the Mount of Olives.

Third, both David and Jesus are very distraught and petition God in prayer.

> **2 Samuel 15:30b, 31b:** [David] weeping as he went, with his head covered and walking barefoot; . . . And David said, "O Lord,I pray thee, turn the counsel of Ahithophel into foolishness."

> **Mark 14:33-35a:** [Jesus] began to be distressed and agitated and said . . ." I am deeply grieved, even to death . . . ." And going a little further, he threw himself on the ground and prayed.

Fourth, both David and Jesus have men that insist they are ready to die for them.

> **2 Samuel 15:21:** Ittai answered the king, "As the Lord lives, and as my lord the king lives, wherever my lord the king may be, whether for death or life, there also your servant will be."

> **Mark 14:30-31:** And Jesus said to him [Peter] . . ."you will deny me three times." But he said vehemently, "If I must die with you, I will not deny you."

Fifth, both David and Jesus are accepting of God's will for them.

> **2 Samuel 15:26:** [David] . . ."here I am, let him [God] do to me what seems good to him."

> **Mark 14:36:** [Jesus] . . ."Father, for you all things are possible; remove this cup from me; yet, not what I want, but what you want."

Sixth, both traitors (Ahithophel and Judas) commit suicide by hanging themselves.

> **2 Samuel 17:23:** When Ahithophel saw that his counsel was not followed, he saddled his donkey and went off home to his own city. He set his house in order, and hanged himself.

Matthew 27:5: Throwing down the pieces of silver in the Temple, he [Judas] departed; and he went and hanged himself.
[All above brackets mine]

The point Crossan makes in laying out these parallels is that Mark's scenario about Jesus' last night stems, in part, from reusing and rebuilding the OT Davidic story; not from anyone's remembrance about what literally happened to Jesus that night. This is not to imply that we have no foundational history of any sort. Not so. As Crossan puts it: "I may judge isolated events to be historical, for example, the betrayal or the flight, but I do not presume that the framing narrative [the event as detailed] is historical."[4] [Brackets mine]

Again, framework prophecy highlights the common tendency by the Gospel writers to create—in the absence of any hard facts—a major story line for Jesus' life by drawing on Old Testament backups. We can observe that the main format of the OT story is being reconstructed in the NT account, even though the characters and many of the details have been changed to accommodate a new situation. The connection between Jesus and David is no accident. As I already stated, he was touted as the prototype of the future Messiah. For that reason, what happens to King David in this OT story now happens to Jesus in the NT story (same house, new furniture). This is why I call it framework prophecy.

One could argue, I suppose, that these converging story lines between the Old and New Testaments are simply coincidental. But what are the odds? Well, according to the science of probability, if you covered the entire state of Texas to a depth of two feet with silver dollars . . . just kidding.

Before moving on to our next category, an intriguing observation about number six came to mind. Perhaps you noticed that Matthew's verse about Judas' suicide was not taken from Mark, as were our other five examples. That's because Mark doesn't have it. With the exception of Matthew, neither do any of the other Gospels. My educated guess here is that Matthew, while copying Mark's Gospel, saw an opportunity to include another feature of the Davidic story that Mark had left out. If you'll remember, Mark (about ten years earlier) had already written his Gospel and Matthew is now copying 90 percent of it as a foundation for his own Gospel. He copies the story about Jesus at Gethsemane sometimes word for word (compare Matthew 26:36ff with Mark 14:32ff). In doing so, he recognizes that Mark is using the OT story about David and Absalom as a supportive backdrop for Jesus' last night. However, Matthew sees Mark's framing narrative as incomplete. He digs deeper into the same OT story (or, he might simply have known it) and puts the finishing touch on Mark's rendition by adding the suicide scene to his own composition.

Another possibility is that Matthew's inclusion of this suicide came from a unique source that none of the other Gospel writers had (what we have already referred to in Chapter 9 as the M source). Whatever the truth of the matter, it is obvious that Matthew is tracing over Mark's apparent use of the Davidic story. Yet unlike Mark, it is also clear that Matthew injects the suicide scene from that OT story into his own Gospel. Matthew's expansion of Mark's story adds drama, a touch of justice, and closure.

Here's a note of interest. Unlike Matthew, neither Mark nor Luke mention the suicide narrative in there Gospels. But Luke does bring forth a conflicting version of that event in his second volume work, The Acts of the Apostles (AKA - Acts). In regards to Judas it reads: ". . . and falling headlong, he burst open in the middle and all his bowels gushed out." (Acts 1:18b) This sounds like Judas fell on his own sword or something to that effect. These conflicting suicide versions between Matthew's Gospel and Luke's Book of Acts, along with the realization that an OT framing narrative has been borrowed to fill in the Jesus story, might help us to understand further why scholars question the "historical" reliability of the New Testament.

If one can acknowledge these anomalies and conflicts, this will help alter the notion that one is reading literal history on all counts. Thereafter, the story can be understood as a mixture of fact and creative imagination. That's what I think Crossan means when he says that he can accept certain isolated events as historical, but does not believe that the framing narrative is historical. In other words, the Passion narrative has been written in such a way so as to convey the trauma that Jesus must have undergone, but not necessarily in the manner described.

Like the very short outfielder that got lost in the grass, let's make sure we haven't gone too far afield. We have labeled the above comparative account as framework prophecy because of its implied prophetic overtone (the David to Jesus Messianic mantle), and also because of its lengthy and sequential use of the OT story about King David and his personal ordeal. Although similar to the other carte blanche raids on the OT by the Gospel writers, this was an extraordinary approach which was much more extensive. For the Gospel writers, it was hoped that the parallel stories of Jesus and David would provide, for informed Jews, some evidence of a Messianic Jesus.

FINAL SUMMATION OF OT PROPHECY
(Chapters 11 & 12)

Most of us grew up thinking of OT prophecy as undeniably fulfilled by Jesus in the New Testament. It is not surprising, therefore, that the 456 predictions of so-called Messianic fulfillment—some of which were listed in the beginning of our last chapter—appeared so persuasive and overwhelming to Dr. Peter Stoner and his 600 college students. But their view of prophecy was extremely naïve. Their KQ on this matter was apparently quite low. They obviously didn't have a clue about the Gospel writer's uncritical cross-reference use of the Old Testament. As we have seen, many of the OT verses used by the NT writers were not at all prophecies, or they were OT prophetic verses that were never intended to be about Jesus.

When one factors in this information, Dr. Stoner's assumptions about prophecy fulfilled are turned topsy-turvy. What appeared to be a rock-solid argument for him and his students turns out to be intellectual quicksand if one is willing to acknowledge the facts at hand. Once again, Dr. Stoner managed only to prove the old adage: "For every complex question, there is usually a very simple, understandable, *wrong answer.*"

Of course, for Dr. Stoner and his students, the Texas silver dollar analogy rang true (as it does with all Jesusgate victims). But they were using counterfeit coin and didn't know it. Ignorance may be bliss, but in this case, it was also misleading, and reinforced a stereotyped view of biblical prophecy that is no longer reasonable or defensible. Dr. Stoner and his students are prime examples of the Jesusgate fallout, and are simply practicing medicine without a license.

Time to move on. Although the upcoming type of foretelling has nothing to do with Messianic prophecy, or the OT, it is nevertheless quite important.

HINDSIGHT PROPHECY

I reserved hindsight prophecy as a category unto itself for the following four reasons. First, this type of New Testament prophecy has no connection to OT verse and, therefore, it is not prophecy about Jesus. Second, although these prophecies are not about Jesus, they supposedly are prophecies made by Jesus. Third, scholars do not believe that Jesus actually made these predictions as biblically portrayed; that is, these are prophecies placed on the lips of Jesus by the NT writer. Fourth, these prophecies create only the illusion of prophecy because the events they foretell have already happened. Say what? All four of these points can be explained by clarifying the fourth.

We usually think of the Bible as having been written in linear fashion, that is, in logical sequence (a then b then c then d, etc.) That's the way most things are written; but there are notable exceptions to this natural flow of unfolding events.[5] Sometimes, for example, certain sections of the Gospels appear to have been written from a 20/20 hindsight perspective. That is, written after the fact, but written so as to imply that the event had not yet taken place, ergo, prophetic hindsight. Therefore, hindsight prophecy cannot truly be prophecy if the Gospel writer is expounding about what he already knows has happened.

To illustrate this problematic "forecasting," let's look at a hypothetical example. If I claimed to predict the fall of the New York World Trade Center Towers *after the event occurred*, this would not be prophecy (duh!). But if no one knew the exact date I made that prediction (before or after the event), the question of whether it was real prophecy or hindsight prophecy, would be up for grabs. Without further evidence to support either side of the argument, resolution would be impossible, although most people would be reasonably skeptical about the prophetic angle (and rightly so).

For the sake of argument, however, let us suppose that *today* you found a document dated 1999, written by an unknown person. To your amazement, the document actually predicted (prophesied) that some calamity would hit New York City within a few years. You might scratch your head and wonder if the letter was genuine; that is, was it really written in 1999, two years *before* the New York Towers were destroyed on 9-11-2001? This makes the so-called prophecy a bit more intriguing. But without some way to verify the document's date, you would still remain skeptical. There are numerous ways one might pursue this kind of puzzle but I will share a method by which scholars conclude that certain so-called prophecies are not at all prophecies.

What I propose next is a no-brainer and you may wonder what the big deal is. It may appear as a pointless example because it will lead us to a foregone conclusion. However, what seems to be a meaningless exercise may nevertheless lead us to a greater insight. Here it is: Harking back to our 1999 document, let us now suppose that the predictions therein are as follows. It tells us that *on the morning of September 11, 2001, terrorists affiliated with Al-Qaeda will crash two jet airliners into the World Trade Center in New York City. The two towers will collapse and nearly 3000 people will perish.*

Without question, something is amiss with this so-called prophetic letter. *It's too precise.* No one could possibly predict future events with that kind of pinpoint accuracy. One must conclude that the document was simply a predated letter describing what the author already knew had taken place. This is nothing short of what I call hindsight prophecy; it is a past event being floated as a future event under the pretense of prophecy. It's a hoax. No reasonable person could conclude otherwise. I told you it was a no-brainer. Here's another example, but this one comes from religion. See what you think.

MORMONISM (The LDS Church)

One of the most blatant examples of hindsight prophecy can be found in the Book of Mormon. No, I'm not purposely picking on the Mormons[6] but the example they provide is just too juicy to let pass. Besides, I'll get to the rest of Christianity soon enough. To set the stage, here is a very brief description of the Book of Mormon and how Mormons believe it came to be.

Mormons believe that *the book was written, at least 600 years before the time of Jesus,* engraved on gold plates by the ancient prophets. According to Mormon belief these engraved plates (which today makeup the Book of Mormon) were condensed by the prophet-historian Mormon and his son Moroni who hid it up to the Lord in or about 421 AD. In other words, the plates disappeared at that time. Considering this timeline, the unabridged Book of Mormon was originally engraved around 600 BC, and then buried By Mormon in 421 AD (about 1000 years before Columbus sailed the ocean blue in 1492).

Not until 1823-27 did these condensed plates reappear. A messenger from God delivered them to Joseph Smith. The plates, Smith said, had been buried in a hill near his home in Manchester, New York. His assignment, as given by God through the divine messenger, was to translate the gold plates into English. He did. As the story goes, the English Book of Mormon came into being and Joseph Smith became the founder of Mormonism. Upon completing his assignment, Smith gave the gold plates back to the messenger from God. That is why today the plates are nowhere to be found. Regardless, Mormons take it on faith that this Book is part of God's divine revelation, even as other Christians (along with Mormons) accept the Bible as divine revelation.

In contrast to the NT, which describes the life of Jesus played out in Palestine under Roman rule, the Book of Mormon claims to be another Testament to the life of Jesus Christ and a record of his dealings with the ancient inhabitants of the Americas (what we now call Central America— Guatemala, Honduras, Nicaragua, El Salvador). Mormons believe that Jesus' ministry to the Americas occurred during the time after his resurrection and before his Ascension (the ascent of Christ into heaven on the fortieth day after his resurrection). Okay, let's get back to hindsight prophecy.

My focus here will be on the opening book of the Book of Mormon called The First Book of Nephi. It is here, supposedly centuries before the time of Jesus, that we find an account of Lehi's family. He has four sons, one of which is named Nephi. Let's cut to the chase. According to the Book of Mormon, the prophet Nephi, *who supposedly had his beginnings in Jerusalem 600 years before Jesus,* engraves on metal plates the following prophecy. (The scene depicted below is that of John the Baptist announcing the coming of Jesus as told by Nephi and the much later Gospel of Mark.)

THE BOOK OF MORMON (Nephi, ca. 600 BC)	THE NEW TESTAMENT (Mark, ca. 70 AD)
8. Yea, even he should go forth and cry in the wilderness: Prepare ye the way of the Lord, and make his paths straight; for there standeth one among you whom ye know not; and he is mightier than I, whose shoes I am not worthy to unloose. (Nephi 10:8)	3. The voice of one crying in the wilderness, prepare ye the way of the Lord, make his paths straight. 7. There cometh one mightier than I after me, The latchet of whose shoes I am not worthy to unloose. (Mark 1: 3 & 7; from the KJV Bible)

[NOTE: I chose the King James Version (KJV) as a comparison to the Book of Mormon because this was the Bible that was in vogue at exactly the same time the Book of Mormon surfaced in 1823-27. Suspiciously, the Book of Mormon reproduces the same wording [as in our above example], the same style, and even some of the same errors found in the KJV. This is all very suspect. Is it possible that Smith created the Book of Mormon, using the KJV as the foundation for his work? Obviously, Mormons believe that Joseph Smith is simply translating, not writing, these ancient plates—plates supposedly written by Nephi around 600 BC.]

Nearly all of us will clearly see that by virtue of its uncanny precision, the above "prophecy" in the Book of Mormon self-destructs. That is, its accuracy makes it unthinkable for us to see it as anything other than hindsight prophecy. When one compares these two texts—one of the many I could have chosen—it is impossible to imagine that Nephi actually wrote it because, whoever did write it, has selectively plagiarized bits and pieces of Mark almost verbatim. How could this be if Mark is 600 plus years off into the future? How could these Mormon verses not be hindsight prophecy?

Therefore, logic dictates that whoever wrote the book of Nephi is living in AD time, unless you want to float the idea that it is first century Mark who is copying Nephi. At least the timeline would be right. But that frog won't jump. We don't have one shred of evidence that would support such a premise. In fact, we have no ancient texts, or plates, or anything to verify that Nephi's engraving or any other parts of the Book of Mormon ever existed prior to the eighteen hundreds when the plates are suddenly revealed to Joseph Smith by the angel Moroni.

If you're still not convinced about hindsight prophecy in the Book of Mormon, listen up. Here are some other very specific predictions pertaining to Jesus, supposedly made by Nephi 600 + years before Jesus was born. He predicts the coming of the Messiah (as a savior & redeemer for the sins of humanity, no less); his virgin birth; his baptism by a special prophet that includes a descending Holy Spirit in the form of a dove; his ministry; his calling of the twelve Apostles; his crucifixion and his resurrection (I Nephi, chapters 1, 10, 11, 14, 19, and more).

For anyone standing outside of the Mormon faith, these precise predictions are reminiscent of our Trade Towers analogy. Such pinpoint details about Jesus are a dead giveaway that someone in AD time has the

NT in hand and is simply repeating knowledge they already possess, not prophesying from BC time as Mormons claim. For that reason, most of us would classify such prophecy as hindsight prophecy; that is, someone has taken information from the Gospels and has created the illusion of prophecy by pretending to foretell events that have already happened. The evidence for this conclusion is quite clear if one's mind is not clouded by religious indoctrination. It's easy to spot hindsight prophecy through common sense inference, *especially when one is analyzing someone else's belief system.*

Of course, Mormons believe otherwise. Here is proof, Mormons would say, that the Book of Mormon is divinely inspired by God. It foretold details about the Jesus story 600 years before the fact. How else could Nephi have made these detailed prophecies without God's guidance? How indeed?

Regardless, without the so-called original plates, the story as to how the Book of Mormon came into being cannot be verified. All we know for sure is that the first copy of the Book was supposedly translated by Joseph Smith, and was written in the same English style and wording as the King James Version of the Bible which was first issued in 1611. However, The Book of Mormon, in its introduction, does present us with eight testimonial witnesses claiming to have been shown the gold plates by Joseph Smith. Assuming these testimonials are true (a debatable point) this still doesn't prove anything except that several people saw some gold plates with what appeared to be ancient writing. Nevertheless, Joseph Smith declares: "I told the brethren that the Book of Mormon was the most correct of any book on earth [Including the Bible?], and the keystone of our religion, and a man would get nearer to God by abiding by its precepts, than by any other book."[7] [Brackets mine]

Whatever the case, here is what Mormons would have us believe. Nephi was a genuine prophet guided by God's influence so as to make him capable of pinpoint prophecy 600 years before the birth of Jesus, and 670 years before Mark's Gospel. Nephi knew what would happen to Jesus because God revealed as much. In short, the Mormon faithful will claim that this is real prophecy, not hindsight prophecy. For them, that is what makes this Book so miraculous. More than that, they will say that the real miracle is in the reading of the Book, where God's presence is truly felt. How else could one explain this great and mighty work?

Unfortunately, the above argument for superiority is quite porous. It's the same line of reasoning that almost all religious groups use when defending their holy texts. For example, aside from the Mormons, it would be difficult to find any other Christians who do not defend the Bible as the greatest work ever written. Only through God's direct intervention could such a miraculous work come to fruition, they claim. More than that, they will say that the real miracle is in the reading of the Bible, where God's presence is truly felt. How else could one explain this great and mighty work?

Most religious Jews feel the same way about the Torah (first five books of the Old Testament). Only through God's direct revelation could such a miraculous work come to fruition, they claim. More than that, they will say that the real miracle is in the reading of the Torah, where God's presence is truly felt. How else could one explain this great and mighty work?

As an example outside of the Judeo-Christian faith, consider the Muslims as they proclaim the Qur'an to be the greatest book ever given to humanity. Only by God's direct revelation through an angel to the prophet Muhammad, could such a miraculous work come to fruition, they claim. More than that, they will say that the real miracle is in the reading of the Qur'an, where God's presence is truly felt. How else could one explain this great and mighty work?

Need I say more? I have other arrows in my quiver, but I'm sure you get the point. If not, you're in real trouble as a reader (or, maybe, just maybe, I'm in trouble as a writer). Okay, it's time to round out hindsight prophecy.

NEW TESTAMENT HINDSIGHT PROPHECY

Hindsight prophecy is not exclusive to the Mormons, and it comes in all shapes and sizes. A good example of what appears to be hindsight prophecy can be found in the Gospel of Mark. In order to understand why scholars suspect the presence of what I call "prophetic hindsight," a short historical sketch is necessary. (I'll keep it short.)

About thirty-three years after the crucifixion of Jesus, toward the close of Nero's reign, Jewish open rebellion erupted against the Romans (66 AD). But the Jewish Zealots (freedom fighters) were no match against the well-trained armies of Rome. The Romans, using catapults and battering rams, finally pushed Jerusalem's defenders back into the sacred Temple area. Even so, their superhuman resistance in defense of the city remains legendary. Amid unbelievable slaughter, the entire city (along with the Temple) was finally burned and destroyed around 70 AD. In fact, the Romans "destroyed the Temple completely, leaving not one stone standing."[8] (Except for the Western Wall.) With this information in mind, we now return to Mark. (Was that short enough?)

For various reasons, most scholars agree that Mark wrote his Gospel around 70 AD. One strong indication for this date is that Mark seems to have some knowledge about the Roman-Jewish war (ca. 66-70 AD). This knowledge appears most evident when he weaves some of the details of that period into his narrative; details that are revealed in the form of what I have termed hindsight prophecy. For example, in Mark 13:1-2 we read:

> As he [Jesus] came out of the temple, one of his disciples said to him, "Look, Teacher, what large stones and what large buildings!"
> Then Jesus asked him, "Do you see these great buildings? Not one stone will be left here upon another; all will be thrown down."

If progressive scholars are correct, Mark has Jesus predicting what Mark already seems to know (about the destruction of the Temple in 70 AD). Additionally, prophetic hindsight appears elsewhere in his writing. Consider, for example, Mark 8:31 and Mark 9:31:

> Then he began to teach them that the Son of Man must undergo great suffering, and be rejected by the elders, the chief priests, and the scribes, and be killed, and after three days rise again. (8:31)

> ... for he was teaching his disciples, saying to them, "The Son of Man is to be betrayed into human hands, and they will kill him, and three days after being killed, he will rise again." (9:31)

These pinpoint predictions that appear in the Gospel of Mark, supposedly made by Jesus, raises serious questions. Mark would have been familiar with the Passion story (the betrayal, suffering, death, and resurrection of Jesus) as proclaimed by the early, oral or written tradition. When scholars consider the above verses, they suspect that Mark has placed hindsight prophecy on the lips of Jesus who is then made to appear as if he is predicting future events; that is, his own betrayal, death, and resurrection, along with the much later destruction of the Temple. If so, Mark certainly made Jesus look as if he had Messianic powers with these precise outcomes. Scholars have no quarrel with Mark's motivation, but in their overall assessment of the situation, they must factor in what appears to be hindsight prophecy.

Whether or not Jesus actually rose from the dead is not relevant here because early Christians believed he did, and that is what makes the words of Jesus appear prophetic in Mark's writing. That also holds true for contemporary Christians, who point to these "prophetic verses" as evidence that Jesus was divine because he knew what was going to happen.

For people standing outside of Christianity, these detailed predictions look suspiciously similar to our Twin Towers analogy or the Book of Mormon. But most Christians will want to make Jesus an exception to the rule; an exception to what common sense generally dictates. They will claim that a divine Jesus could not help but know the blueprint details of his own demise. In other words, what seems to be an obvious case of hindsight prophecy will not apply to Jesus because he is unlike all others. But as we all know, this is the same argument used by every other religious body in the world. It's always about the supremacy of our holy leader, our holy book, our revelation, and our doctrine. Faithful believers almost always play the "supernatural" card. This puts God up their sleeve, and helps to sustain the uncompromising belief in the ultimate superiority of their culturally acquired religion that, in turn, leads them to irrational thoughts and actions. This brings us straight back to the primary characteristics of Jesusgate: presumption and expediency.

Here's what I tell my college students. We should not apply the rules of logic, common sense, or the scientific method to other religions, if we are not willing to apply them to our own. If, for example, we encounter the story of Vishnu—one of the Trinitarian gods of Hinduism—who on different occasions assumes human form in order to help humans, we will by virtue of our general KQ conclude that such stories are mythological in nature. As Christians, however, what will we conclude when we contemplate the virginal birth of Jesus, his ability to walk on water, or his miraculous return from the grave? I can't speak for everyone, but generally, when the bias of "religious certainty" is instilled through the cultural process of indoctrination, there will undoubtedly be an absence of honest inquiry and, therefore, and absence of truth.

Our following chapter will focus on the Virgin Birth of Jesus. This is another one of those Christian doctrines in need of clarification.

THE CHURCH IN THE WILDWOOD

There's a church in the valley by the wildwood
No lovelier place in the dale
No place is so dear to my childhood
As the little brown church in the vale.

The United Methodist Church (UMC) is wide-ranging in its theological makeup. It is inclusive because it is based on pluralism (a condition or system in which theological differences willingly coexist). In other words, the Church as a whole is comprised of conservative, moderate, and liberal congregations or a combination thereof. Conveniently, ministers can be assigned to churches that are in keeping with their theological inclinations.

After spending nine years in youth ministry—that was my specialty—I requested a pastorate (church). I was a member of the California United Methodist Conference and was assigned a small church (par for the course as a first assignment) in Vallejo, California.

It wasn't exactly the church in the wildwood, but it did sit on the outskirts of the town. I had asked for an "open pulpit," which are code words for a more progressive church. After all, I didn't want to become a Jesusgate preacher. I wanted a church in which I could share what I had gleaned from my education without getting crucified on first hearing. I was, however, savvy enough to tread carefully. My opening sermons were strictly G and PG, so to speak. I spent the first six months of my ministry just getting to know my congregation and vise versa. In the process, I discovered that most of my parishioners were quite conservative (not what

I had asked for). No matter, everything was going great. Our rapport was wonderful and the congregation doubled in size. It was time to ratchet up my sermons.

I can honestly tell you that my message on that fateful Sunday morning was quite benign. It certainly wasn't one of my X-rated, or even R-rated, sermons. But it doesn't take much to draw fire when the people you're addressing are sporting conservative antennae. Following the close of the service, I knew something was terribly wrong when some of my congregants descended on me like a flock of starving vultures looking for a fast meal. Evidently, during the course of my sermon, I had made a verbal misstep (at least in their thinking). One question led to another and before I knew it, they wanted to know if I believed in the Virgin Birth (which had nothing to do with my sermon). I answered directly and honestly, "I don't take it literally." My answer was too blunt. In a blink of an eye, friendship was out the window and all bets were off. I had answered like an honest minister, not a politician. I should have answered like a politician.

My Virgin Birth miscue quickly spread like the rumor of dead rats in Kentucky Fried Chicken's meat. (As a word of caution, the rat rumor was totally wrong.) Containment was impossible as my congregants continued to jabber away. Soon after, they called in my D.S. (District Superintendent) for a special meeting of the Administrative Board (the governing body of the local church). It was during this meeting that someone stood up, pointed me out and shouted, "he's the anti-Christ!" When the D.S. supported my views (based on the pluralistic nature of the UMC), my accuser stomped out of the room (gosh, that sounds familiar).

This whole affair split the church in half. Fortunately, we had grown sufficiently enough to absorb the loss of those disenchanted members. But is it any wonder that ministers today are reluctant to update their congregants beyond the warm and cozy boundaries promoted over the centuries by yesterday's, "go along to get along," clergy?

This was not my first or last encounter with congregants who had their religious KQ stifled by the malfeasance of Jesusgate clergy. Just so you'll know, I have not relented in my efforts to fight against the headwinds of religious illiteracy. My struggle reminds me of that song by Pete Seeger, *Against the Wind.* I can only identify with the refrain— *against the wind*—because the song is really about a drifter who lives life irresponsibly. Even as he gets older, he continues to run against the wind. That is the part of the song I can relate to because I am older now and still running against the wind. It's a haunting refrain and I suspect that most freethinkers can relate.

To be clear, the wind I face—and other educators face—is the hurricane force of religious illiteracy, created primarily by the clergy majority (professional Jesusgaters) who continue to default on their educational responsibilities. They are unwilling or unable to inject the findings of biblical criticism into their church curriculum. As a result, they have wittingly or unwittingly become part of the Jesusgate majority.

However, as I have already indicated, some ministers do introduce their congregants to the findings of biblical criticism. Also, ministers are not solely to blame for the knowledge gap between scholar and layperson. As illustrated through my own experiences, laypeople can be quite dogmatically unequivocal when theological issues are on the table. They can also be confrontational and provocative. As a consequence, this dampens the spirit of most ministers who are then forced to be more calculating. They become more guarded for fear of condemnation. The end result is the loss of any meaningful dialogue between themselves and the laity (specifically on the findings of biblical scholarship). The real losers in this unfortunate cycle are the laypersons that are then deprived of any educational benefits that might have liberated them from their pre-seventeenth century religious mindset.

Not surprisingly, laypersons become the Jesusgate proxies of popular Christianity because they're not hearing anything new from the clergy. For the past three hundred years or so, almost all Christians have been on a diet of pabulum. Where's the beef? Where are the findings of mainstream scholarship that would help curtail religious naiveté in our churches and, therefore, help to reduce our overall societal ignorance about Christianity?

I do not wish to imply that all of these clergy are not involved with life-giving service. Their contribution to humanity, for the most part, has been invaluable. Even so, the Achilles heel of ministry, it seems to me, has been its massive failure to deliver even a glancing blow against religious illiteracy. It may not have been possible to do this prior to the Enlightenment of the seventeenth century, but there's no excuse for this situation to have lasted for more than three hundred of years.[1] It's really a shameful time in the life of the Church, second only to the centuries of the witchcraft craze.

I say this because the failure to expose our congregants to the findings of biblical criticism does, in some ways, make our society dysfunctional—dysfunctional in the sense that it impedes our social and scientific progress. Everything from abridging women's rights, going to war, lashing out against gays, obstructing stem cell research, anti-Semitism, misguided foreign policy, you name it. I realize, of course, that other factors play into these troubling issues. Religion is not the sole culprit. But it shouldn't be any part of the problem; it should be part of the solution.

It's obvious that we live within the confines of a Jesusgate society. This is most apparent in the way Christianity is portrayed on television (by televangelists), by mega-churches with their charismatic leaders, by millions of unsuspecting Christians across the land (regardless of their denomination), by ordinary citizens and politicians of all persuasion. In fact, I consider most politicians to be suspect when they feign religious understanding, and simultaneously exhibit a complete lack of religious KQ. What a mess! This "popular Christianity" is so far removed from the knowledge we now possess, it would be comical were it not so tragic.

However, I am an optimist. Besides, you cannot suppress the religious KQ indefinitely. In reference to Jesusgate, I honestly believe this too shall pass, although not in my lifetime because the resistance to biblical criticism is well entrenched. Even now I can hear the outcry from the Jesusgate crowd: "Do you presume to criticize the great Oz? . . . Pay no attention to that man behind the curtain."

Well, we know how that turned out.

WHAT TO EXPECT NEXT

This chapter will deal with the doctrine of the Virgin Birth. Generally, Christians believe that Jesus was born of a virgin, or that his birth entailed the miraculous. The majority of Christians still interpret this birth narrative literally, although a good number of progressive and moderate Christians do not. Mainstream scholars, certainly not. Aside from the biological absurdity that the story connotes, this next chapter will help us to see why scholars have determined that the VB is an unsupportable doctrine, a primitive notion that requires reinterpretation.

[NOTE: I will continue to err on the side of caution by way of redundancy. I suspect that this repetitive style will be helpful to those who are unfamiliar with Christian development and the dating sequence of the New Testament.]

Chapter 13

THE BIRTH OF JESUS

For reasons that will soon be clear, I begin with a fact that almost everyone knows: Jesus was not born on December 25th and no one knows the actual date of his birth. It is commonly understood that Christians chose the December date because it coincided with the celebrated birth of the god Mithra who was worshipped by the Aryans of ancient Persia (modern day Iran). Mithra was adapted into Greek as Mithras (add the s) before making its way to the Roman Empire (the popular god of soldiers). This was the assumption for most of the twentieth century, although it is now being challenged as to whether Mithra and Mithras is one and the same god.[2] However that controversy pans out, in ancient Persia, Mithra was associated with the sun god.

A more compelling argument for choosing December 25th revolves around the Roman sun god. He was referred to as Sol Invictus (the Unconquered Sun) or, more fully, Deus Sol Invictus (the Unconquered Sun God). This victorious image was envisioned by the ending of the winter solstice (the shortest day of the year, December 21st or 22nd), when the sun appeared to recover its vigor. Thus, the Romans celebrated the sun's victory and observed its rebirth on December 25th.

There was a time during the third century AD when the religion of Sol Invictus rivaled Christianity for the allegiance of the Roman world. But as Christianity gained momentum over this rival religion, "it became a custom to use the old festival day for the celebration of the birth of Christ. In this way the church undertook to Christianize a celebration deeply rooted in Roman culture."[3] Truth be known, there were several pagan gods that were *supposedly* born on December 25th (including the Roman god Attis, the Greek god Dionysus, and the Egyptian god Osiris).

When this information came to light, it created quite a stir. But for Christians today, these details don't matter. They simply respect December 25th as the symbolic date for Jesus' birth. No one really cares about the precise date, or even that the 25th was borrowed from pagan religion. The issue is totally benign in the minds of most. But why is this tidbit of information so readily accepted? This now leads us to an interesting point of which we should take notice.

It is easy to see why people became so accepting of this detail from scholars. It does not really threaten the essential image of Jesus. The information is noninvasive, it does not pinch the nerve of faith; it does not wreak havoc with one's religious core. There is nothing here to defend and nothing here to dishearten. No biggie. To use a basketball phrase, "no harm, no foul."

Yet, what happens when scholars come back to us with particulars that undermine or threaten more sensitive beliefs about Jesus or the Bible—beliefs that we have cherished as bona fide truth? Do we continue to listen, or do we suspend our rational judgment of the scholar's knowledge? Historically speaking it has been the latter because the things that people consider sacred are the very things that they consider unalterable, and irrefutable. And when one is sucked into this religious black hole, there is little hope for escape. The following Jesus birth narrative will test that proposition. We begin with an obvious statement:

IT TAKES TWO TO TANGO

For many Christians, the doctrine of the Virgin Birth (VB) is little more than a lovely story that never happened; that is, the virgin aspect of it never happened. Still, there are two huge exceptions that represent the Christian majority worldwide: (1) Although some Catholic scholars and lay people no longer accept the VB as a literal event, it is still a basic teaching for the majority of Catholics worldwide and, (2) it is a basic belief for millions of evangelical Protestants who still view the Bible in literal mode.

In contrast, mainstream scholars do not believe that Jesus was born of a virgin, or that his birth entails the miraculous. These scholars are not alone. They are joined by millions of non-evangelical lay Christians.

These lay Christians, however, have rejected the VB not so much because they know what the scholars know, but because they cannot escape its biological absurdity. After all, it takes two to tango (unless were talking about the three branches of the federal government, and we can't even get them out on the dance floor.) Biology aside, the following points will help us to see why scholars have determined that the VB is an unsupportable doctrine, a primitive notion that needs reinterpretation. We'll begin by looking to see how this VB tradition developed chronologically within the New Testament.

THE EARLY BIRD GETS THE WORM, ONCE MORE
(Paul's writings, ca. 50-64 AD)

It was the Apostle Paul who spearheaded the earliest written record of Christianity. Paul's point of entry is crucial because his writings are the closest in time to Jesus (and the oral tradition about Jesus). He certainly *predates* the much later Gospels (ca. 70-100 AD). Therefore, the early bird factor will take precedence. Our investigation must begin with Paul— looking to see if Paul makes any mention of this "miraculous" birth.

We discover very quickly that Paul makes no mention of the VB in his body of work. One might consider this to be a serious exclusion by Paul if, indeed, he had any knowledge about this remarkable event. It appears that he didn't. In Galatians 4:4 he simply says that Jesus "was born of a woman." Here we have at the inception of NT writing, in one of the first NT books (ca. 50 AD), a modest declaration that Jesus was born of a woman (good guess). Paul is silent about a virginal birth for Jesus. It stands to reason that if Paul had known anything about such a miraculous birth, he would have proclaimed it. Although the argument from silence is not conclusive, scholars must factor in this observation as part of the evidence when evaluating the origins and accuracy of the VB story.

WE'RE NUMBER ONE (The Gospel of Mark, ca. 70 AD)

Paul dies around 67 AD. A few years later Mark's Gospel is penned (the first of the four Gospels to be written). We are now nearly forty years past the crucifixion, and at least seventy years past the birth of Jesus. And still, there is no mention of the virgin birth. Why not? This is an important question because Mark is not only the earliest Gospel to be written, but as we have seen, it is considered by scholars to be the most historically reliable of the Gospels.

As in Paul's case, it is highly unlikely that such a profound oral or written VB tradition, if it existed, could have slipped by the author of Mark unnoticed. It is important to note that Mark was the first NT writer to attempt a chronological narrative about Jesus' life (what he did, where he went, what he said). The significance of this point is that Mark had no way of knowing that anyone would follow suit with the Jesus story. Think about it. At that point in time, his *narrative* Gospel—to the best of our knowledge—was the only one that existed. It's not like he could relax and assume that this matter would be taken care of by somebody else. He had no clue that the Gospels of Matthew, Luke, and John were coming down the historical pike many years later. So it stands to reason that he would be careful to write down everything he thought to be important. Certainly, he would not allow such a profound assertion as the VB to go unmentioned if he thought it to be true or if he knew anything about it.

Thus far, these observations do not invalidate the VB, but they begin to raise serious questions. For the moment, it is enough to say that for scholars, the silence of Paul and Mark on this issue, speaks volumes. With this silence noted, we move on with our analysis of the Virgin Birth and its evolution within the Christian tradition.

WE TRY HARDER (The Gospel of Matthew, ca. 80 AD)

Finally, the VB makes its debut in the first chapter of the New Testament's lead-off book, Matthew. Although Matthew's Gospel appears at the front of the NT, it was nevertheless composed about sixteen years after Paul's final letter, about ten years after Mark's Gospel. We also need to remember that Matthew is writing about fifty years after the crucifixion, and about eighty years after Jesus' birth.

Obviously, we are now well into the Christian tradition. Why does the VB appear at this moment in time? From what, where, or how does the author of Matthew inherit this idea? He didn't hear it from Jesus because he never knew Jesus (besides, we have no evidence that Jesus ever made this claim). Matthew didn't get the VB idea from Paul because Paul doesn't seem to be aware of it. It didn't come from Mark since he also is silent on this matter. He didn't get it from the Gospels of Luke and John, as they were not yet written and, of these two, only Luke includes it. *[NOTE: Luke's birth story varies greatly from Matthew and is probably the result of an ongoing embellished evolution, post-Matthew by five or ten years.]*

Maybe Matthew received the VB account from the M Source (explained in chapter 13), or the oral stories about Jesus that floated around early on. In fact, these oral stories were passed from person to person long before they were committed to written form. But this brings us back to Paul, who died ca. 67 AD. He stands like a giant redwood between the crucifixion (early 30s AD) and Matthew's Gospel (ca. 80s AD). Paul, after all, was the most important Jesus advocate of his time (or any time, for that matter). And let's not forget Mark who precedes Matthew by about ten years. Again, it is highly unlikely that such a miraculous birth story could have bypassed these major players unnoticed, or that either of them would have ignored it.

We are left with the impression that Matthew's VB narrative, which suddenly appears about eighty years after Jesus' birth, signals a new strand of religious thought not previously held. He is the first to proclaim it and we have no evidence to support the claim that it was part of the earliest Jesus tradition. So why did Matthew pursue this line of thought? Aside from the mystery religions that promoted virgin births, how did he justify this pagan belief? We must ask again, from whence did he access the VB concept?

Recalling Chapter 11, we know that Matthew took great liberties with the OT in order to persuade his audience that Jesus was the fulfillment of "prophecy." In fact, we have already used the VB story as an illustration of Matthew's creative license—the fish out of water prophecies. Now it's time to dig deeper.

We previously acknowledged that Paul's writings and Mark's Gospel—our earliest written sources—make no mention about a virginal birth. We don't know why Matthew came up with the VB story. Was he influenced by the mystery religions and their virginal birth stories? Did he latch on to some oral or written tradition to which Paul and Mark had no access? Did he push the concept in order to qualify Jesus with other notables of his time who supposedly had been born of virgins (for example, Alexander the Great, Socrates, Caesar Augustus, to name a few)? Indeed, almost anyone who was anyone had to be born of a virgin; it was almost a mandatory, entry-level requirement for any superstar résumé. There are other possibilities as to why Matthew promotes the VB; but how does Matthew attempt to make the story credible?

To justify his claim for a miraculous birth, Matthew needs an authoritative source. Matthew solves this problem (as we have already seen) by quoting one of the most venerated sources of his time—Isaiah (7:14). This rendering from Isaiah reappears in Matthew 1:22:

> "Look, the virgin shall conceive and bear a son, and
> they shall name him Emmanuel," which means, "God is
> with us."

So there it is. Matthew is reaching back long before Paul to support his VB assertion. Matthew claims that around seven hundred years before Jesus was born, Isaiah predicted this miraculous event. It seems that Matthew has inherited the idea from the most authoritative source possible at that time. He didn't need—or, perhaps even want—Paul, or Mark; they were too contemporary. In Matthew's day, these men are certainly important, but not yet the luminary standouts that historical hindsight will make them. Even their written works are not yet considered sacred. No, for Matthew, in the first century, Isaiah was the real heavyweight. Thus, Matthew quotes from the OT Book of Isaiah: "Look, the virgin shall conceive".... At first glance Matthew's position appears to be solid. But wait! (as they say in sales). So, what could be wrong with Matthew's ironclad approach? There are three big problems.

First (in Chapter 11), we came to understand that Matthew yanked this prophetic verse (Isaiah 7:14) out of its original context (a fish out of water prophecy). That is, he took Isaiah's short-term prophetic sign from God as assurance for King Ahaz's deliverance, and turned it into a misapplied long-term Messianic prophecy about Jesus.

Second, Matthew presents the pregnancy in Isaiah's story as a future event. Isaiah tells us that the woman is already pregnant ("Look, the young woman is with child ....")

Third, we also came to recognize that Matthew used the Greek word "parthenos" (virgin), rather than using the original OT Hebrew word "almah" (young woman) when he translated Isaiah 7:14. It appears that Matthew may have misquoted Isaiah. But how could this happen? The most accepted scholarly answer to that question is as follows.

THE SEPTUAGINT (LXX)
(76 Trombones Led the Big Parade [more or less])

The Septuagint is the translation of the Hebrew Bible (the OT) into Greek—the international language of Matthew's day. This translation (from Hebrew to Greek) was started around 250 BC, and took a couple of hundred years to complete (although scholars are not agreed on the times that certain portions were translated). Its purpose was to make the Hebrew Bible available to Greek-speaking Jews who could no longer read the Hebrew language (that would be most Jews).[4]

Legend has it that about seventy Jewish scholars translated the first five OT books (called the Torah or Pentateuch) of the Hebrew Bible into Greek in just seventy-two days. In fact, the term, Septuagint, is a Latin word meaning "seventy" and often abbreviated by the Roman Numerals LXX. When you think about it, this layout is a bit humorous. You have the *Hebrew* Bible translated into *Greek,* titled in *Latin* (septuaginta, "seventy"), and capped off with *Roman* numerals . . . go figure. The legend also contends that this Greek translation was divinely inspired because the end product coincided word for word with the original Hebrew text. For modern scholars this last aspect of the legend is a bit of a stretch, although the Torah (first five books) is considered well translated.

Nevertheless, no translation can capture the whole of the original, neither word for word nor its complete essence. Certainly, anyone who is bilingual understands how difficult it is—sometimes impossible— to translate the nuance and meaning of words from one language to another. Thinking back, I can still remember a few of my grandmother's nifty Spanish jingles: "En bocas cerradas, no entran moscas," or, "El que anda en la miel, algo se le pega." In the order presented, the English translation would be as follows: "In mouths that are closed, flies will not enter," and, "He who walks through the honey, is bound to get stuck with something." Having somewhat of a grasp on Spanish, I can tell you for certain that something significant has been lost in translation; these silver proverbs have been tarnished.

Likewise, a translation never produces a perfect match. By virtue of this reality, every language conversion is inferior to the original. The LXX is no exception. In fact, we believe that Jewish scholars, while translating the Hebrew text into Greek, perhaps inadvertently created a theological nightmare that, in some respects, altered the course of history. A possible miscue became a VB ballistic missile that eventually blew-up in the faces of future generations. Here's what appears to have happened.

When Jewish translators reached Isaiah 7:14, they apparently altered the text. The original Hebrew rendering of Isaiah specifically states that a *young woman* (not virgin) is with child. The Hebrew word used here is "almah," which *almost always* means "young woman." Although the term almah has on rare occasion been used to imply the idea of virginity, it is highly improbable to be so here. If Isaiah had wanted to convey the idea of a miraculous birth, he would have used the specific Hebrew term "betulah" (virgin), not almah (young woman). But it really *doesn't matter* how one translates the word almah. We know from other details already mentioned, that this was not about a long-range Messianic prediction capped off with a supernatural birth story.

For reasons unknown, the Jewish scholars took the Hebrew term almah (young woman), and translated it into the Greek word "parthenos" (which is the usual Greek word for virgin). The more accurate translation should have been "neanis" (the usual Greek word for young woman). Anyway, the term almah in the Hebrew Bible became parthenos in the Greek Bible (Septuagint or LXX). This blunder—if it was a blunder—created a host of problems still argued today by scholars of every persuasion.

Although the above scenario I have laid out does not draw unanimous consensus, it does draw general consensus. Accordingly, the following reflects what most scholars believe happened. Whatever the truth makes little difference, as we shall see. All right, let's get back to Matthew's VB assertion and see how most scholars think he played this out; or, in the paraphrased words of Oliver Hardy to Stan Laurel: Well, here's another fine mess you've gotten me into.

About 80 years after Jesus' birth, Matthew is composing his Gospel. Obviously, Matthew's goal is to cast Jesus in the most impressive manner. He wants to bring Jesus into this world at the highest entry level. To do so, he parades Isaiah out as "prophetic proof" that heralds the birth of Jesus in a miraculous way. Please note, however, that Matthew now has access to two different versions of the OT: (1) the original Hebrew Bible and, (2) the Greek Septuagint (or, LXX). Scholars are uncertain as to how fluent Matthew was in the Hebrew language. The Jews of Palestine spoke mainly Aramaic, and the Jews outside of Palestine spoke mainly Greek; that's why the Jewish scholars translated the Hebrew Bible into

Greek in the first place. So, if the person we call Matthew, like so many in his day, couldn't read Hebrew, then he had to use the Greek Septuagint as his source for the Isaiah rendering. Most scholars believe he did.

The reason they come to this conclusion is because they know—almost to a certainty—that Greek was Matthew's primary language. He wrote his Gospel in Greek, and, according to scholars, it's a very fine Greek, indeed. He knew Greek, and he knew it well. Even though we do not have any of the original Gospels, the copies we do have gives no evidence to indicate that they were composed in any other language but Greek. For the scholar, these clues indicate that the author of Matthew lived outside of Palestine and was writing to a Greek-speaking community (probably for Jews or early Christians with Jewish backgrounds).

My point is threefold: First, during and after Christianity arose, the Greek Septuagint became the go-to source for reading the OT, not the Hebrew Bible because most people couldn't read Hebrew (the truth is, most people couldn't read anything). Second, Matthew (in all probability) spoke, read, and wrote in Greek. Accordingly, and this is my third point, Matthew probably accessed the Isaiah rendering from the Septuagint which he could easily read. But remember, the Jewish scholars had translated the Hebrew word from almah (young woman), to parthenos (virgin) in the newly translated Greek Septuagint (LXX). Apparently, then, Matthew is quoting from the LXX, and not the original Hebrew Bible when he writes: "Look, the *virgin* shall conceive . . . ."

As already noted, whether Matthew could read the Hebrew text in conjunction with the Greek LXX is not certain. If he could *not* read the original Hebrew Bible, there was no way for him to recognize the Septuagint's version of Isaiah 7:14 as a variant reading. If that is the case, we cannot fault him for the transcription he made. If, on the other hand, he could read the Hebrew text, then he deliberately ignored the original dominant use of the Hebrew word almah (young woman), in favor of the Septuagint's rendering of the Greek word parthenos (virgin). In that case, what we see here is Matthew simply being Matthew—playing fast and loose with the material at hand to foster his own passionate belief in Jesus as the Messiah.

As one would expect, not very many Jews bought into Matthew's line of thinking. Demigods, virgin births, and sin saving Messiahs, were concepts unacceptable to the Jewish mind. They repudiated such ideas. In contrast, the Gentiles (non-Jews) were saturated with this type of folklore and could easily embrace the idea of a human-divine Jesus. It made perfect sense to them.

What's important here is to realize that the Christian movement was becoming dominantly *Gentile*—where Hellenism (the Greek language, customs, ideals, spirit, mythology, and religious beliefs) permeated the Mediterranean world. So it really didn't matter that the Jews balked at Matthew's ideas because the Gentiles were taking over the Christian movement (in huge numbers) and they certainly could buy into the VB concept. They were myth oriented, primed and ready. It was the perfect storm. To coin a baseball phrase, they were the cleanup batters. (We will revisit this issue later in more detail when we take a close look at Paul and his work with the Gentiles.)

NSYNC OR OUT OF SYNC

It is obvious to scholars that the historicity of Matthew's VB story is somewhat doubtful (at least from an analytical literary perspective). This inference is based on the triple whammy that Matthew left us.

First, he quotes the Isaiah prophecy, originally directed to King Ahaz, as if that prophecy pertained to the coming Messiah. It did not. Unless you agree with Matthew that the entire OT is a wide-open document with applications far beyond those intended by its authors, it is highly unlikely that Isaiah 7:14 could be applied to Jesus.

Second, Matthew further complicates this "fish out of water" prophecy by overlooking—for whatever reason—his primary source, the Hebrew Bible. In so doing, he eliminates the original rendering of young woman, and replaces it with virgin as found in his secondary source, the Greek Septuagint (LXX). Matthew's editorial tinkering (be it accidental, intentional, or out of ignorance), certainly hit the mythological bull's-eye of the Gentile mind. This is most important because it is in the Gentile territories that the growth of Christianity explodes.

Matthew's third whammy swirls around the biblical contradiction he creates between the OT and his own NT Gospel.

The OT reads: "... the *young woman is with child* and shall bear a Son..." (Isaiah 7:14)

> The NT reads: "... the *virgin shall conceive* and bear
> a son ..." (Matt. 1:23) (Italics mine)

Aside from the "young woman" to "virgin" rendering, you will notice that in the OT version, the young woman is already pregnant; but in the Gospel of Matthew, the pregnancy is presented as future life. No matter how you read these two versions, they are out of sync. It's a very serious biblical contradiction.

Some religious groups cannot tolerate the apparent disagreement between Isaiah's "young woman," and Matthew's "virgin." They'll eliminate the discrepancy by changing Isaiah's "young woman" to "virgin" thereby making the OT appear to be in sync with the New Testament. This helps to avoid any embarrassing inconsistencies. By doing so, however, they have altered the original Hebrew text. This is *expedient,* but misleading. Your better translations do not attempt to gloss over this disparity. (Look for biblical translations that reasonably reflect the original Hebrew language of the OT, and the Greek language of the NT (such as, *The New Oxford Annotated Bible, The New Revised Standard Version* or, *The Jewish Annotated New Testament*.) I mentioned previously that Catholic scholars have now moved in this direction. New Catholic Bibles will now reflect the young woman rendering rather than that of the virgin in the Isaiah verses of the Old Testament. The New Testament will retain the word virgin because that's what Matthew wrote.

HONEY, I'M HOME

In summary, scholars look askance at the Virgin Birth story for the following reasons: (1) there is no mention of the VB in the earliest Christian tradition (Paul's writings), (2) there is no mention of the VB in the first written Gospel we call Mark, (3) the VB concept is suspiciously late in the evolving Jesus story, (4) it seems that Isaiah's prophecy to Ahaz was misapplied to Jesus by Matthew, (5) it seems that Matthew, for whatever reason, substituted the Greek Septuagint wording of virgin over the primary Hebrew text wording of young woman, (6) the recognition that numerous VB accounts were part and parcel of the first century mythological landscape, and (7) Jewish scholars are in accord with mainstream Christian scholars on this issue. Consider, for example, these following comments from a most prestigious Jewish publication (*The Jewish*

Annotated New Testament): "Thus for the Hebrew text of Isa 7.14 . . . the prophet is saying, 'The young woman is pregnant . . . .' There is no reason to presume her pregnancy was miraculous."[5]

Scholars—using the rules of investigative analysis as applied in all disciplines—are prone to conclude that the VB is historically improbable. Many Christians will certainly disagree. They will argue that God was responsible for this miraculous birth. It was no accident that Matthew found Isaiah's prophetic proclamation to King Ahaz. They would then conclude that even if Isaiah didn't have a clue about the extended meaning of his writing, God would bring it to fruition seven hundred years later with a new purpose, a Messianic purpose. Furthermore, they would then reason that with God's help, the Hebrew word for "young woman" would be translated as "virgin" in the LXX (Septuagint), regardless of what Isaiah originally intended. Finally, they would then reason it was no accident that when Matthew was writing his Gospel, well, God made sure that he chose the LXX rendering.

Because of my own Jesusgate upbringing, I can empathize with this line of reasoning. For those who still follow along these lines of thought, I would urge caution. Humans are so creative in their attempts to circumvent the obvious. That's the main weakness of the Jesusgate syndrome; it is one of the real drawbacks of popular Christianity, or any religion that primarily relies on tradition, authority, and presumption while, at the same time, ignoring any evidence to the contrary. This is blind faith. Furthermore, too often religion is based on imagination, wishful thinking, and extreme possibilities that are too incredible to entertain. Sure, almost anything is possible; but to accept a line of reasoning that is less evidential than another, leads one to mentally suspend what is most probable. I'm reminded of that song from the Eagles—one of the few they didn't write—*Already Gone.* The song pertains to a broken relationship, but it can be spun metaphorically here. The young man is telling his "girlfriend" that she can look up to the stars and still not see the light. (It's another way of saying you can't see the forest for the trees.)

Before closing this chapter, I think it advisable to briefly explain why such a bizarre concept as a virgin birth (bizarre for our time) could so easily take root in first century soil. Most of us could answer that question in general terms. But we need to be specific.

Basically, the answer is that people of the first century had a very low KQ in every subject you can imagine. Accordingly, they were sometimes unable to make critical distinctions between superstition and reality. As we explore virgin births a bit further, keep in mind that superstition is usually only recognized in retrospect.

ROSEMARY'S BABY

Rosemary's Baby was a 1968 hit movie directed by Roman Polanski. The story focuses on a young housewife (played by Mia Farrow) who is raped by an evil spirit. As the story goes, her baby boy turns out to be the son of Satan. I suppose this was entertaining theatre, but that's about it. What is interesting here is the idea of sexual intrusiveness by a supernatural entity. This is reminiscent of the virgin birth story in our New Testament. Of course, *Rosemary's Baby* is the diametrical opposite of Jesus' birth. That is, Mary's pregnancy comes from the Holy Spirit, and the child she carries is the Son of God. For sure, this is a monumental difference. Still, the concept of pregnancy outside of the natural order is central to these two stories. But in this case, "birds of a feather do not flock together." That is to say, on the one hand most people will rationally conclude that pregnancy via a demonic presence is superstitious nonsense; yet, on the other hand, millions upon millions of religious devotees readily believe that pregnancy via a supernatural agent has already happened (albeit a positive one).

The literal belief in the Virgin Birth is probably the result of continuous exposure to the idea, so as to render its impossibility, possible. Indigenous mythology is not easily recognized if one has been raised to take it literally. Sometimes you have to be on the outside looking in, in order to make an objective observation. For example, one Buddhist tradition claims that Maya—mother of the Buddha—was impregnated through her side by a white elephant. A Christian would have little trouble categorizing Buddha's Virgin Birth story as mythology, pure and simple. In contrast, a Buddhist would probably classify the Virgin Birth story of Jesus as mythology, pure and simple.

It's easy to recognize someone else's mythology, isn't it? However, neither of these ancient, mythological concepts could be sold to an enlightened people today if they were hearing it for the first time. That is precisely why hardly anyone takes seriously the plot of *Rosemary's Baby*. Although you can still play with the concept as pure fictional entertainment, you cannot convince *informed* people that a supernatural birth is possible. Not today (except, of course, for the one that happened within their own religious tradition thousands of years ago).

THE VIRGIN BIRTH SYNDROME

In ancient times, some stories, be they ever so outrageous, were difficult to recognize as true, untrue, or half true. Sometimes folks were successful in making these distinctions, but generally not. Still believable in those days were the numerous tales about deities, or supernatural beings, impregnating women. These tales were especially strong in the Greek and Roman traditions. Take for example the mortal mother of Heracles (known to the Romans as Hercules), who, supposedly was impregnated by the Greek god Zeus.

But virgin births were also ascribed to historical persons such as: Plato (424-347 BC), perhaps the greatest philosopher of Western culture, Heraclides of Pontus (ca. 387-312 BC), was a Greek astronomer and philosopher, Alexander the Great (356-323 BC), a Macedonian king who conquered most of the world known to the ancient Greeks, Augustus (27 BC-14 AD), was the first emperor of the Roman Empire, and on it goes. Many other notables could be added.

The point is this: the above greats are said to have had mothers made pregnant by divine agents. For example, the Greek god Apollo was supposedly responsible for the births of the above named Plato and Augustus. Supernatural births were in vogue. "There are eight million stories in the Naked City."[6]

But the impregnation of women by divine beings was also a familiar theme within the biblical tradition. Aside from Matthew and Luke's Virgin Birth story, in the OT we find that ". . . the sons of God saw that they [the daughters of men] were fair; and they took wives for themselves of all they chose," and ". . . the sons of God went in to the daughters of humans, who bore children to them." The offspring from divine-human intercourse came to be known as "warriors of renown" (Genesis 6:1-4, brackets mine). This theme is also echoed in certain non-biblical Jewish writings (Book of Enoch) when heavenly angels were thrown out of heaven because they lusted after the daughters of men and sinned with them. The offspring of these unnatural encounters were called "mighty men," "demons," or "giant spirits."[7]

Of course, Matthew, in contrast to the lustful activity just mentioned, creates and elevates Mary's supernatural pregnancy. He writes that Mary "was found to be with child from the Holy Spirit" (Matthew 1:18b). Unlike Rosemary's baby, this is a Hallmark visitation. However, it is obvious from our findings of that period that the Christian VB story was not an isolated event. Impregnation by a supernatural entity was not unfamiliar to the first century mind. The mythological soil of that time was quite fertile, which made these stories special, but not unique.

So it was that a miraculous birth would be expected on the résumé of any would-be hero. Origen (ca. 185-254 AD), one of the most distinguished of the early church fathers, certainly thought so. He attempts to separate Jesus from the pack by trying to explain away the similarities between Jesus' birth and pagan divine births. But he unwittingly makes the same case against the VB by virtue of his reasoning. For example, in regards to Plato's miraculous birth via his human mother and the god Apollo, Origen writes:

> And yet these are veritable fables, which have led to the invention of such stories [supernatural births] concerning a man [Plato] whom they regarded as possessing greater wisdom and power than the multitude, and as having received . . . better and diviner elements than others, because they thought that this was appropriate to persons who were too great to be human beings.[8]
> [Brackets mine]

What in the world is Origen thinking? Doesn't he realize that he is applying the same illogic to Jesus that others applied to Plato; that is, that supernatural births are ascribed to persons who are thought to be too great to be human beings? Of course, Origen believes Jesus to be greater than Plato and therefore believes that Jesus is entitled to a supernatural birth whereas Plato is not. Isn't Origen expressing here the Jesusgate characteristic of *presumption*?

Incidentally, in this same section of his writing, Origen argues for the virgin birth of Jesus based on his understanding that vultures don't copulate. He *wrongly* believes that the female vulture is capable of creating life and giving birth without any male interaction. He then argues that if a female vulture can produce life independently of a male, certainly God could do the same for a woman. (If this doesn't help us to see the value of a higher KQ, nothing will!)

As we noted earlier, Mary's virgin birth was probably Matthew's way (with Luke following suit) of establishing parity for Jesus alongside the other superstars of his day. This was not only a familiar ploy in the ancient world, but also a necessary one. Indeed, these status symbols went far beyond divine births. If the Greek god Dionysus could turn water into wine, then Jesus better be able to match the deed (which he does). If the Greek god Poseidon could drive his chariot across the water, then Jesus should be able to raise the ante by walking on the water (which he does).

Regardless of any writer's motivation to beef up an individual's stature, virgin birth stories were everywhere in ancient times, and therefore, considered the norm; they were thought to be plausible. A major contributing factor to that belief was sheer ignorance.

BIOLOGY

To be more specific, the other side of the antiquity coin that fueled the plausibility of a virgin birth was a dismal lack of biological knowledge. Through no fault of their own, the ancients had a very low KQ in biology. Today, in terms of procreation, we know what goes together like a horse and carriage, and it isn't necessarily marriage; it's the sperm and the ovum—you can't have one without the other. Even if you argue that a woman can remain virginal by means of in vitro fertilization or artificial insemination, you would still be in need of the male sperm. This is why the ancient claims for divine-human births are seen today as mythological stories of a less enlightened time.

In those days, as we have already shown, biological knowledge was insufficient (to say the least). Virgin birth stories were partially concocted by the misconception that women played no part in the creative process. More precisely, the woman made no substantial contribution in the creation of the child. She was merely the vehicle—receptacle—into which the male injected his seed. The male was the giver of life the woman was simply the incubator.[9]

These were commonplace assumptions based on limited perception. The semen was obviously visible while the female egg, as far as anyone knew, was nonexistent. (The existence of the ovum was not discovered until 1724.) Thus, the best Oscar that a woman could win was that of

"Supporting Actress." The "Best Actor" award always went to the male because the sperm was the all-important factor. After all, no one knew about genetics. They didn't know about the X and Y, chromosomes. Most importantly, no one knew that the sperm was teaming up with an ovarian egg that carried *half* of the embryo's genetic code.

As a result of this low biological KQ, first century people were able to entertain their mythology as being plausible. They had very little science to the contrary. Their reproductive notions were limited to what they could see; ejaculation was visible, ovulation was hidden. Therefore, it was not so far-fetched to believe that a woman, adding "nothing" to the creative material, could be impregnated from any source of intelligence (human or otherwise). They were free to speculate that any spirit or angel could place a bun in the oven, so to speak. Now does anyone believe that if the people of the first century understood biology as we do today, that anyone could have convinced Joseph as to the innocence of Mary's pregnancy, albeit by the Holy Spirit? Could any woman today sell that story to her husband?

The KQ makes a world of difference, doesn't it? They had their mythology without our biology. We have our biology without their mythology.[10] Except, of course, for the millions of Christians who are still unable to recognize myth within the NT story line.

Our next two chapters will focus on the divinity of Jesus.

Intro to Chapter 14

AMERICAN IDOL
Top of the World

What's an idol? Figuratively, it's a person or thing that is greatly admired, loved, wanted, adored, or revered, and draws extreme devotion. Throw in some fame and fortune and you've got it made (or so the story goes). I'm reminded of Karen Carpenter's song, *Top of the World*. To be an idol would certainly put you there.

Why do so many millions watch TV's *American Idol*? The reason is simple: It has an electrifying range of drama, emotion, anticipation, and viewer participation second to none. It's not your run of the mill talent show. Furthermore, the contestants are not only incredible vocalists, but they know what's at stake—nothing short of stardom, wealth, and mega-tons of self-esteem. To win is to win big, really big. To lose is to lose big, really big. This becomes evident over the passing of weeks as one by one the contestants are emotionally skinned alive, agonizingly pealed away from the remaining winners. It's brutal. Host, Ryan Seacrest, delivers the riveting line: "America voted. . . ." There is no way for any of these youngsters to hide their raw emotions when he either makes them "safe" for another week of competition, or, dismisses them outright. The same holds true for the competing shows, *The X Factor* and *The Voice*. It's captivating theatre because everybody understands what's at stake.

Very few of us will ever approach the borders of celebrity status, much less cross into that promise land. However, because we have imagined or dreamed of such glory, we can, on some level, vicariously empathize with these winners and losers, but not totally. Fortunately, I got a taste of that star world.

Can you really imagine what it's like to be written about in magazines nationwide and see your moniker on the glittering marquees of showplaces like the once famous Hollywood Palladium? That's one of the first places Phil and I appeared before I gave up on personal appearances due to my educational responsibilities.

Can you imagine how it feels to hear your voice booming out of a Top-40 radio station? The first time I clicked on a Los Angeles station and heard one of our records, it nearly blew my mind. I was cruising down the boulevard in my beat-up '52 Ford when suddenly a D.J. played our record, *Here I Stand*. I almost slammed into a telephone pole. I wanted to jump out of the car and shout to anyone within earshot that it was our song. I was bouncing all over the front seat. I rolled down the window and yelled at the driver alongside of me: "Hey," I shouted, "tune in to KFWB, it's my song." I was delirious with joy. I think I scared him or he thought I was nuts because he sped off before the light turned green.

Once you're an idol, be it ever so brief, it's an amazing feel. Of course, I can only speak from my success with the Rip Chords, which is somewhat limited relative to the success of many others. In any case, the following personal anecdote is taken from my previous publication, *Created Equal: A Case for the Animal Human Connection*.[1]

> Three thousand screaming teenagers packed the municipal auditorium. Excitement mounted as show time drew near. Dick Clark's "Caravan of Stars" was about to unfold in Bakersfield, California (1964). From the wings I could see the jam-packed audience in random motion. It was an electric moment as teens clamored for a glimpse of their rock idols.
>
> Dick Clark walked briskly across the stage, and everything broke loose. A thundering explosion of applause, squeals, and screams merged into mega-noise. It was pandemonium. Through this turbulent uproar, Dick Clark introduced the first act—Diana Ross and the Supremes. His words ignited yet another boisterous response of whistles and screams. The building rocked.

Several minutes later it was our turn.[2] With micro-
phone advantage, Dick Clark's mellow voice rose above
the fanfare: "And now ladies and gentlemen, from
Columbia Records, the fantastic Rip Chords." Once
again the teens cried out with shouts of approval.

What a night! *[NOTE: For clarification, be sure to
see Endnote #2.]*

The ultimate idol must rest within the religious arena. It is here that
the concept of the idol can literally move from the human dimension to
the supernatural dimension. In Chapter 3 of this writing I mentioned
that the prominent scholar, Dr. Robert W. Funk, boldly declared that
Jesus was in need of a demotion. This was based on his belief that attrib-
uting divinity to Jesus had made him a superhuman idol. This in turn led
to the conception of Jesus as a god, which, he believed, was a runaway
assessment of Jesus the man. Many scholars would agree with Dr. Funk,
although the idea runs counter to the Christian majority, both inside and
outside of the Jesusgate world.

IMPORTANT NOTE:

In preparation for our upcoming chapter, I need to give a cautionary
statement about the word, "mythology," because it can have a misleading
connotation. We have already touched on mythological aspects earlier in
this work but a more definitive word is in order. The following is a general description of mythology, not applicable to all times and situations.

In the field of religion, this word is usually applied in hindsight; that
is, what we call mythology was, in the past, our theology. For example,
when people worshipped the "Sun God," that was their theological reality. When, however, through scientific advancement the sun god proved
to be an illusion, we turned around and labeled it as mythology. But that
myth was not perceived as a myth at the time people embraced it—it
was perceived as a vibrant theological truth. So, when one sees the term
"mythology," one needs to keep in mind that we're really speaking about
the *theology* of that time, and that those people did not consider their
beliefs to be mythological any more than we do ours. Two thousand years
from now, advanced people may be looking back at our belief system
and . . . you guessed it: given enough time, I'm sure that our theology

will be viewed by future generations as mythology. Thus, we must avoid becoming unconsciously condescending and disrespectful of ancient worldviews simply because they are not realistic as compared to current knowledge. This shouldn't happen anyway if one truly understands the value of *some* mythological constructs. Myth sometimes serves a very positive function, as we shall see.

WHAT TO EXPECT NEXT

The following chapter explains the importance of recognizing the relative nature of worldviews. It explores the prevalence of mythology in ancient cultures—both pagan and Jewish—and clearly illustrates why the demigod genre (a person thought to be partly human and partly divine) was so widely accepted. It appears quite probable that the mythological imagination of the first century left an indelible imprint on Christological belief.

Chapter 14

THE DIVINITY OF JESUS
(Part One)

Was Jesus divine? Was he a mortal being? Was he literally the Son of God? Was he somehow God in the flesh? Was he one of these things, some of these things, or all of these things? Traditionally—following the Councils of Nicea (325) and Chalcedon (451)—the church's testimony has been that Jesus was *all of these things*. These are Christological claims that are more or less proposed in the doctrine of the Trinity.

Still, in the eyes of many scholars, Jesus was never divine. According to them, he was very much mortal and not the *literal* Son of God. We need to explore some more of the dynamics that bring scholars to this unconventional viewpoint—unconventional as compared to what Jesusgaters preach and teach. *This is not to imply that everyone who believes in the divinity of Jesus is a Jesusgater. There are some ministers and scholars who openly write about, or discuss with their congregants, the findings of higher criticism, and yet maintain their faith in Jesus as being divine. They simply draw different conclusions based on the same information that others interpret differently. In so doing, they cannot be classified as Jesusgaters as they do not restrict the flow of mainstream scholarship. However, these individuals, in the opinion of mainstream academia, do not represent the most convincing arguments in the overall assessment of higher criticism.*

Be that as it may, we have already unveiled numerous reasons why scholars might be doubtful about the divinity of Jesus. But there is yet more to consider. Metaphorically, let's begin with those tuneful lyrics from American composer Jimmy Webb, as recorded by the Fifth Dimension: *Up, Up And Away (my beautiful, my beautiful balloon)*.

MY BEAUTIFUL BALLOON (MY WORLDVIEW)

A worldview can be defined as the way our mind perceives reality, or, more precisely, what we think reality is (how we see the world in which we live; our perception of life on all levels). Remember the RQ (Reality Quotient)? We all have one.

Primarily, it is our family and surrounding culture that shapes our RQ, our worldview. This leads to conformity of behavior and uniformity of belief. Most of what we perceive to be true—whether it is or not—is fashioned during the earliest years of our lives. The imprint of our familial and cultural tattoos are deeply ingrained and, in many respects, permanent. Harking back to our adage, *you cannot reason but from what you know*, clearly demonstrates that our KQ is the lynchpin of our IQ + KQ = RQ equation. However, what you know—or think you know—is what you've been told by the cultural forces that surround you. This leads the majority of people to a less desirable adage: "You cannot reason but from what you've been taught" (unless, of course, you upgrade your KQ).

Social indoctrination is two-sided: On the positive side it unites us into a cohesive whole; on the negative side it will limit our horizons on many levels. The following story will clarify the latter point. "Up, up and away my beautiful, my beautiful balloon."

On August 5, 1998, Steve Fossett, in his second attempt to be the first person to fly solo around the world in a hot air balloon (talk about a worldview), fell short of his mark. He ran out of luck over India. As he descended from the clouds near a rural hamlet, the locals thought him to be one of their long-expected gods. Without a doubt, their reality quotient (RQ) was totally out of whack, driven by a very low KQ about the natural order. This was a very normal *wrong* conclusion for a people living out their isolated existence at a level of pre-scientific knowledge.[3] This simple but vivid example introduces us to several characteristics common to all worldviews.

First, worldviews are shaped by place and time—the location and era into which one is born. We have no control over these critical factors. They shape a person's point of view. The worldviews of our time are burned into our psyche by cultural flamethrowers. No one escapes the initial blast. These scorched implants reflect our numerous beliefs and attitudes about religion, politics, social behavior, education and the like. In short, anything and everything about life in general. If, for example, Fossett had landed in an urban part of India, god status would not have been bestowed. If he had landed in England, a simple "nice try mate," would have ensued. Thus, it is not just the passing of time that separates one worldview from another, but also one's place on the planet. Philosopher of religion Mark C. Taylor puts it this way: "What one thinks is deeply conditioned by where one thinks."[4] To sum it up, *we do not choose our beliefs; the beliefs of our time and place choose us.*[5]

A second characteristic of worldviews is that they are emotionally and socially unifying. That is, people are held together by the glue of conformity so as to belong, to fit in, to be accepted, and to be loved. In this sense, people go along to get along. Moreover, through osmosis, they become emotionally and mentally anchored to their surrounding cultural base. They are in effect, programmed to live according to the blueprints they have been handed. Very few of us ever develop significant *my prints*. It is extremely hard for people to think outside of the box because they seldom realize they're in a box. Also, it's hard to go against the grain or think independently from crowd mentality. That is why there is animosity between Arabs and Jews; between North Koreans and South Koreans; between Democrats and Republicans (I had to get them in there).

A unified worldview continues to elude us in spite of the global influence of the Internet, smart phones, TV, computers, McDonald's, and Tigger. Of course, total worldview consensus is literally impossible because of deep-rooted religious, political, and social beliefs and practices. This diversity is not necessarily a negative. It can add color and celebration to the human family; we don't want total assimilation. Nevertheless, universal worldviews regarding civil rights, human rights, animal rights, and going green, are essential to the welfare of all living things on this planet. Only through unrestricted and unbiased educational consistency can we hope to achieve anything close to worldwide consensus on some of these crucial issues.

Third, worldviews are almost always determined by the quality and equality of education (or the absence thereof). Twenty-first century knowledge is not evenly distributed. A diminished KQ in liberal arts is the result of educational disparity not only between cultures, but the sub-cultures within a culture, say, for example, between inner city kids and upscale suburban kids. But it's not just about economic class. Racial worldviews, as another example, can develop, even if people are economically well off or equally educated. Consider the wide-ranging differences of opinion between Blacks and Whites over the O. J. Simpson case. How could two worldviews within the "same" culture be so diametrically opposed? The answer is clear: The experience of the one is not necessarily the experience of the other, even when there is parity between the two.

A fourth common characteristic of worldviews is that they are generally a composite of numerous worldviews. One's overall worldview would probably incorporate the following: a social worldview, a theological worldview, a scientific worldview, a morality worldview, a nationalistic worldview, an ethnic or racial worldview (which in part explains the O.J. controversy), and so forth. Very much like the game of Pick-up sticks we played as children, some of these worldviews will mingle, overlap, and blend into general convictions. Others will remain in juxtaposition (side by side) with no meaningful interaction. For example, a person who claims to be religious but remains a racist is a person who does not allow the teachings of religion—love of neighbor—to override his prejudicial worldview.

Depending on our ability to integrate these differing beliefs, depending on when and where we are born, depending on parental and peer influences, depending on the subject matter and our educational background, these worldviews may be highly evolved so as to produce a healthy RQ (in line with reality), or quite inaccurate and even ludicrous (as was my youthful hope to play tailback for the USC Trojans). Whatever our situation, we all exhibit both positive and negative (good or bad, right or wrong) worldview positions. Additionally, if we trace back over our personal histories, we will notice that most of our worldviews have always been in flux.

This brings us to our fifth and final point. Worldviews are not static, be they personal or collective. Over time, they are modified by life experience and new information. I certainly am light years away from my adolescent days when I held a simplistic view of an infallible Bible. Beyond our own personal beliefs, community worldviews may hold sway for hundreds or even thousands of years, but they ultimately bow to the forces of new knowledge. For example, Ptolemy's views on astronomy held sway for nearly 1400 years but eventually gave way to the Copernicus/

Galileo astronomical model during the sixteenth and seventeenth centuries. Astronomer Edwin Hubble redefined this model in the twentieth century. So on it goes.

With these points in mind, we are now ready to begin our inquiry as to how and why the Church was able to place Jesus inside the hot air balloon of divinity, and why many scholars today are trying to bring him back to earth.

ANCIENT PAGAN WORLDVIEWS

To understand why Jesus might be considered divine, one needs to comprehend the worldviews of his time. Into what kind of world was Jesus born? In our survey of the virgin birth we noted a world brimming with ancient mythological imagery. Correspondingly, in Chapter 4 we noted the mystery religions with their mythological worldviews, including that of the demigod. In the absence of any knowledge to the contrary, mythological concepts were both popular and believable. It would be an understatement to say that Jesus was born into a pre-scientific age.[6]

We have seen that the existence of a demigod—which to us seems far-fetched—was very plausible to the first century mind. But how could it be otherwise when such ideas circulated throughout the Greco-Roman world. These people were no less intelligent as compared to us today. But their KQ levels on numerous subjects were obviously deficient (through no fault of their own). As a consequence, they were universally influenced by the worldviews of their time in the same way that we are influenced by the worldviews of our time.

So it is that when scholars analyze secular Greek documents, they find many of the same terms we thought were exclusive to the NT ("Lord," "Savior," "Son of God"). Unquestionably, these terms—which invoke the supernatural—were not unique to Christianity and were very much in vogue prior to Jesus.[7] Furthermore, as I mentioned earlier, the Greeks bestowed divinity on such notables as Plato, Pythagoras, Alexander the Great, and many others. The prevalence of belief in this divine-mortal mythology is reflected in the most famous work of Greek biographer and essayist, Plutarch (46-120 AD), *Parallel Lives*, in which divinity is bestowed on both Greeks and Romans. Speaking of the Romans, their historical documents give off the same mythological vibes as that of the Greeks, vibes that also permeate the New Testament.

Syncretism—the cross-fertilization of myth and other ideas between different religions—was quite prevalent (as we saw with the mystery pagan religions in Chapter 4).

As one example of Roman metaphysics (supernatural speculation), consider Octavian's victory over Mark Antony at Actium in 31 BC; thereafter, Octavian was proclaimed "bringer of good news" (evangelion), "savior," and "manifestation of Zeus." Temples were erected to worship him and the calendar of Asia Minor (modern day Turkey) was "revised so as to begin the year with the birthday of the god and savior of the whole human race." By decree of the Roman Senate, Octavian received the title of Augustus that also implied he was more than mortal.[8]

Beginning with Augustus, this led to the imperial cult: the worship of the Roman emperor as divine. They were worshipped primarily as demigods. Some Roman emperors actually came to believe their own press clippings. Take for example Emperor Caligula (ruled from 39-41 AD), who accused the Jews of being disrespectful of his divinity. Caligula, you see, believed himself to be Zeus in human form. No, he wasn't crazy (well, maybe just a little), but he was definitely immersed in the worldview of his day . . . and that's the point of our present discussion. Again, we do not choose our beliefs; the beliefs of our time and place choose us.

The Roman Empire, with Christianity in tow, represents the tail end of a long mythical tradition as regards the popular acceptance of "human divinity." (Was that an oxymoron?) We must also remember that ancient religions fostered the concept of the demigod, even before the Greeks and Romans. The entire geographical region from Europe to India was colored by mythological expression. Mythical stories were being honed within Mesopotamia (today's Iraq) and Indian cultures. In Mesopotamia, for example, the Sumerian people—which predate the classical Greek civilization and the Roman Republic by about two thousand years—developed the mythological Epic of Gilgamesh; an epic poem that became part of the story line for the much later, Noah's Ark in the Book of Genesis (but that's another story, see Appendix D). Gilgamesh, the supposed Sumerian King of Uruk (ca. 2500 BC), is portrayed as being two-thirds god, and one-third mortal. I believe this is the oldest written account on record of a demigod (written in cuneiform on twelve clay tablets).

In India, Hinduism presents us with a modified version of the mythological demigod. It's beginning predates the Classical Greeks by about

500 years. In it's later development, the Hindu god, Vishnu, is said to have assumed human form (called an avatar) nine times, including that of Krishna and the Buddha.[9] The concept of the demigod[10] came to be commonplace not only in Mesopotamia and India, but as we noted earlier, also in the pagan mystery religions of the Mediterranean region, the birthplace of Christianity. Therefore, the role that these mythological worldviews may have played in Christological development cannot be ignored.

JEWISH WORLDVIEWS

Mythical worldviews were not exclusive to Gentile (non-Jewish) cultures, but were also imbedded within Jewish writings dating back to the very beginnings of the Hebrew Bible. In Genesis, you have several mythical stories such as the Creation story, Noah's Ark, Jonah and the Whale (big fish), the Tower of Babel, and so forth. The majority of scholars believe that some of these stories are post-Exilic writings (538 BC).[11] Throughout the OT we hear about angels and witches and all kinds of weird happenings. Take for example the story of Balaam, a well-known legendary visionary who has a pointed discussion with his jackass. In this scenario, Balaam thinks that his donkey has been disobedient when, in fact, the donkey has taken precautionary action to save him from harm. Misjudging the donkey's action as insubordination, Balaam strikes his four-legged friend three times. Standing on all fours, the innocent donkey cries out:

> ". . . What have I done to you, that you have struck me these three times?" Balaam replies to the donkey, "Because you have made a fool of me! I wish I had a sword in my hand! I would kill you right now!"
> [Where's PETA when you need them?]
> But the donkey said to Balaam, "Am I not your donkey, which you have ridden all your life to this day? Have I been in the habit of treating you this way?"
> And he said, "No." (Numbers 22: 28-30)
> [Brackets mine, obviously]

This talking donkey story reminds me of *"Francis the Talking Mule,"* who was a mule celebrity featured in seven movie comedies in the 1950s. Francis shared top billing with the then famous actor, Donald O'Conner. Come to think of it, Francis reminds me of that long-ago TV sitcom, *Mister ED*, the talking Palomino horse. He and Wilbur (his owner) were always having chitchats nobody else could hear. Mr. Ed wouldn't talk unless they were alone. The situations these two got into were hilarious. Now that was a funny show.

Don't get me wrong here. I'm not making fun of the mythological donkey in the Balaam story. Certain types of myth are not only desirable, but also necessary for human adjustment and growth. They teach us lessons we otherwise might miss. According to Joseph Campbell,[12] "myth has four primary functions: (1) a mystical function—to awaken our spiritual consciousness about the universe and our relationship to it; (2) a scientific function—to offer an image of the universe in accord with present scientific knowledge; (3) a cultural function—to help validate, support, and imprint the norms of our society; and (4) a practical function—to help us adjust emotionally and mentally as a means to relate usefully throughout our lives."[13] In other words, myths provide some of the maps by which we live. We'd probably go mad without them or live in a nagging state of anxiety.

The point is, mythical worldviews—both Gentile and Jewish—were popular expressions prior to and during the time of Jesus. No one should disagree with that point. Mythology was everywhere and served to offer a lopsided image of the universe in a world not yet balanced with scientific knowledge.[14] Nevertheless, *at least one sharp distinction must be drawn between Gentile mythology and Jewish mythology.*

The Jews of Palestine were under Roman domination. But they were also under the influence of Greek culture (called Hellenism). Even so, they did not accept the Greco-Roman demigod concept. In part, the Aramaic language they spoke, along with their strong religious heritage, served as a buffer zone between themselves and Greco-Roman influence. However, for those Jews living outside of Palestine it was a whole different story, but we'll get to them shortly (these out-of-Palestine Jews are referred to in the NT as "Greek speaking Jews").

Here's my point. Aside from the Jesus story, *the concept of the demigod is totally absent in Jewish tradition.* The closest thing to it would be the appearance of a few angels incognito (disguised as humans). But those would not be demigods in the "partly human, partly divine" definition of that word. Think about it—there is not one example in Jewish history where this demigod element is invoked. There is plenty of OT mythology (as we saw with the talking jackass, and angels incognito) but there is no demigod mythology.

Jesus was a Jew (a fact curiously overlooked by many). Jesus was born a Jew, lived as a Jew, and died a Jew. However, when his followers came to believe in his resurrection, that was the beginning of "Christianity" (albeit, still part of Judaism). It was also the beginning of a new way of thinking. Would Jesus now be tagged as a demigod? Apparently, he was to some degree. The concept was captured within Paul's writing, and within the much more sophisticated doctrine of the Incarnation (as suggested some 60+ years after the death of Jesus in the prologue of John's Gospel). This evolving shift toward Gentile belief created a new Jewish-Christian worldview that would change the course of history. Slowly but surely over the course of a few centuries, Jesus would be deified beyond that of a mere demigod as formulated in the Trinitarian doctrine at the Council of Nicea in 325 AD. He became part of what can only be defined as an oxymoron—a monotheistic Godhead.

The question of the divine-human nature of Jesus would eventually separate Jewish Christians from other Jews. This subgroup of Christian Jews would eventually introduce a totally new understanding of the Messiah. It was strictly a new interpretation of the Messiah's role, based on the immediate need to explain the unexplainable death of Jesus. After all, the Messiah, according to Jewish tradition, was never intended to die a shameful and humiliating death, and certainly not as a saving act for the sins of humanity. He was supposed to be a warrior in the same manner as King David of old, to help liberate the Jews from the domination of foreign powers.

Before Christianity, there was no Jewish belief that the Messiah would come to save his people by virtue of his own execution and thereby make atonement (pay the price) for the sins of the world so as to reconcile God with humankind.[15] That was strictly a Christian interpretation in order to explain the awkwardness of his death and, consequently, his failed mission to liberate the Jewish people. The role and nature of the Messiah had to be redefined. As a solution, Jesus the Messiah became, in part, a "demigod." More than that, he became part of the Godhead and the Savior of humankind so as to lend meaning to an otherwise blown assignment—a blown assignment in terms of Jewish Messianic expectations.

As we saw earlier, this Messianic transition was accomplished by using OT verses to bolster this new Messianic explanation. But these verses, according to many scholars, were taken out of context. Whether or not you agree with the scholars, one thing is certain: a few Jewish Christians were constructing a new worldview, a new theological model that conflicted sharply with mainstream Judaism. Their attempt to reconstitute Jewish thought was significant because it stood in opposition to Judaism's core beliefs—core beliefs that rejected demigod mythology or anything that resembled it. So it's not surprising that the Jewish majority did not buy into the new Messianic reconstruction of emerging Christianity. In fact, the whole idea of the Incarnation (the Logos aspect of God becomes flesh in the person of Jesus) was an affront to the Jewish mind. As we have seen, it wasn't that Jews were myth free, but this was a bridge too far. Aside from not catering to the demigod mythos, there are other reasons why the overwhelming majority of Jews rejected this new Messianic interpretation.

We have already noted that the Messiah's role did not include dying for the sins of the people. The *traditional* expectation of the coming Messiah was used only in reference to the *human* "son of David" whom God would raise up to restore the glory days of King David and who would liberate and defend the Jews against any enemy. We also observed that Jewish history (prior to Jesus) never fielded a demigod. They did, however, flirt with the idea.

By Jesus' time, modified versions of Messianic belief had emerged in post-Old Testament literature. Some of these versions pictured a Messiah as a *divine being* who would lead the Jews to victory against their enemies. Some scholars believe that this new Messianic twist was the result of repeated defeats by foreign powers, especially the Romans. In other words, the Jews came to the conclusion that the military odds against them were so great, not even a Messianic warrior from the Davidic line would be capable of turning the tide. Nothing short of a divine Messiah would guarantee a miraculous intervention by God. However, This latter version was not universal. Some believed that God would literally send a military leader, while others believed that the coming of the Messiah would constitute a supernatural event.[16]

However, even this "divine" Messiah being from god would never have been equated with *being God* or even being a part of God. There is a huge difference between believing Jesus was a godsend as opposed to believing he was part of the Godhead—a Godhead that the Jews didn't even believe existed. *Monotheism, by definition, excludes the idea of Godhead because the term Godhead implies multiplicity rather than singularity. Monotheism is the oneness of God, not a triune god as in the Trinity. You can't speak of a "Godhead" without dismissing monotheism. That is why I see the term, "monotheistic Godhead," as an oxymoron. On the other hand, Christians try to get around this multiple Godhead rendering by stating that the three are in one.*

This is vitally important: *first century Jews were strictly monotheistic in the classical definition of that word.* At the most, they might view any Messiah as a God-given supernatural entity; but it would be highly unlikely that they would elevate him to the level of sharing God status as explicitly given by the prologue in John's Gospel, or as defined nearly 300 years later in the doctrine of the Trinity at the Council of Nicea. It is here that Jesus and God are defined as being of the same substance (defined, I might add, by Gentiles, not Jews). Nevertheless, some early Jewish Christians did lean in this direction, as evidenced by Paul and other NT writers. But these modest beginnings mushroomed into full-blown doctrines, as put forth by the Councils of Nicea and Chalcedon centuries later.

Whatever the truth of the matter, the majority of Jews would balk at the notion of demigod theology, much less any suggestion of Godhead status for Jesus. If the fledgling Christian movement was to survive, it had to go elsewhere. It did. It went Gentile.

Even so, we need to search further to see how Jesus, a Palestinian Jew, came to be equated with the Greco-Roman worldview of the everyday first century demigod? Even more so, what chain of events bore him to the status of Godhead? Obviously, Constantine at Nicea represents the near tail end of this process. But it was writings of Paul that kicked it off. This will be the focus of our next chapter.

AMERICAN IDOL (ALMOST)

We're back to *American Idol*. During its seventh season, a young woman by the name of Carly Smithson gave her rendition of *Superstar*. The song came from the classic rock opera, *Jesus Christ Superstar,* which was written by Andrew Lloyd Webber, with lyrics by Tim Rice. It had its first staging on Broadway in 1971. The lead song, "Superstar," was a powerful song. Carly made a good choice. But she didn't survive the cut. In spite of what I thought was a stellar performance, Carly was voted off the show (4-23-08). I can't prove it but I suspect a bit of religious backlash. She was, after all, singing a song that didn't conform to Christian dogma. Instead of posing theological assurance about Jesus, the lyric was a bit confrontational. In some circles, that's paramount to being unfaithful. Then again, maybe that wasn't the problem. Maybe it was her tattoos. Maybe both. It's hard to say without the voting demographics.

If you don't know the lyrics, you'll have some trouble catching the power of that song. Because of copyright laws I can't offer a lyrical sample of *Superstar*. If you have the CD, or Internet access, listen to it. It's a somewhat controversial song. Basically, *Superstar* questions Jesus's identity and mission, along with the place and time of his arrival. It also highlights political and interpersonal stuggles—struggles that are not in the Bible.

Over the course of a few hundred years, the early church debated some of the same questions that are posed by the Jesus Christ Superstar rock opera. Reaching a general consensus was anything but a smooth process (as we saw in Chapters 4 & 5). No doubt, Jesus, and the story about Jesus, was an enigma for early Christians. Eventually, they hammered out doctrinal statements that today we accept as Christian orthodoxy. But did these early Christians get it right? Could they get it right owing to their limited perspective? Okay, I know, this is where someone starts to holler about the guiding influence of the Holy Spirit. But what does the evidence tell us as opposed to the many faith-based assumptions people make? That's what the historical scholar is after. Some of you will remember the catch phrase from Sergeant Joe Friday on TV's *Dragnet*, "Just the facts, Ma'am."

Accordingly, scholars and hopefully this book, attempt to present: just the facts. However, that's not the whole story. Every writer will spin the data in one-way or another. The most you can hope for is that the writer is trying to be objective. I have given you plenty of information and I hope some down-to-earth extrapolation (to sensibly calculate, infer, or predict from the data at hand). In concert with this attempt, this chapter will continue to explore some of the possible explanations for how Jesus came to be hailed as divine by the followers who believed in his resurrection. Since the Gospels are, at the very least, second generational writings, we will find the earlier works of Paul most helpful.

However, we must be mindful that the Bible is not always comprehensive in scope. Furthermore, as higher criticism continues to point out, the answers we garner only raise more questions. Not only that, but almost any belief can be argued from opposite sides simply because the Bible gives credence to opposing views. Consider the contradictions between the Book of Acts (written by Luke) and some of Paul's Letters, or those disagreements found between the four Gospels. Examples of biblical discord are numerous. Was Jesus crucified at 9:00 AM on the Day of Passover as reported by Mark's Gospel (15:25), or around noon on the day before Passover (known as the day of Preparation) as reported in John's Gospel (19:14)? Was he born in a house as recorded in Matthew's Gospel (2:11), or was he born in a manger as recorded in Luke's Gospel (2:12,16)? Did Judas hang himself as described by Matthew (27:5), or is Luke's version of Judas' self-disembowelment correct as recorded in the Book of Acts (1:18)? Needless to say, one should not fall into the trap of trying to prove one's point simply by quoting a particular scripture as if that settled the issue.

Hopefully, people are not only forming their convictions based on a holistic view of the Bible, but on other disciplines as well; that is, biblical criticism, along with the social, natural and behavioral sciences, and a host of others. All things considered, where does the preponderance of the evidence take us? Herein I am simply looking at the facts, indications, pointers, and markers that we have from biblical studies and other disciplines. In short, the divinity of Jesus is a complex issue that should not be confined to the biblical text. That is why the historical records of the early centuries that surrounded Jesus are so important (for example, the pagan mystery religions or the Christological controversies we examined in Chapters 4 and 5).

Nevertheless, the NT remains the focal point of Christology. Therefore, we now turn our attention to Paul's writings—writings that *preceded the Gospels* and spearheaded the early discussion of Christological concerns. No matter how one views Paul, there is no denying that his impact on Christianity remains indelible, as we are about to see. He is sometimes referred to as the second founder of Christianity. In preparation, I will close this introduction with the following anecdote.

WHEN WORLDS COLLIDE

As a child, I sat spellbound watching the riveting 1951 sci-fi movie, *When Worlds Collide*. There wasn't much action until the very end, but that was remedied by a great story line with Academy Award winning special effects.

The plot revolves around the frightening discovery by scientists that a giant rogue planet, they name Bellus, is hurtling through space on a collision course with Earth. Scientists also notice an earth-sized sister planet—they call Zyra—orbiting Bellus. They calculate that this orbiting satellite will not hit the Earth. It offers the human species the hope of survival if they can only reach it.

In a desperate effort to do just that, a rocketed "Noah's Ark" is hurriedly constructed. Of course, there's not much room for passengers, and that's the rub. When doomsday Bellus arrives with its sister planet Zyra in tow, panic breaks loose. In the final frantic moments before the collision, it appears that the rocket won't even get off the launch pad because people are falling all over each other trying to get to it. But it manages to lift off with the chosen few, just before the Earth and Bellus obliterate each other. Whew, close call. The rocket ship with its limited human and animal cargo gets away safely and lands on the planet Zyra, which has not been involved in the catastrophic collision. The old Earth passes away, but a new beginning is at hand on an altogether different world. But life will never be the same.

WHAT TO EXPECT NEXT

We know how the question of the "divine-human" nature of Jesus had bedeviled the early church. We know how Jesus was ultimately defined in 325 AD at the Council of Nicea under Constantine. But long before these events, at the very inception of the Christian movement during the first century, there was a collision of worldviews the likes of which the world had never seen; a collision that still reverberates today. It started with Paul.

Chapter 15

THE DIVINITY OF JESUS
(Part Two)

[NOTE: The words "Hellenism" and "Greco-Roman" as defined in Chapter 8 will be used interchangeably because of their thematic demigod similarities. Therefore, Hellenistic mythology, Greco-Roman mythology, Gentile mythology, Pagan Mythology, or other such combinations, will be considered as synonymous. However, as we have seen, Jewish mythology did not promote demigod concepts.]

Similar to our Intro story, this chapter reflects the earthshaking collision, not between planets, but between religious worldviews of the first century. On the one hand we had the strictly monotheistic Jewish worldview; on the other hand we had the overwhelming Gentile Greco-Roman worldview of the mythological demigod (which included the idea for the mobility of gods in human form between heaven and earth). These worldviews, not unlike our Bellus and Earth analogy, were on a first century collision course. The impact would profoundly change the course of human history. Life would never be the same. To fully understand the upcoming segments, three points of clarification are necessary.

First, this chapter is primarily based on the writings of the New Testament. I want to remind the reader once again that the discipline of biblical criticism does not regard the Gospels as historical documents; they are seen as declarations of faith. Nevertheless, there is general consensus among scholars that the 27 NT books in combination are sufficiently reliable for reconstructing the early Christian movement. Still, we cannot pretend to know precisely what happened, but only what appears to have happened. For that reason, the following scenarios must be considered in terms of probabilities, not absolutes.

Second, for those who may not know, Paul's original name was Saul of Tarsus (in Asia Minor/Turkey). He is referred to as Saul in the Book of Acts (The Acts of the Apostles) until after his conversion experience (Acts 9:3-8; 13:9). To avoid confusion, I will always revert to the name of Paul regardless of how the biblical text reads.

Third, here are a few facts about Paul, who was central to the growth of Christianity, and is the main character of this chapter. Paul was a Jew. He was a Roman citizen. He was well educated. He was a Pharisee (a Jew steeped in the strict observance of the Jewish law). He was a dedicated and violent guardian of the Jewish faith. That's probably why he hated Christians. He hunted and persecuted them to the point of death. Then one day on his way to Damascus (in Syria), he had a supernatural encounter with the risen Christ and was converted to Christianity. Thereafter, he became one of Christianity's greatest personages. What all this has to do with the divinity of Jesus will be evident in what follows.

THE ASCENT OF CHRISTIANITY

Following the crucifixion of Jesus, his resurrection and ascension into heaven, as described by the Gospels, the Apostles (disciples) were gathered at Jerusalem, the center of Jewish faith. These Jewish followers of Jesus did not divorce themselves from Judaism "as they spent much time together in the temple . . . ." (Acts 2:46b). In its Palestinian beginnings, then, Christianity, as we think of it today, did not exist. The Apostles were Jews. These leaders, and any other Jewish followers of Jesus, were simply becoming another sect (or school) of Judaism (as had been the case with the Pharisees, Sadducees, and Essenes). None of these devotees had any intention of starting a new religion. They just wanted to bring folks around to their way of thinking.

[NOTE: The word "Christians" seems to occur no earlier than ca. 44 AD when the disciples are first called by that name in Antioch, Syria (Acts 11:26).[1] However, I use the term Jewish Christianity (or Jewish Christians) because at this time Christianity was not independent from Judaism. It was a sect of Judaism and would remain so until it broke away around 70-80 AD. Some scholars argue that there were not yet two separate religions called "Judaism" and "Christianity" until after the end of the first century.]

It wasn't long before these Jewish Christians breached the limits of toleration with their unwavering insistence that Jesus was the Messiah and that he could save his people from sin, and in him was the promise of eternal life. This last point really rankled the Sadducees, they had never believed in the concept of an afterlife. In short, the Apostles (especially the disciple Peter and the newly converted Paul) became pebbles under the saddle of Jewish orthodoxy. Slowly but surely things got ugly. It wasn't long before the Apostles were being chastised and flogged by fellow Jews; yet they persisted with their out-of-bounds preaching and teaching (Acts 5:40-42).

This young "Christian" sect of Judaism survived early Jewish disapproval and continued to grow in strength until persecution finally pushed them out of the Jewish womb (ca. 70-80 AD). This was after Peter and Paul's demise. But I'm getting ahead of myself. Let's get back to the early rise of Jewish Christianity and the transformation of Jesus the man to Jesus the divine.

Around 45-50 AD, the newly developing Jewish Christian community organized a missionary offensive. It was decided that there would be two missions: one for their Jewish brethren (to be conducted by Peter), and one for the Gentiles (to be conducted by Paul). Ready, set, go!

As we learned from our last chapter, the majority of Jews did not buy into this new movement. Jewish Christianity sounded way too liberal with its presentation of a savior god who saved people from sin, and promised life eternal. For whatever reasons, when compared to Paul, Peter's overall campaign to win converts was apparently uneventful (a notable exception would be Peter's preaching on the Day of Pentecost [originally, a major Jewish harvest festival] where according to Acts, 2, 3000 Jews were converted). Nevertheless, the real growth of Christianity and its eventual triumph must be credited to Paul's missionary efforts.

> For the next decade the Church's history is dominated by Paul and his fellow apostles . . . .Their activities amounted to a vast proselytizing mission in Gentile country, carried out with the utmost vigor. . . . They aimed at preaching the Gospel from one end of the Mediterranean to the other . . . .[2]

At this juncture, one must recognize that although Christianity begins in the Jewish heartland (Jerusalem), the momentum of its growth and development radically shifts to the other Greco-Roman territories beyond Palestine (for example, Syria, Asia Minor, Greece, Cyprus, etc.); lands that are dominated by Gentiles. Understanding this pivotal relocation is crucial. It is here that the collision between the Jewish religious worldview and the Gentile religious worldview, occurs. If one does not comprehend the significance of this collision (KABOOM!), one will never grasp the transition from Jesus the man to Jesus the Christ (the divine Messiah).

As we are about to see, the religious worldview of Judaism was no match against the overwhelming number of Gentiles that were converted by Paul and his co-workers—Gentiles who were raised in the territories dominated by the demigod myth. The outcome of this theological clash can be metaphorically seen in Marv Newland's 1969 hilarious cartoon, *Bambi Meets Godzilla* (it's less than two minutes long, Google the title). Anyway, Jewish monotheism got crushed. Here's what appears to have happened.

[*Reminder*: In Paul's time, all of the Mediterranean and extended territories are now part of the Roman Empire. But we also call them Greek territories because earlier they had been conquered by Alexander the Great and were still influenced by Greek culture (known as Hellenism). As a consequence, Greek language was the international language of the day (aside from Palestinian Jews who spoke Aramaic). Latin was also present in the Mediterranean area because of Roman influence, but Greek was predominant. For various reasons, sometimes these territories are referred to as Greco-Roman.]

THE ASCENT OF JESUS

From the very get-go, Paul had a problem in the Greek territories outside of Palestine. Here was his problem: How does one explain Jesus as the Messiah to the Gentiles? Paul's difficulty was not with the Greek speaking Jews who lived in these non-Palestinian regions. They understood him well enough when he took the Hebrew word *Messiah* and replaced it with the Greek word *Christ*. "Jesus the Messiah" and "Jesus the Christ" were synonymous terms. *But the Greek Gentiles didn't get it.* The title Christ (Messiah), which represented a statement of faith in the saving mission of Jesus to restore the kingdom of Israel, was of little interest to the Gentiles. They couldn't care less about the Messianic hope and the national cause of Judaism. Eventually, therefore, *Jesus the Christ* became a proper name, *Jesus Christ*.[3]

Because the word Christ did not carry the same importance for Gentiles as it did for Jews, Paul supplemented his preaching with the word *Lord*. The term *Lord*—as a reference to God—was familiar to Jews and Gentiles alike, but with very different application. In Jewish circles, Lord and God—as in monotheism--were synonymous. To call Jesus Lord was to equate him with God. Although the term Lord was applied to Jesus in the early Jewish Christian community, the extent of its use is questionable as it would have been unacceptable to Jewish Christians who had been trained in the strict monotheism of Judaism.[4] That is why Paul and the other Apostles, according to Acts, were, at the very outset, in conflict with their Jewish brethren.

In contrast, the term Lord (Kurios, in Greek) had a broader application for the Gentiles. In their religious worldview, it commonly referred to a god, any god, especially to the gods of the mystery religions. For example, in the worship of Osiris and Dionysus, Kurios (Lord) was the everyday designation for the savior-god.[5] That's why scholars believe that when Paul used Lord in reference to Jesus, it is likely that the Gentiles looked upon Jesus as a savior-god, akin to many of their own. Purposely or not, Paul's use of this term in Gentile territory was the equivalent of a five-car pileup on the Hollywood freeway during rush hour (which nowadays could be any time of the day). That is, the mythological demigod may have been handed off to the evolving Gentile Christian movement.

None of this would matter but for the fact that the Jesus-as-Lord message preached by Paul in these non-Palestinian territories, was being accepted by great numbers of Gentiles and very few Jews. Obviously, the majority of Jews balked at the idea of calling Jesus, Lord, that is, equating Jesus with God. In contrast, it made perfect sense to the myth oriented Gentiles, and they were converting in mass. In short, the Jesus story was moving like wildfire across the Mediterranean world and, with it, the understanding of Jesus as Lord (demigod; savior-god). Consequently, it was in Gentile soil that Christianity germinated in ways far beyond anyone's imagination. Whether or not the Greek speaking Christian Jews and Gentiles carried Christianity far beyond its original intentions is still hotly debated. What did Paul think about Jesus? I'll get to that shortly.

There were other reasons for this expanding Gentile Christian base. Early on, Paul had argued for the inclusion of Gentiles into the Jewish Christian movement without being subject to some of the requirements of the Torah (the first five books of the OT that included Jewish law). If you wanted to become part of Judaism, which at that time included Jewish Christianity, there were some pretty stiff prerequisites for joining up. All converts to Judaism—whatever its configuration—were subject to these requirements. For example, dietary laws (what you could and could not eat) were mandatory. Also front and center, in a manner of speaking, was the commandment to be circumcised. Male Jews were circumcised as a sign of the Covenant (an agreement) established between God and Abraham in the Book of Genesis:

> God said to Abraham ... This is my covenant, which you shall keep, between me and you and your offspring after you: Every male among you shall be circumcised. You shall circumcise the flesh of your foreskins, and it shall be a sign of the covenant between me and you. (17:10-11)

A very wise and sensible Paul wanted these sacred obligations lifted. He instinctively knew that male prospects wouldn't convert to this evolving religion if the entry level required circumcision. The idea of adult circumcision would bring any man to a screeching halt. You think? Giving up certain foods was hard enough, but circumcision was a deal breaker. Needless to say—but I'll say it anyway—if Paul had not convinced his brethren in Jerusalem to chill out on these requirements, Gentile conversions would have dwindled down to a few masochists. You can bet on it. As it turned out, however, Paul had his way. The mandatory laws of circumcision and food restrictions were lifted, and the Gentiles came to Jewish Christianity like bees to the nectar.

In short order, there were many more Gentile Christians than Jewish Christians. As I have already indicated, the importance of this transforming shift—from Jewish culture to Gentile culture—cannot be overstated. Therefore, read the last two sentences over again.

There is little doubt that the Judeo Christian movement was significantly influenced by the early infusion of mass numbers of Gentiles. It is more than plausible to believe that these Gentiles, along with Paul's help, steadily pushed Jewish monotheism toward the demigod mythology of the Greco-Roman world. This metamorphosis was unstoppable as the sheer number of Gentiles piled on to one end of the mythological see-saw. Inevitably, Jewish Christians not only lost control of the seesaw, but they also lost control of the Jewish Christian playground. Inevitably the Jews withdrew and rightly so: By their reckoning, Jewish monotheism was being replaced with Gentile demigod mythology.

It was Paul who started the ball rolling down that mythological road so well traveled by people of the first century. Nowhere in Paul's writing, for example, is there a more powerful statement to that effect than the one found in Philippians 2:5-8 where he clearly states that Jesus was "in the form of God ... but emptied himself ... being born in human likeness ... in human form ...." This is mystery religion imagery, the savior god moving between heaven and earth.

This supernatural portrait of Jesus was not lost on those who survived Paul. After he died, it was the Gospel writers—especially "John"—who pushed the divinity envelope. But catch this, the Gospels were not written by orthodox Jews, they were written by newly converted Christians (probably living outside of Palestine). These people would have no problem interpreting Paul's description of Jesus as a demigod, regardless of what Paul actually intended. Why not? They lived and breathed the demigod worldview of Hellenism (Greek culture), and Hellenistic Jews were far more liberal than their Palestinian counterparts. Hellenistic Jews spoke Greek and did not have the advantage of an Aramaic linguistic buffer. As it turned out, the Gospels and all other non-Pauline writings came after Paul's demise (ca. 67 AD) and were penned by people who lived under the Hellenistic umbrella, both Jews and Gentiles alike. To what degree they were influenced by Hellenistic mythology is now debated among scholars. One thing is certain, these later writings—especially the Gospel of John—sharpened the image of Jesus as a Redeemer, who, via a miraculous birth, descended to earth from above, fulfilled his mission as a savior-god and then ascended to be with God.

Incidentally, it's possible that the Gospel writers succeeding Paul never saw his writings. For example, we can't be sure that any of the Gospel writers ever read Philippians. It's not like Paul's letters were present throughout the empire, not to mention the fact that at this point in time his work is not even considered to be sacred literature. Regardless of whether it was Paul, oral tradition, or whatever, scholars are inclined to believe that it was the demigod mythology of the Hellenistic Gentile world that made the most significant impact on the earliest development of Christology (the belief in Jesus as both human and divine).[6]

However exact in detail the above scenario may, or may not be, one thing is certain: Christianity, sponsoring a supernatural Jesus, broke away from its Jewish moorings and became a Gentile force to be reckoned with. Although Paul designed the spaceship that propelled the Jewish Christian satellite into orbit, it was the Jewish rocket boosters that were jettisoned away, falling back to the Temple launch pad that had supported the initial blastoff.

THE TWO FACES OF PAUL

So what did Paul think about Jesus? Did he believe Jesus to have been God in the flesh, or something less miraculous but nevertheless divine, perhaps an agent from God? In defining Jesus, was Paul inclined to lean toward the Jewish worldview of monotheism, or the Gentile worldview of demigods? He was, after all, a Jew, and a Pharisee no less. He was also a non-Palestinian Jew, born and raised in the Hellenistic world of Asia Minor (modern day Turkey). So, what did Paul think about Jesus?

There is no easy answer to these questions because the evidence is inconclusive. Scholars must be cautious. Nevertheless, there are indications that Paul had mixed feelings and was inconsistent in his portrayal of Jesus. On the one hand he boldly applied OT verses to Jesus in which the word Lord meant God. A prime example is Romans 10:9-13, where Paul quoted the promise of the prophet Joel that ". . . everyone that calls upon the name of the Lord shall be saved." Here, Paul uses the word Lord (meaning God) in reference to Jesus.[7]

On the other hand, Paul subordinates the Lord Jesus Christ to God the Father. God is superior to the Messiah. This is obvious in I Corinthians 11:3 ". . . and the head of Christ is God." Here, Paul characterizes the authority of Christ as secondary to that of God.

Whether or not Paul viewed Jesus as God, or a part of God, is unclear. His ambiguity is best illustrated by the text I partially quoted earlier. Here is the broader reading of Philippians:

> Let the same mind be in you that was in Christ
> Jesus, who, *though he was in the form of God,* did not

THE DIVINITY OF JESUS

regard equality with God as something to be exploited, but emptied himself, taking the form of a slave, being born in human likeness. And being found in human form, he humbled himself and became obedient to the point of death—even death on a cross.

Therefore, God also highly exalted him and gave him the name above every name, so that at the name of Jesus every knee should bend, in heaven and on earth and under the earth, and every tongue should confess that *Jesus Christ is Lord, to the glory of God the Father.* (2:5-11)

[Italics mine]

Paul's ambiguity about God's relationship to Jesus runs rampant in the above verses. He says that Jesus "was in the form of God," (whatever that means), but in verse 11 he says "that Jesus Christ is Lord, to the glory of God the Father." The use of the term *Lord,* in this context, cannot be taken to mean God because it wouldn't make any sense (Jesus Christ is God, to the glory of God?). Also, the phrase that Jesus "did not regard equality with God as something to be exploited" (or, *grasped,* as some versions have it) can be interpreted in several ways. What is Paul trying to say? The Oxford Annotated Bible states that, "*In the form of God, equality with God,* may refer to divine status, or simply preexistence as a heavenly being."[8] In my opinion, it is clear that Paul considers Jesus to embody some aspect of divinity, along with some form of preexistence. But the issue of *equality* between God and Jesus remains vague.

The point is: These and other verses clearly show that Paul was the first to reflect in his writing a theological perspective that ran parallel to the god-man mythology of the ancient world. Was Paul embracing the demigod concept of Hellenism and the mystery religions or was this theological similarity a coincidence? Put another way, if demigods had not been popular at the time that Paul lived, would he have come up with this Jesus equation? Is this syncretism (borrowing) or coincidence? Again, you cannot reason but from what you know: what Paul knew was Jewish monotheism, and the demigod worldview of first century Hellenism. So, do we see in Philippians a Paul who is trying to straddle the fence, or strike a compromise of sorts? It appears, but not to a certainty, that Paul is trying to reconcile Jewish monotheism with Gentile pagan mythology. What do you think? What does the evidence imply?

Whatever the truth of the matter, one thing is certain: In Philippians, Paul seems to categorize Jesus as a demigod with perks; he presents him not as a minor deity, but as a divine entity with special qualities more akin to God himself, who, by the way, has now assumed human form. This advent is pivotal because the rest of the NT is not yet written. Paul's writing will set the theological tone for whatever follows. And what follows are the Gospels—Gospels that progressively raise the Christological bar. Even if the Gospel writers were unaware of Paul's writings, demigod mythology was in the air.

What also follows is a decreasing Jewish influence with a rapidly increasing Gentile presence in Christian communities outside of Palestine that willingly embrace the god-man traditions of the Greco-Roman world. Here is another example of Paul's *ambiguous conflation* of monotheistic Judaism and what smacks of pagan belief (taken from 1 Corinthians 8:4-6). Paul is writing to Hellenistic Christian Jews in the church at Corinth, Greece.

> Hence, as to the eating of food offered to idols, we know that "no idol in the world really exists," and that "there is no God but one." Indeed, even though there may be so-called gods in heaven or on earth—*as in fact there are many gods and many lords*—yet for us there is *one God*, the Father, *from whom are all things* and for whom we exist, and one Lord, *Jesus Christ, through whom are all things* and through whom we exist. (Italics mine)

If Paul were here I would ask him two questions about these verses: (1) is there more than one God and, (2) do the Father and the Lord share equal billing or, is the Lord subordinate to the Father?

Another intriguing but mysterious reference about Jesus comes from Colossians 1:15-20 that may not have been written by Paul.[9] (Scholars question the authorship of Colossians.)

> He is the image of the invisible God, the firstborn of all creation; for in him all things in heaven and on

earth were created, things visible and invisible, whether thrones or dominions or rulers or powers—all things have been created through him . . . . For in him all the fullness of God was pleased to dwell, and through him God was pleased to reconcile to himself all things, whether on earth or in heaven, by making peace through the blood of his cross.

As was the case with Philippians, there's a zillion ways to spin the above verses. Still again, however, we find an embellished "demigod-like" figure. Similarly, the question of equality between God and Christ remains ambiguous. What does Paul mean when he refers to Jesus as "the firstborn of all creation"? There seems to be a self-contradictory nuance that runs throughout (God and Jesus are equal, but they're not equal). And it really doesn't matter who penned these verses; it only matters that we recognize them as verses that are cast within the mold of first century mythology.

Let's dig a little deeper as to why Paul (thirty to forty years before the prologue in the Gospel of John) pictured Jesus as a divine preexistent being "in the form of God," who "emptied himself" into "human form." This picturesque mythology, although compatible with his time, *was not compatible with Judaism.* There is no question in my mind that he is fiddling with both Jewish and Gentile beliefs. But why did Paul dip his brush into the pagan palette to paint his portrait of Jesus? There are at least three reasons that may have pushed Paul toward those mythical colors.

First, we must remember that Paul, as a faithful Jew, vehemently and violently persecuted the Jewish Christians until his conversion to Christianity. Although Paul recounts in Galatians (1:15-17) that God revealed his Son to him, the most popular conversion story comes from Acts (9:3-8). This version is probably somewhat embellished since it was written about thirty-five years later by the author of Luke, long after Paul's demise. Anyway, according to this text, Paul saw a bright light, fell to the ground, heard the voice of Jesus, and was blinded for three days. (Without invoking a supernatural causation, these would be classic symptoms of a schizophrenic hallucination: hearing, seeing, or feeling things that are not there.)

For the moment, however, let us assume that Paul, who is a well-educated and highly intelligent man, now believes—regardless of cause and effect—that he has envisioned Jesus as a risen redeemer (both Galatians and Acts agree on this point). His traumatic encounter is with Jesus, not God, although he does assume that God is behind this revelation. Nevertheless, this unearthly encounter that Paul experienced would certainly be in keeping with Gentile beliefs, especially the savior gods of the mystery religions. His Jewish background grounded him in monotheism, but his mystifying encounter with a dead Jesus brought him face to face with an opposing worldview. He must have struggled with the polarizing contradiction between the demigod model and the strict monotheism of Judaism. I don't see how Paul could escape making that comparison. Did this insight help frame his Philippians discourse? If so, that explains some of the ambiguous and vacillating comments within his writing.

This dovetails us right into our second point regarding what might have caused Paul's mythological leanings. We spoke of Paul's need to portray Jesus in a manner of importance that the Gentile mind, his target audience, could appreciate. (When in Rome, do as the Romans do.) His continued use of the Greek word Kurios (Lord) was a good beginning, but his writing of Philippians was the clincher. It seems to me that he tried to graft the pagan demigod genre of his day onto the very heart of monotheistic Judaism. Paul's theological surgery was a practical move as he tried to woo Gentile listeners. However, it led to at least one unintended consequence: For the Gentiles, the graft took; for the Jews, the patient died. In other metaphorical words, it appears that Paul painted a portrait of Jesus by conflating two different worldviews onto the same canvas that, in turn, brightened pagan mythology but subdued Jewish monotheism.

The third reason I believe Paul leaned toward the demigod model is a touch more speculative, but I think quite plausible. The fact is that Philippians was one of Paul's last letters to be written (ca. 60-64 AD). He is near the end of his ministry. This means that Paul had been serving these Gentile communities for about ten to fifteen years. As most of us know, significant changes in one's outlook can occur in that space of time; belief is not static, it tends to evolve. Paul could have been influenced not only by looking back on his otherworldly conversion experience, but also by the pagan mythology that surrounded him. At the beginning of his declared mission, the sensible use of Kurios in Paul's writing to reach the Gentile mind remains clear. His desire to convert Gentiles was front and center. Fair enough. However, we must not forget to factor in the ongoing process of cultural osmosis (the natural process of gradual or unconscious assimilation of ideas and knowledge). It may be that he absorbed some of the Greco-Roman mythology that surrounded him. It was a rational progression of mental and spiritual insights that one would expect, brought about by time, experience, and the pagan culture that encircled him. In other words, I think there were a number of broad and diverse influences, which over an extended period of time (this didn't happen overnight) eventually led Paul to his wide-ranging theological mix. So, I don't believe it's by chance that Paul's most definitive, yet mystifying, portrait of Jesus ("though he was in the form of God . . . but emptied himself . . . being born in human likeness . . . in human form") emerges in one of his last letters, Philippians.

Conjecture aside, Paul's impact on Christianity's development was monumental. Next to Jesus, he remains the most important Christian personage and is often referred to as the second founder of Christianity. Some people take it up a notch by claiming that without his missionary efforts, along with his Epistles, the Christian movement would have waned and disappeared like so many other wannabe movements. Not only did he help spread the developing faith across worldwide boarders and communities, he was also heavily responsible—along with Gentile influence—for shaping the Christological model. To help illustrate his enormous contributions, the following sports analogy will vividly demonstrate the potency of Paul's evolving theology as he mingles his Jewish outlook with Gentile beliefs in the fertile myth-seeded lands beyond Palestine.

STUDENT BODY RIGHT

The University of Southern California (USC), more often than not, heats up the gridiron with a gifted, breakaway tailback; these days they seem to have a plethora of them. These phenomenal runners can sometimes help their team win a national title or, for themselves, a Heisman Trophy (an annual award given to the outstanding football player in the US). Having had seven tailback Heisman Trophy winners, USC is often referred to as Tailback U. The best of the Trophy tailbacks would include:

Mike Garrett (1965), O.J. Simpson (1968), Marcus Allen (1981) and Reggie Bush (2005). Win or lose, USC tailbacks create excitement.

One of the team's favorite plays is called "student body right" (or left). When the play is called, the quarterback makes a handoff to the tailback who is in motion and who is now gliding along the right side of the offensive line. Looking for daylight, the tailback breaks quickly through whatever hole the offensive line opens up. The play is unstoppable. (But somebody forgot to tell that to the Texas Longhorns when they beat the USC Trojans for the national championship in the 2006 Rose Bowl). Anyway, these Trojan tailbacks, more often than not, delivered the game. Keeping these thoughts in mind, let's jump back to Paul.

When the Jewish Christians gave the missionary ball to Paul, he was, in a manner of speaking, a USC tailback executing a "student body right" into Gentile territory. He hit that geographical line in full stride and, like any great open-field runner, never looked back. He also broke every tackle until his execution by Roman officials around 67 AD, but he had already scored the winning touchdown. Paul's run to the goal line was unstoppable. He obviously had leadership and literary skills, was intelligent, well educated, and dedicated. His willingness to restructure his worldview was very accommodating. On his way to the winning touchdown, he finessed his way past the Jewish linebackers by eliminating the OT dietary and circumcision laws that threatened his missionary thrust into the Gentile end zone. Paul's quick thinking, his willingness to compromise on theological issues, and his passion to convince were overpowering. These are the facts, as we know them, without invoking supernatural considerations.

However, let's not forget pagan mythology and its possible influence on Paul as he made his long run; it perhaps was equally overpowering. It seems that the Gentiles may have scored a touchdown of their own. Hey, maybe it was they who won the game after all. Maybe our Christology is in part, a sophisticated reflection of pagan mythology. It was just a thought.

QUESTIONS GALORE

Was the divinity of Jesus pushed along, perhaps redefined, by the god-man mythology of the ancient world? Was Christianity transformed by the overwhelming hometown advantage of a Hellenistic stadium?

Did Paul doublespeak his Christology so as to reconcile Gentiles to the new faith? Did his unmatchable success in winning Gentile converts, tilt Christian beliefs far beyond their original intentions? Did the Jesus story eventually metamorphose through a Gentile prism that somehow derailed Jewish monotheism? Did Paul's personal theology incorporate both Jewish and pagan worldviews? Did the Christians of the first, second, third, and fourth centuries have a unified understanding of Christology? Did they all agree as to what Paul and the other NT authors meant in their writings about Jesus?

These and many other questions abound. They have been there from the very beginning. As I have already made clear, the early church didn't have the answers either. For centuries they fought and argued over how to define the human and divine natures of Jesus. They even argued as to whether Jesus was at all divine or at all human. The Christological issue remained front and center for centuries. We must not forget the momentous contribution on this issue by the Emperor Constantine at the Council of Nicea in 325 AD. The Christological matter wasn't really put to rest until the Council of Chalcedon in 451 AD. Even so, the issue became only partially dormant. Periodically, like a smoldering volcano, Christological magma rises to the surface. These occasional eruptions are inevitable because trying to grasp the conceptual mystery that surrounds the nature of Jesus (the Christ) is nigh on to impossible. Therein is the ultimate question with the ongoing elusive answer.

However you ponder the historical record being unraveled by biblical scholarship, however you answer the above questions, or however you see the scenarios I have laid out, it's not important that we have universal agreement as to how all this happened. That would be impossible, anyway. What is important is to look beyond the simplistic answers provided by the Jesusgate crowd who continue today, as they have throughout history, to present Jesus in the most dogmatic and uninformed manner. Thus, I strongly believe that it's incumbent upon all of us to push for the truth. We must look beyond the adamant assertions made by the Jesusgate crowd. And, we must not allow our religious indoctrination to override any rational consideration of the evidence forthcoming from higher criticism or any of the other fact-finding disciplines of our time.

WHAT TO EXPECT NEXT

The upcoming chapter incorporates some of my particular beliefs. It is a personal reflection about religion, atheism, and other matters that may be of interest to the reader. It also proffers a word of encouragement to those who seek to further their journey of discovery.

The upcoming Epilogue will also incorporate some interesting information on what we sometimes refer to as the "godless" countries. Can one be happy without God? I suspect that most of us would answer no. Although the answer is highly subjective, we do have some studies that shed light on the issue. However, other cause and effect factors should also be considered.

CHAPTER 16

EPILOGUE

I guess it's time to cap this project. I trust the read has been meaningful and enlightening. But it would be unconscionable if I left you with the impression that we had exhausted the findings from biblical criticism. Not hardly. This work sought only to create a framework of knowledge. I encourage the reader to pursue the quest. Before I end this one-way conversation, a few personal comments are warranted.

It is true, of course, that my spiritual journey has been heavily influenced by the intake of formal and informal education. The education I speak of is not solely that of biblical criticism, but also the disciplines of cultural anthropology, geology, astronomy, astrobiology, biology, psychology (my major in college), world religions (what I now teach in college), and so forth. You will see, therefore, that my heartfelt thoughts and my overall KQ have been shaped by the integration of these many disciplines. I cannot overemphasize how important the acquisition of knowledge has been in my life, except to reiterate the words of the sage: *You cannot reason but from what you know.* Throw in some experience and contemplation—presto, here I am. I also will not underestimate the importance of the Church through these many years, and its overall impact on my life (this would obviously include my seminary training which left an indelible imprint).

To reiterate, the acquisition of knowledge has been the mainstay of my religious modifications and my worldview in general. Nevertheless, as we all know, KQ is not the only component of the human equation. Also, knowledge by itself does not necessarily equate with being the better person. As I tell my students, I may know everything there is to know about religion (which I don't), and still be spiritually and morally bankrupt. I recognize that this writing has not touched on what it means to be spiritual or religious. But that was not my purpose. Neither have I offered any insight as to how one might be spiritually inclined without being religious. For example, cannot the atheist or humanist be equally loving and responsible as the most dedicated believer? I believe so, and, if so, what does that mean? That would take another book.

Harking back to my Introduction you will remember my first sentence: "This is not a religious book; it is a book about religion." My purpose was to spotlight the knowledge gap that exists between the scholar and layperson. It was also to spotlight Jesusgate as the reason for that knowledge divide. Furthermore, this book sought to highlight some of the scholar's findings so as to offset the travesty of Jesusgate, and the religious illiteracy it has created. To that end I have been faithful and, hopefully, with a small measure of success. I'm changing gears.

It was with great interest that I read through Richard Dawkins' book, *The God Delusion*. This self-proclaimed atheist—whom I greatly respect—has written a powerful book, a 2006 *New York Times* Bestseller. I am not an atheist or even close to being one. In this regard, Richard Dawkins and I are light years apart. What we share in common, however, is the belief that religious systems do not reflect the most rational explanations. Accordingly, his book properly undermines the many notions of religion and emphasizes the words of Ralph Waldo Emerson: "The religion of one age is the literary entertainment of the next."[1]

As for Dawkins' chosen path of atheism, I have no problem or concern with his well-thought-out convictions, even if they should prove to be wrong. In my opinion, anyone who believes that this well-informed atheist is doomed under the doctrine of religious retribution is lacking discernment. It would be ludicrous to believe that Dawkins, who, unlike most people, has fully engaged his intellect and knowledge in a concerted effort to unravel the mysteries of life, would now be eternally punished by some higher authority should his conclusions be faulty. That would make any so-called god that I can imagine, quite shallow and very mean-spirited, certainly not one of compassion and justice. In any case,

I have no concerns about his atheism except to say that I disagree. I will explain further.

Although "God" is still very much a part of my belief system, I do not define God in the traditional sense of any religion I know. In fact, I am not at all comfortable with that term. At worst, I believe that "God" is an antiquated expression and, therefore, inadequate; at best, it's a mythological reach for the ultimate Mystery that vibrantly resonates within our imaginings. As I stated in Chapter 1, I believe that the fog of religion is thicker than the fog of war. I say this not only because of the Jesusgate disaster, but because I no longer believe that religious doctrines are adequate reflections of reality, regardless of the religion. In other words, I believe that the Mystery is real, but I can no longer see the image of that Mystery as reflected through the religious models of our time. In fact, I do not believe there is any meaningful correlation between what our religions surmise, and what actually constitutes that Mystery. I do believe, however, that these religions are humanity's way of seeking out that Enigma, be they ever so far off the mark in their attempts.

As a result, I view the religions of the world as deficient attempts— but perhaps necessary ones—to describe what we cannot comprehend. I also cannot deny the positive contributions that religion has made to the whole of humanity. Yes, religion has its dark side, no denying. But that is simply because people have a dark side, and religion is composed of people. What else would you expect?

Anyway, the only thing I know about God is that I really don't know anything about God. As far as I'm concerned nobody else does either, although most religions claim that certainty. But I'd rather wrestle with the unknowable then be mentally bushwhacked by religious dogmatism. Throughout history, such dogmatism has led people down the path of no good. I'm always a little wary about people who claim to know the will of God, talk to God, or vice versa. Presumption and expediency can create havoc. The following line sums it up quite nicely: "It's not [only] the things we don't know that get us into trouble; it's the things we do know that just ain't so."[2] I got the impression—perhaps incorrectly— that President George W. Bush suffered from this religious malady. Lets face it, most of our society—and most of the world, for that matter—is trapped within the confines of religious presumption.

The Jesusgate influence continues to foster religious illiteracy. Our human potential, either collectively or individually, cannot be reached by lingering in the womb of delusional thinking, no matter how comfortable. Based on the findings of biblical criticism and other educational disciplines, it is time to revise, rethink, reinterpret, and perhaps re-mythologize the doctrinal side of Christianity (for example, the Virgin Birth, the Incarnation, the Resurrection, and the Second Coming). We should also rethink traditions that regard the Bible as ultimate authority, and perhaps the long-held belief of a personal God that watches over us, sends his son to save us from sin, and delivers us from the fires of hell. I'm not saying I know the answers to these difficult issues, but I know they need to be seriously challenged and, at the very least, discussed.

As for the ethical and moral teachings that religion promotes, that's another category altogether. That distinction has to be drawn. In my opinion, many of those teachings are quite valuable. Consider, for example, the overarching concept of love that at the very least incorporates kindness, mercy, justice, charity, and forgiveness within the human family. I think these admirable directives are reflected in almost all religions. In some of the Eastern religions—Hinduism, Buddhism, and Jainism—that sensitivity is extended to the animal kingdom at large (a sentiment I certainly agree with). But these characteristics can also be found in those outside of the religious order, for example, Humanists. In fact, I recently read a book titled *Good Without God,* written by Greg M. Epstein, the Humanist Chaplin at Harvard University. Epstein is an atheist but, as was the case with Dawkins, I'm not worried about this man's personal journey of discovery.

Epstein's book promotes the values and ethics of religion minus the theology. It proposes that one can have purpose, compassion, and community, without the trappings of religion, and he's right. The evidence shows that one *can* be "good, without God." But can one be *happy* without God? To answer that question, let's take a look to see how some of the "godless" countries of the world are doing. Consider, if you will, the excellent book review by Louise Bayard on sociologist Phil Zuckerman's book about Scandinavia, *Society Without God: What the Least Religious Nations Can Tell Us About Contentment.* (Scandinavia includes Norway, Denmark, and Sweden.) Here is a partial quote of Bayard's review of Zuckerman's book.

> . . . he tells of a magical land where life expectancy
> is high and infant mortality low, where wealth is spread

and genders live in equity, where happy, fish-fed citizens score high in every quality-of-life index: economic competitiveness, healthcare, environmental protection, lack of corruption, educational investment, technological literacy . . . well, you get the idea.

. . . what makes Scandinavia particularly magical is what it lacks. "There is no national anti-gay rights movement," writes Zuckerman, "there are no . . . school boards or school administrators who publicly doubt the evidence for human evolution . . . there are no religiously inspired 'abstinence only' sex education curricula . . . there are no groups lobbying schools and city councils to remove Harry Potter books from school and public libraries . . . ."

Not to put too fine a point on it, there's no God. At least none that would pass muster with evangelical Americans. As few as 24 percent of Danes and as few as 16 percent of Swedes believe in a personal deity. (In America, that figure is closer to 90 percent.) In Scandinavia, belief in life after death hovers in the low 30 percent range, as opposed to 81 percent in America. Some 82 percent of Danes and Swedes believe in evolution, while roughly 10 percent believe in hell. Their rate of weekly church attendance is among the lowest on Earth. [*Bayard's review of Zuckerman's book was taken from the Internet.*]

As an added note, the United Nations Human Development Index 2011, declared Norway to be the world's happiest country, followed by Australia, the Netherlands, and the USA. The Index measures happiness in different countries based on factors such as income, education, health, life expectancy, economy, gender equality and sustainability.

But again, I do not agree with the exclusion of the supernatural, whatever that might entail. However, I do agree that our energies should be directed toward the welfare of the human family; that should be our prime directive, not the worship of some deity. I was tempted to explain my religious worldview in this last chapter but quickly realized it was the beginning of another book. Perhaps later, if time allows. I'm no spring chicken but I'm still a chicken with some spring. Anyway, what's most important is not what I believe or don't believe. The purpose of this writing was to close the informational gap between scholar and layperson. It is incumbent on each of us to pursue the quest. In that spirit, I have decided to end this work with a word of encouragement to all who are on the road to discovery. I will reprise some of the words from my earliest book, along with editorial modifications.[3]

THE ROAD NOT TAKEN

Two roads diverged in a yellow wood,
And sorry I could not travel both
And be one traveler, long I stood
And looked down as far as I could
To where it bent in the undergrowth;

Then took the other, as just as fair
And having perhaps the better claim,
Because it was grassy and wanted wear . . .

Robert Frost (1874-1963),
American Poet

The fork in the road described so eloquently by Robert Frost in his poem *The Road Not Taken*, clearly illustrates the dilemma of decision-making. As life unfolds, such fork-in-the-road decisions must be made. No matter which path we follow, we leave behind still another path—the road not taken.

When that decision is made, and if the angle of the fork is not too great, those who have chosen the other road may be kept in sight for some time until the ever-widening split obscures them. Whether these roads move apart quickly or slowly, the result is the same; the experiences of the one become isolated from the experiences of the other.

At times, while moving forward on our chosen path, we may glance back with a curiosity about the road not taken and wonder, "What if?" We made our decision, however, and there's no turning back. We are committed to following the road we chose, and our experiences thereon will determine whether we made the right choice—or at least a good choice.

Theologically, I know many will choose a different road than mine. Some because they are less informed, others because they are more informed. And their road to them is as real as mine is to me. It would be foolish and presumptuous of me to believe that this book has laid out the ultimate explanation about the religious issues discussed herein. No individual, no school of thought, no educational discipline, no government, no religion, can corner the market on truth. We can, however, search for clarity through these various sources. Therefore, I cannot help but believe that my theological path is appropriate for me because its direction was influenced by religious studies, and the collective knowledge from other fields of study, not to mention my own experiences and ruminations.

My personal journey aside, there is no argument that the findings from biblical criticism and other disciplines of study have raised perplexing questions—questions that can only be viewed as adding more mystery to the Mystery. These unresolved questions, with their serious overtones may not bring aid and comfort to the reader. But as I have already stipulated, this work seeks only to create a framework of knowledge, a starting point for discussion. One must continue to wrestle with these thorny issues and perhaps, along with other seekers, help lend perspective to these troubling insights.

For the present, we must resist the easy answers streaming from the Jesusgate crowd. Their negative response to this work is anticipated. Importantly, however, we must avoid relying on simplistic answers that no longer correlate with twenty-first century knowledge. Biblically stated, we must not put new wine into old wineskins. All to often, our fear of the stark truth has led us to denial. Even some Christian scholars, in an attempt to salvage traditional beliefs, have tried to force square pegs into round holes—an attempt to preserve the foundation of a religious system badly shaken and cracked by the continuous jackhammer impact of emerging knowledge.

In the pursuit of truth, freethinkers must find their own way through the maze of learning and spirit. Any outside authority such as the state, the church, the Bible, our peers, our parents, may indeed point us in the right or wrong direction. Yet, the responsibility for what we choose to believe remains with us. But there can be no substitute for personal perseverance. Opinions and viewpoints without a raised KQ are basically worthless, debilitating, and sometimes dangerous.

If, after examining the bulk of the evidence, we adopt beliefs that conflict with "the powers that be," we must summon the strength to keep faith with our growing awareness. Some may accuse us of arrogance or perhaps heresy, especially if we choose to adopt beliefs that run counter to religious tradition. But we must hold fast to our chosen course, our chosen road.

The satisfaction derived from this quest will depend on the maturity, strength, courage, and resolve of the seeker. Such character traits are essential for this journey since it will also be difficult and painful. Pain is likely whenever we are forced to reexamine and, perhaps, jettison ideas that we once thought to be sacred. When one is separated from one's religious blanket, the surrounding temperature can take a precipitous drop. I suppose it wouldn't be so difficult if the pain were swift and brief, but this is not generally the case for those recovering from Jesusgate addiction. The personal struggle for growth involves long-term doubt, emotional anguish, and requires courage to abandon the familiar, comfortable, but convoluted answers of the Jesusgate herd. However, there can be no other way, for change is essential to a vibrant existence. Without change there is stagnation and, ultimately, decay and death within the human spirit.

According to John S. Dunne (Professor of Theology at the University of Notre Dame), the key to renewal and growth is the "seeking and finding" we experience at each new stage of life: infancy, childhood, adolescence, adulthood, and maturity. This is true, Dunne says, if we perceive our lives as a journey for discovery, and if we expect each new plateau not merely to repeat what we know, but to give us new insights and new perceptions.[4]

Similarly, world renowned, psychologist Dr. Carl R. Rogers (1902-1987) states:

> Life at its best, is a flowing, changing process in which nothing is fixed . . .
>
> When I am thus able to be in process, it is clear that there can be no closed system of beliefs, no unchanging set of principles which I hold.
>
> Life is guided by a changing understanding of and interpretation of my experience. It is always in process of becoming.[5]

In the process of becoming, we must search deep within ourselves to discover the great reservoirs of faith. We will need a more tenacious faith than previously held because the Mystery will remain unclear, and also because all of the props and security of popular Christianity will be gone. We will discover that the most cherished and accepted religious dogmas of our upbringing are no longer attuned to our evolving level of awareness. Forever lost will be the absolute assurance of a "divine" Jesus or an all-authoritative Bible. Indeed, there will be times when we will long for the warm shelter of our Jesusgate tradition in which simple, unquestionable answers soothed the troubled soul. Even so, we cannot return to that system any more than we can return to the innocence of a childhood Christmas.

Our chosen path may also lead to feelings of isolation. We may find that our ability to relate to the system and the people that nurtured us will diminish substantially, not only because we are different but also because they cannot tolerate our difference. They will feel uneasy about our chosen path, and will view our expanding consciousness as an aberration. The seeker's fate is well illustrated by the creative words of Kahlil Gibran:[6]

> *Said the Eye one day,* "I see beyond these valleys a mountain veiled with blue mist. Is it not beautiful?"
>
> *The Ear listened, and after listening intently awhile, said,* "But where is any mountain? I do not hear it."
>
> *Then the Hand spoke and said,* "I am trying in vain to feel it or touch it, and I can find no mountain."
>
> *And the Nose said,* "There is no mountain, I cannot smell it."
>
> *Then the Eye turned the other way, and they all began to talk together about the Eye's strange delusion. And they said,* "Something must be the matter with the Eye."

Still, we will find the rewards of our journey are commensurate with the trials endured. As we become the *eye* of our spiritual quest, we will also perceive a reality beyond the one that surrounds us. No longer will we be fettered by religious dogma and mind conformity. Instead, like a bird on the wing, we will soar into open skies and, hopefully, experience new vistas of insight. This will be possible only if we allow the continuing light of knowledge to illuminate our minds, and if we take seriously the implications and responsibilities of love.

Importantly, I am indebted to my Christian heritage. I cannot imagine my life without the loving Christian community that nurtured me through my formative years. The experience was invaluable, in spite of the Jesusgate influence. I believe that Christianity—and other religions also—carry some core values for us that must be maintained. Therefore, I would be at fault to leave you with the impression that Christianity is an enemy. It is not. However, It should be clear from this writing that the Jesusgate element is a negative force that must be reckoned with; it fosters religious illiteracy that leads to attitudes of exclusiveness, dogmatism, arrogance, presumption, adverse expediency, and stifles human progress. Not unlike the Berlin Wall, the Jesugate blockade must fall. It will. It will fall with or without the cooperation of the clergy.

For myself, I am grateful for the journey thus far. It has not been easy, but that is what has made it special and valuable to me. And I feel deeply confident, as echoed in these concluding words from *The Road Not Taken*:

> *I shall be telling this with a sigh*
> *Somewhere ages and ages hence:*
> *Two roads diverged in a wood, and I—*
> *I took the one less traveled by,*
> *And that has made all the difference.*

Appendix A

THE WEAKEST LINK

As already stated, evangelical scholarship is not used by public institutions of higher learning worldwide. The reasons are as follows.

First, evangelicals are driven by an all-consuming presupposition (something that is assumed beforehand at the beginning of a line of argument). It is this: They take for granted—*in advance of their research*—that the Bible already possesses the unquestionable truth. This dominating assumption is super-glued to the belief that *all* biblical verses are a God-given revelation. Therefore, the Bible is to be regarded as a *perfect* revelation from beginning to ending, above anything. This belief has led to the misguided view that the entire Bible is flawless. Technically, this view is known as the doctrine of Inerrancy or Infallibility (without any error). They generally take the Bible literally. The Bible is seen, therefore, as a collection of sacred e-mails from God that are considered unfailing, timeless, and universally valid. Their thinking is as follows: (1) God is perfect! (2) The Bible comes from God! (3) Therefore, the Bible is perfect! This simplistic argument appears logical but the issue is much more complex. For one thing, it fails to consider the human prism through which the biblical message was filtered or, perhaps even created.

The assumption of possessing ultimate truth (and thereby ultimate authority) is woven into all belief systems that claim to have received special revelation from some higher power. For Christians, that special revelation would be the Bible, for Jews, the Torah,[1] for Muslims, it would be the Qur'an, and so on. But when one accepts any "holy" book as an uncontestable authority, this cannot, by any true academic standard, be the starting point of honest inquiry. This brings us to my next concern.

A second reason I do not rely on fundamentalist scholars is because they are prone to employ a flawed methodology (mode of operation). Their investigative procedures are slanted to ensure support for their chief presupposition, which is, biblical infallibility. Of course, no one is totally free from biased leanings. But more than any other group, they screen and manipulate only those bits and pieces of evidence that will help substantiate their preconceived notions, while ignoring the full weight of scholastic input. In other words, evangelicals have a tendency to seek out micro bits of evidence to validate their assumptions rather than allowing the macro spectrum of evidence to speak for itself. This narrowed approach dabbles with the partial; it is not holistic. They cherry-pick.

As a result, these conservatives will dismiss an entire system of thought—such as the Theory of Evolution[2]—because it does not provide an answer for every unsolved mystery it raises. But evolution, as an organizing, scientific principle for explaining the development of life, remains convincingly so in the scientific community. And yet Fundamentalists reject this scientific model on the basis of its imperfection while simultaneously disregarding its overwhelming coherence. Worse yet, they will then substitute their own so-called biblical answer (camouflaged as Creation Science or Intelligent Design), which, in every way measurable, falls far short of the solid evidence they have dismissed.

When the findings from biblical science (or any scholarship) prove to be the most plausible, their acceptance cannot depend on whether they measure up to the "holy" writings (as it was for the apes in the sci-fi blockbuster, *Planet of the Apes*). Knowledge must not—as fundamentalists are prone to do—be rejected, be ignored, be rationalized, or somehow be forced to "harmonize" with religious belief. This leads only to unfounded doctrinal absurdities, intellectual contortions and, subsequently, to the loss of academic integrity. That is why their scholastic efforts are not recognized as being the most compelling, objective, or reliable. That is also why mainstream educational institutions of higher learning do not rely on their scholarship.

For the reasons I have stated, mainstream educators view fundamentalists as the weakest link in the educational chain. As noted, no scholar in any field of thought is totally unbiased. But slanted views become insurmountable when they are the driving force behind the investigator's procedure. Striving for predetermined results, as if one were shaping clay on the potter's wheel, does not yield academic excellence; it yields only what one forces it to yield.

In the main body of this text, I have already stated that not all conservative scholars fall within this restrictive model I have described. Many are dedicated, highly intelligent, and are neither presumptuous nor expedient. Nevertheless, I believe that the preponderance of the evidence puts them on the wrong side of history. Time will tell, as it always has.

Appendix B

WOMEN AND TEXTUAL CRITICISM

In Chapter 7 I focused primarily on the Gospels. I will redirect the early bird method toward the Pauline Corpus (the NT letters written by Paul or those traditionally attributed to him). I won't drag this out but I think it's important to visualize how some of the scribes injected their biased views into the scriptures through simple rewrites of the text. In this case, it has to do with women. Incidentally, the following is not intended as a thorough discourse on Christianity's subordination and dehumanization of women. Ample sources exist on this topic.

WOMEN AND TEXTUAL CRITICISM

Before we get to the nitty-gritty, I will address a serious misconception about Paul's so-called sexist remarks as found in the following passages.

I CORINTHIANS 14:34-35	I TIMOTHY 2:11-13
Women should be silent in the churches. For they are not permitted to speak, but should be subordinate, as the law also says. If there is anything they desire to know, let them ask their husbands at home. For it is shameful for a woman to speak in church.	Let a woman learn in silence with full submission. I permit no wamn to teach and have authority over a man; she is to keep silent.

The problem here is that mainstream NT scholars agree that *Paul never wrote these gender-biased comments.* In 1 Timothy's case they believe the entire book was written pseudonymously (written by someone else, using Paul's name). This conclusion is based on the following solid evidence.

First, the vocabulary differs sharply from Paul's; that is, the author of 1 Timothy uses Pauline words in a non-Pauline sense. As one example, Paul's use of the word "church" throughout his writings refers to individual congregations, but in 1 Timothy it refers to the church universal. Second, the literary style differs sharply from Paul's. For example, "Paul writes a conversational, lively Greek, with gripping arguments and emotional flare-ups, and he introduces real or imaginary opponents and partners in dialogue." But 1 Timothy is written "in a formal, meditative style."[1] Third: "The people, geography, and situations in the letters cannot be placed within the lifetime of Paul."[2] Fourth, neither 1 Timothy, nor the few lines from 1 Corinthians will mesh with Paul's egalitarian attitudes on women as expressed in most of his other writings.

Speaking of 1 Corinthians, which Paul did write, some scholars believe that the few sexist comments, as seen above in the Corinthians' passage, were transplanted from 1 Timothy (the wording and intention is quite similar). That is, they were inserted into Corinthians by the same author who wrote 1 Timothy, or a later scribe who agreed with 1 Timothy's biased content. But as we noted, this gender bias does not square with most of Paul's other writings:

> Paul elsewhere talks about women leaders in his churches without giving any indication that they are to be silent. He names a woman minister in Cenchreae, women prophets in Corinth, and a woman apostle in Rome. Even more significantly, he has already indicated in 1 Corinthians itself that women are allowed to speak in church, for example, when praying or prophesying . . . How could Paul allow women to speak in chapter 11 [of 1 Corinthians] but disallow it in chapter 14? Moreover, it is interesting that the harsh words against women in 1 Corinthians 14:34-35 interrupt the flow of what Paul has been saying in the context. Up to verse 34 he has been speaking about prophecy and he does

so again in verse 37. It may be, then, that the intervening verses were not part of the text of 1 Corinthians but
originated as a marginal note that later copyists inserted
into the text after verse 33 . . . . However the verses came
to be placed into the text, it does not appear that they
were written by Paul but by someone living later, who
was familiar with and sympathetic toward the [nega-
tive] views of women advanced by the author of the
Pastoral epistles.[3] [1 and 2 Timothy and Titus are called
the Pastoral Epistles] [Brackets mine]

This is not to imply that Paul wouldn't get kicked in the shins if he
were to be confronted by today's feminists. There are verses in that same
11th chapter of 1 Corinthians that are more problematic than helpful.
For example, verse 3 is troublesome: "But I want you to understand that
Christ is the head of every man, and the husband is the head of his wife,
and God is the head of Christ." If you dissect this verse carefully you will
find an established hierarchy of authority, from the greatest to the least.
God is highest, then Christ, then man, and, at the bottom, woman. Also,
verse 7 doesn't sound very positive when Paul writes that man "is the
image and reflection of God; but woman is the reflection of man." Verses
8 and 9 are also a problem: "Indeed, man was not made from woman,
but woman from man. Neither was man created for the sake of woman,
but woman for the sake of man." All of these verses lend themselves to
spousal abuse—be it physical or emotional—as some husbands use them
as an excuse to run rough shod over their wives and other females for that
matter.

In spite of these apparent Pauline deviations, most scholars can glean
from Paul's *overall work* that, more often then not, he certainly leaned
toward equal rights and opportunities for women. In fact, in verses 11
and 12 of that same 11th chapter, Paul finally comes around with a more
positive slant: "Nevertheless, in the Lord woman is not independent of
man or man independent of woman. For just as woman came from man,
so man comes through woman; but all things come from God." Also, in
Galatians 3:28, Paul writes: ". . . there is no longer male and female . . . ."

Nonetheless, Paul provided enough negative fodder for anyone who
is gender biased to maintain their position if, indeed, they are not willing to take a good look at the larger picture. It's been that way since the

get-go. As proof, textual criticism, with its cross-checking of manuscripts down the historical timeline, illustrates that the later scribes wasted no time distorting Paul's writing in favor of their patriarchal bias. Let's take a look-see.

Aside from the above verses we have examined, consider the following examples. Notice how scribes reworded Paul's positive comments about women so as to neutralize them, or added opposing views to Paul's overall work. These verses expose the narrow-mindedness of the later copyists as they attempted to undermine Paul's egalitarian view of women and their authoritative positions in his emerging churches. I have taken Dr. Bart D. Ehrman's following scriptural examples, and his comments, verbatim. *[NOTE: most of the misleading alterations that follow have been corrected in our newer biblical translations.] [Brackets mine except for the one that appears in Col. 4:15. Parentheses are original to Ehrman's examples.]*

> **Acts 17:4:** the original text spoke of *"prominent women"* among Paul's converts; some scribes changed the text, however, so that now these converts are described as *"wives of prominent men"*—thereby giving men, of course, the spotlight.

> **Acts 18:** several times in this chapter Paul speaks of Priscilla (a woman) and Aquila (a man) as a prominent Christian couple in Corinth [Greece]. Scribes sometimes reversed the names to Aquila and Priscilla (e.g., v. 26), so that women would be placed in a secondary role. On other occasions scribes simply dropped her name altogether, so that only the man was mentioned (e.g., v. 21). [Verse 21 cannot be correct since neither name appears; I believe Ehrman was referring to verse 2, or possibly verse 18. I remind the reader that both names have been reinstated in our modern translations. However, some of these translations—such as the New King James Version—continue to list the names in the incorrect order of Aquila and Priscilla, rather than vice versa (e.g., v. 26).]

Col. 4:15: originally the author spoke of a church meeting in the home of a woman named Nympha ("Nympha and the church in her house"); one scribe changed the name so that now it was a man who hosted the church ("Nymphas [a man's name] and the church in his house").

Rom. 16:7: in the original text Paul sends greetings to Andronicus (a man) and Junica (a woman), who are called his "compatriots and foremost among the apostles" (so that the woman Junica was designated as a leading apostle). Some scribes, however, made a slight change in the text so that now Paul greets Andronicus and Junica as "his kin,". . . now Junica has been stripped of her apostleship!

Other changes of this sort occur throughout the tradition. If nothing else, they show that some Christian scribes in later times did not approve of the high profile women occasionally enjoyed in the early churches.[4]

[NOTE: These changes also show the value of our early NT manuscripts when compared to the later editions. We otherwise would not be able to make these insightful observations.] [Brackets mine]

Appendix C

NEW TESTAMENT AUTHORS

Only two of the four Gospels could pertain to Jesus' disciples. That would be Matthew, the tax collector who is mentioned in the Gospel that bears "his" name. The other is John. Although the name John does not appear in the Gospel of John, tradition offers him up as the composer; believed to be the son of Zebedee, and mentioned only in the Gospel of John as the "beloved disciple."

As for Mark and Luke, scholars of all stripe agree that neither of these two were disciples of Jesus. The NT does not list them as disciples, and Luke admits as much about himself in his opening comments (Luke 1:1-3). Therefore, our focus for the moment will be on the question as to whether the disciples Matthew and John could have authored the Gospels of Matthew and John. We begin with Matthew.

MATTHEW

It was the church historian Eusebius (writing in the 300s AD), who quotes Papias (one of the early church leaders working ca. 130 AD) as naming the disciple Matthew as the author of the Gospel we now call Matthew. Papias also claimed that the Gospel had originally been composed in Hebrew. But for various reasons, scholars today look askance at those declarations.

First, there is an issue about Papias' reputation as a writer. Papias' writing, *Interpretations of the Sayings of the Lord* (in five books), has utterly disappeared. It has survived in remnants and also in the form of quotations made by other writers who followed. Judging from the comments of his "contemporaries," Papias was not highly regarded in spite of his literary efforts. For example, neither the early church historian Eusebius, nor the early Church Father, Irenaeus, viewed his judgments with confidence.

Second, the claim by Papias that the Gospel of Matthew had originally been written in Hebrew doesn't make any sense; Jesus and his disciples spoke Aramaic, not Hebrew. Thus, it is doubtful that Matthew, the disciple, would have spoken and written in Hebrew. And even if we grant him this improbability, why would he pen the Gospel in Hebrew—a language that was not easily spoken or read by the common Jew (or by any non-Jew, for that matter)?[1] If one is trying to get a message out, common sense dictates that one must write it in the vernacular (the language) of the people. That's why I'm writing this book in English. Papias' claim for Matthean authorship would have been more credible had he argued that the Gospel of Matthew had originally been composed in Aramaic, rather than Hebrew. He seems to have made a mental error while attempting to shore up authority for the text.

JOHN

As for the Gospel of John, it was the last of the four Gospels to be written (ca. 90-100 AD). Christian tradition designates John, the son of Zebedee,[3] as a disciple of Jesus, and as the author. Once again, this attribution comes from Eusebius in the fourth century when he quotes in retrospect Irenaeus (ca. 180 AD) as having made that claim. This "early" speculation is somewhat prompted by the Gospel itself. Mentioned within the text is an unknown person by the name of the "disciple whom Jesus loved" (John 13:23; 19:26; 21:7; 21:20). Even today, many believe that this "beloved disciple" is John. They believe he refrains from identifying himself for fear of appearing arrogant; that is, arrogant if he declared himself to be the disciple whom Jesus loved. Regardless, here are some of the reasons why mainstream scholars do not attribute this Gospel to the disciple John.

To begin with, the text itself betrays the author as someone other than the disciple. The passage in question—John 21:20-24—reads: "This is the disciple who is testifying to these things and has written them, and we [that is, someone other than the disciple himself] know that his testimony is true."⁴ If John were writing this, he would not be using "we" and "his" as it appears here. Even the conservative scholar, Raymond E. Brown, acknowledges that most scholars no longer believe that any of the Gospels were eyewitness accounts to the ministry of Jesus.⁵

A second indication that the disciple John might not have written this Gospel is that the Book of Acts (written by the author of Luke) tells us that John, the son of Zebedee, couldn't read or write (the literal meaning of the Greek phrase, "uneducated and ordinary," as found in Acts 4:13).⁶

In that last paragraph, notice that I said, "John might not have written this Gospel." I do not use an isolated scripture as indisputable evidence to make an inflexible judgment or opinion. (That's called proof-texting.) That's because I do not accept the Bible as infallible. In other words, whoever wrote Acts could be mistaken about John's literary capabilities, that is, it doesn't prove that John was really illiterate. After all, the historical accuracy of Acts itself is questionable. For example, did Paul consult with the Apostles (the original disciples) before going out into the mission field? In Galatians 1:17 (which Paul wrote), he definitely says no. But Acts 9:26ff (which Luke wrote), says that Paul did. And what about the serious conflict between Paul and the Apostles in Jerusalem as claimed by Paul in Galatians 2:14. In contradiction, Acts, claims nothing short of total harmony from the beginning to the end of Paul's mission (Acts 15:1-24).⁷ One of these sources is wrong. I'm betting on Paul because he's writing about himself while the author of Acts is writing from hearsay about thirty years after Paul's death.

But in regards to our original comment in Acts about John's illiteracy, we cannot know with certainty that this reference in Acts proves the point simply because it's biblical. Although the reference to John's illiteracy in Acts is not conclusive, it is nevertheless another piece of the puzzle that scholars must consider. In this case, there is good reason to assume that the author of Acts got it right because scholars know that 85 percent to 90 percent of the people living in the first century were illiterate. So what are the chances that a company of fisherman could actually read and write?

Similar to our other three Gospels, there are many reasons as to why scholars do not accept the traditional notion that John the disciple (or any other eyewitness) authored the Gospel of John. Again, suffice it to say that the general consensus of scholarship on the Gospel of John is twofold: (1) the Gospel of John was not written by the disciple John or any other eyewitness and (2) the author of John remains anonymous.

As for Luke and Mark, we have already established that there is no hint of discipleship or eyewitness status in the New Testament. Besides, as already noted, Luke admits that he is neither a disciple nor an eyewitness. Even so, I'll give a brief comment on Luke at the close of this Appendix. As for Mark, he may not have been an eyewitness, but tradition makes him a special case. Let's take a closer look.

MARK

Traditionally, it was believed that John Mark was the secretary of the disciple Peter. According to 1 Peter 5:13, (a letter supposedly written by the disciple Peter), Mark is on hand with Peter in Rome. Tradition also declares that this mentioned Mark eventually wrote the Gospel of Mark. Although Mark himself was not an eyewitness to the events he records, he obviously would be well qualified to write a biographical work about Jesus if, indeed, he collaborated with Peter. Early Christians assumed that he had received most of the information (what to write) directly from Peter; secondhand information to be sure, but that would make this Gospel only one step removed from Peter's firsthand experiences with Jesus. It was the next best thing to the real thing.

This traditional view is bolstered by the church historian Eusebius, writing in the fourth century, who reports that Papias, who lived in the early part of the second century (here we go again), maintained that Mark was the secretary of Peter and later wrote the Gospel of Mark. Eusebius also quotes Clement of Alexandria[8] to the effect that Mark accompanied the disciple Peter on his journey to Rome. Furthermore, in both the Book of Acts and the letters ascribed to Paul, Mark is named as an associate of Paul (Acts 12:25; Col. 4:10), and, John Mark is identified as a member of the Jewish Christian community in Jerusalem (Acts 12:12).[9]

When we bring this information together, we get the following snapshot: John Mark belonged to the first Christian community in Jerusalem and, at least for a while, accompanied Paul on his travels. He also associated himself with the disciple Peter and went to Rome with him as his secretary. Eventually, John Mark wrote the Gospel of Mark after receiving firsthand information about Jesus directly from Peter. That's how the popular version goes.[10]

But scholars no longer accept this scenario. Here again we find a "fly in the ointment." [That's a strange cliché: a fly in a bowl of strawberries, probably; a fly on a cow chip, for sure; but a fly in the ointment... I don't think so.] Anyway, there's more than one fly in the ointment here; there's a bunch of flies in the ointment. Several questions arise: (1) Did the disciple Peter actually write First Peter (1 Peter) where John Mark is mentioned? (2) Did John Mark actually go to Rome with Peter and was he actually Peter's secretary? (3) Are all of these "Marks" sprinkled around in the NT actually the same person, and did any one of these Marks actually author the Gospel of Mark, as many Christians will argue? Most scholars believe *no* on all counts. Here's why.

First, scholars have ample evidence to show that the disciple Peter did not write 1 Peter, and that Peter's association with John Mark mentioned therein is purely imaginary. For example:

> "The situation indirectly described by the letter [1 Peter] ... points to a time after Peter's death. The language, style, content and thought world seem inappropriate to Peter the ... fisherman and missionary to the Jews ... The excellent and sophisticated Greek, the lack of references to the life and teachings of the earthly Jesus, the Christological emphasis on the cosmic Christ ... point to a disciple of Peter writing in the name of the revered apostle."[11] [Brackets mine]

Second, the claim for Markan (John Mark) authorship first came from ... you guessed it ... Papias, as reported by Eusebius. Aside from what we have already mentioned about Papias, it is enough to say that scholars consider Papias unreliable because he is eager to attribute eyewitness (or near-eyewitness) guarantees to the Gospels without any substantial evidence, and without any apparent knowledge or concern for how these books developed through decades of oral tradition.[12]

As for Clement of Alexandria, if Eusebius got it right in quoting him to the effect that Mark accompanied Peter to Rome, it still doesn't make it so. After all, if Papias was on shaky ground, why should we give Clement, who was born long after Papias, more credibility on this issue? He obviously bases his opinion on the belief that 1 Peter was written by the disciple Peter and, therefore, accepts at face value verse 5:13 (that

Peter and Mark were together in Rome). But as scholars have indicated (see above), it is highly unlikely that the disciple Peter wrote First Peter, and that undercuts the probability that Mark and Peter were ever together in Rome.

For the sake of argument, however, let's assume that the disciple Peter is the author of First Peter. It still doesn't tell us who this Mark is. Nothing is said in 1Peter about this Mark being Peter's secretary or anything about his having written the Gospel of Mark.[13] Again, better arguments have surfaced in our previous chapters as to why it is highly improbable that the disciple Peter gave firsthand information to the author who penned the Gospel of Mark.

LUKE (Luke-Acts)[14]

[NOTE: It is almost universally agreed by biblical scholars that the Gospel of Luke and the Book of Acts (The Acts of the Apostles) were composed by the same person, ergo, Luke-Acts.]

As was the case with our previous Gospels, the author of Luke-Acts was not an eyewitness to the events he narrates. Traditionally, however, he was considered to be an eyewitness and was identified as "the beloved" physician who accompanied Paul on some of his missionary journeys. This Luke is presumably the same Luke named in several of Paul's letters.

Still, scholars doubt that the author of Luke knew the apostle Paul firsthand because he shows no knowledge of Paul's letters. Furthermore, they consider some of Luke's comments incongruous had he really been an observer of Jesus's ministry; ". . . scholars have criticized the writer of Luke for inaccurate geographical notations, description of persons and events, and illogical stories. For example, Anna, a prophetess in Luke, is portrayed as having lived in the temple (Luke 2:36-38). According to all the evidence collected about the Jewish Temple in Jerusalem, women were not allowed to enter it. They stood outside the gates with the Gentiles, or non-Jews."[15]

Appendix D

EPIC OF GILGAMESH

The Epic of Gilgamesh is an ancient flood story that originated with the Sumerian people of Sumer, an ancient region in the lower part of Mesopotamia (known today as Iraq). This Epic was written around 2500 BC (about 1600 years before the Old Testament was started). It is similar to the account of Noah's Ark found in the Book of Genesis. For example, the gods decide in anger to send a flood upon the earth; this calamity is revealed to one man; the man is instructed by the gods to build an ark; when the rains come his family and animals are brought into the ark; the waters cover the earth; humanity is lost; the birds are sent forth from the ark to confirm a receding flood; the ark lands atop a mountain; offerings are made to the deities.

Of course, there are many great differences between the stories of Gilgamesh and Noah. Nevertheless, the parallels between the two are obvious. Therefore, it appears that the OT writer borrowed some of his material from this ancient pagan text. The following excerpts indicate as much.

EPIC OF GILGAMESH (ca 2500 B.C.)	NOAH'S ARK (ca 950 B.C.)
I opened the window and the light fell upon my face . . . I sent forth a dove and let her go. The dove flew to and fro, but there was no resting place and she returned. I sent forth a swallow and let her go. The swallow flew to and fro, but there was no resting place and she returned. I sent forth a raven and let her go. She . . . came not back. [1]	Noah opened the window of the Ark . . . and sent forth a raven and it went to and fro . . . Then he sent forth a dove . . . but the dove found no place to set her foot, and she returned to him to the ark . . . Then he waited another seven days, and again he sent out the dove from the ark . . . the dove . . . did not return to him any more.[2]

A TAD OUTSIDE THE BOX by Ernie Bringas

ENDNOTES

(Endnotes may sometimes begin within
the intro section that precedes the main chapter.)

PROLOGUE: THINGS YOU SHOULD KNOW

[1] The *New Interpreter's Bible* is generally regarded by academia as the scholar's bible. Any library with a good reference department will carry these numerous volumes.

[2] *The New Interpreter's Bible, Vol. VIII*. Nashville: Abingdon Press, 1995, pp. 2 & 9.

[3] Technically, these groups are not identical. But I will use these terms interchangeably because they have similar, conservative views about biblical authority. For further information, see *The Perennial Dictionary of World Religions*, (HarperSanFrancisco).

[4] Although AD is commonly interpreted and accepted as "after the death of Christ," AD literally comes from the Latin, Anno Domini, which means, "in the year of our Lord."

CHAPTER 1: PREPPING FOR JESUSGATE

[1] James D. Smart, *The Strange Silence of the Bible in the Church*. Philadelphia: Westminster Press, 1970, pp. 66-67.

[2] Robert W. Funk, *Honest to God*. HarperSanFrancisco, 1996, p. 53.

[3] Bart D. Ehrman, *Jesus, Interrupted*. San Francisco: HarperOne, 2009, pp. 1-2.

[4] *When Faith Meets Reason*, Edited by Charles W. Hedrick. Santa Rosa, CA: Polebridge Press, 2008, p. xi.

[5] Rod Serling was the American TV host and writer for the *Twilight Zone*.

CHAPTER 2: JESUSGATE

[1] Dag Hammargkjold, *Markings*. New York: Alfred A. Knopf, 1964, p. 66.

[2] Of the five major religions of the world (Hinduism, Judaism, Buddhism, Christianity, Islam), Hinduism is far and away the most tolerant. Hindus believe that all religions are viable and that each religious path, although unique in character, leads to the same spiritual finality.

[3] Hans Kung, *Christianity*. New York: Continuum Publishing Co., 1994, p. 184.

Also: Charles Henry Lea, *A History of the Inquisition of the Middle Ages*, Vol. 1. New York: S.A. Russell Publishers, 1955, p. 213.

[4] Walter Nigg, *The Heretics*, edited and translated by Richard and Clara Winston. New York: Alfred A. Knopf, 1962, p. 236.

[5] Williston Walker, A History of the Christian Church, New York: Scribners, 1959, p. 231.

[6] Rebecca Moore, *Voices of Christianity*: *A Global Introduction*. New York: McGraw-Hill, 2006, p. 265

[7] Paul Johnson, *A History of Christianity*. New York: Atheneum, 1976, p. 309.

[8] John A. O'Brien, *The Inquisition*. New York: Macmillan, 1973, p. 122.

[9] Henry Kamen, *The Spanish Inquisition*. New York: American Library, 1965, p. 204. Also: see the 1997 Yale University Press publication, pp. 269-76.

[10] P. Johnson, *A History of Christianity*, p. 309.

[11] T.H.L. Parker, *John Calvin: A Biography*. Philadelphia: Westminster Press, 1975, p. 59.

[12] Ernie Bringas, *Going by the Book: Past and Present Tragedies of Biblical Authority*. Charlottesville: Hampton Roads Publishing Company, Inc., 1996, p. 121.

[13] Bart D. Ehrman, *Lost Christianities*. New York: Oxford University Press, 2003, p. 180.

CHAPTER 3: SCHOLAR SHOCK

[1] James Schafter, "Moon Science," *Popular Science*, October, 1978, p. 90.

[2] In 1985 the Jesus Seminar was established by a distinguished group of scholars led by Robert W. Funk and John Dominic Crossan (co-chairs). More than any other group, they have sought to share the findings of biblical analysis with the laity.

[3] Taken from *The Fourth R*, 11.4. Santa Rosa: Westar Institute, July/August, 1998.

[4] Ibid.

Also: John Shelby Spong, *A New Christianity for a New World*. New York: HarperCollins, 2002, pp. 3-6.

[5] Taken from *The Fourth R*, 11:4, July/August, 1998.

Also: Marcus J. Borg, *Meeting Jesus Again for the First Time*. New York: HarperCollins, 1994, pp. 23, 29, 36, 118.

[6] Borg, *Meeting Jesus Again for the First Time*, pp. 31-36.

[7] Ibid. p. 4.

[8] It is important to remember that in some religious circles, higher education is not required for ministry. As I have already mentioned, this is part of the Jesusgate problem.

[9] Robert W. Funk, *Honest to Jesus*. New York: HarperCollins Publishers (A Polebridge Press Book), 1996, p. 5.

[10] John Shelby Spong, *Why Christianity Must Change or Die*. New York: HarperCollins, 1998, p. 214.

[11] If I remember correctly, this quote came from one of John Shelby Spong's books, and he was quoting one of his seminary professors.

CHAPTER 4: JESUSGATE 1

[1] I don't mean to sound like an expert on classical music, because I'm not. This info came from the Wikipedia Encyclopedia.

[2] *It's never too late, baby* by Ken Barnes, USA TODAY, April 24, 2002.

[3] Bart D. Ehrman, *A Brief Introduction to the New Testament*, 2nd Edition. New York: Oxford University Press, 2009, pp. 14-16.

[4] Ibid. pp. 15,16.

[5] Bart D. Ehrman, *The New Testament: A Historical Introduction to the Early Christian Writings*, Third Edition. New York: Oxford University Press, 2004, pp. 32-33.

6 Timothy Freke & Peter Gandy, *The Jesus Mysteries*. New York: Harmony Books, 1999, p. 4.

7 Rebecca Moore, *Voices of Christianity: A Global Introduction*. New York: McGraw-Hill, 2006, p. 69.
Also: Bruce M. Metzger, *Historical and Literary Studies*. Leiden, Netherlands: E.J.Brill, 1968, p. 19.
Also: Marla J. Selvidge, *Exploring the New Testament*, 2nd Edition. New Jersey: Prentice Hall, 2003, pp. 30-34.

8 Bradley P. Nystrom & David P. Nystrom, *The History of Christianity: An Introduction*. New York: McGraw-Hill, 2004, p. 60.

9 Timothy Freke & Peter Gandy, *The Jesus Mysteries*, p. 57.

10 Bruce Metzger, *Historical and Literary Studies*, p. 19.

11 *Cybele, Attis and Related Cults: Essays in Memory of M.F. Varmaseren*, ed. by Eugene N. Lane. New York: E.J. Brill, 1996, pp. 40-41.

12 Timothy Freke & Peter Gandy, *The Jesus Mysteries*, p. 35.

13 Ibid. pp. 57 & 271.

14 *The New Interpreter's Bible*, Vol. VIII, p. 25.

15 Justin Martyr, ?—165 AD, was a Christian philosopher and writer.

16 St. Irenaeus, 125-202 AD. Bishop of Lyons in Gaul; writer.

17 Tertullian, ca. 160-220 AD. He was an outstanding third-century theologian and writer.

18 Bradley P. Nystrom and David P. Nystrom, *The History of Christianity*. McGraw-Hill, 2004, p. 54. (NOTE: David S. Noss and Blake R. Grangaard, *A History of the World's Religions*, 13th Edition. New Jersey: Pearson Education, 2012, p. 430—states that Christianity became the imperial state religion in 383.)

CHAPTER 5: JESUSGATE 2

1 Ernie Bringas, *Created Equal: A Case for the Animal Human Connection*. Charlottesville: Hampton Roads Publishing Company, 2003, pp. 100-101.

2 Harvey Cox, *The Future of Faith*. New York: HarperOne, 2009, p. 59.

3 Bart D. Ehrman, *Lost Christianities*. New York: Oxford University Press, 2003, p. 113.

4 Walter Bauer (1877-1960) was an eminent German scholar of massive knowledge and comprehension. His Greek dictionary (often

updated now) remains the standard tool for students who study New Testament Greek, the first language in which the NT was written.

5 Bart D. Ehrman, *Lost Christianities*, p. 173.

6 David S. Noss and Blake R. Grangaard, *A History of the World's Religions*, 13th Edition. New Jersey: Pearson Education, 2012, p. 431. Noss's source was: Joseph Cullen Ayer, Jr., *A Source Book for Ancient Church History*. New York: Charles Scribner's Sons, 1913, p. 501.

7 L. Michael White, *From Jesus to Christianity*. New York: HarperCollins Publishers, 2004, p. 409.

8 *The New Oxford Annotated Bible*, third edition. New York: Oxford University Press, 2001, pp. 147-148NT.

9 Jaroslav Pelikan, *The Christian Tradition (A History of the Development of Doctrine)*, Vol. 1, The Emergence of the Catholic Tradition (100-600). Chicago & London: The University of Chicago Press, 1971, pp. 172-73.

10 Ibid. p. 173.

11 Lewis M. Hopfe and Mark R. Woodward, *Religions of the World*, 11th edition. New York: Vango Books, 2009, p. 266.
Also: W.H.C. Frend, *The Early Church*. Minneapolis: Fortress Press, 1982, pp. 128, 137-38. (NOTE: most scholars portray Constantine's involvement with Christianity as problematic; that is, a question mark remains as to how deeply he was committed to Christianity relative to Sol Invictus.)

12 W.H.C. Frend, *The Early Church*, pp. 139-40.

13 Tertullian, *Against Praxeas*, Chapter 2 (". . . one cannot believe in One Only God in any other way than by saying that the Father, the Son and the Holy Ghost are the very selfsame Person.").

14 W.H.C. Frend, *The Early Church*, p. 140.

15 Ibid. pp. 140-41.

16 *Creeds of the Churches*, edited by John H. Leith. Garden City, New York: Doubleday and company, 1963, pp. 30-31.

17 David S. Noss and Blake R. Grangaard, *A History of the World's Religions*, p. 431.

18 *Dictionary of World Religions*, Keith Crim, General Editor. New York: Harper & Row, 1989, p. 339.

19 *Creeds of the Churches*, edited by John H. Leith, pp. 35-36. (Quoted verbatim but for the exclusion of Greek terminology.)

[20] Karen Armstrong, *A History of God*. New York: Ballantine Books, 1993, p. 117.

[21] David S. Noss and Blake R. Grangaard, *A History of the World's Religions*, p. 431.

[22] Elaine Pagels, *The Gnostic Gospels*. New York: Vintage Books, 1989, p. 142.

Also: Harvey Cox, *The Future of Faith*, pp. 58-60.

[23] At this historical time period, the leadership of the Roman Catholic Church is composed only of priests. Protestant ministers (who themselves become Jesusgaters), do not appear until the first half of the 16th century (1500s).

[24] Bart D. Ehrman, *Jesus, Interrupted*. New York: HarperOne, 2009, p. 215.

CHAPTER 6: JESUSGATE 3

[1] *When Faith Meets Reason,* Edited by Charles W. Hedrick. Santa Rosa, CA: Polebridge Press, 2008, p. xi.

[2] Bradley P. and David P. Nystrom, *The History of Christianity: An Introduction*, pp. 167-68.

[3] Ibid. p. 283.

[4] Ernie Bringas, *Going by the Book*, p. 79. Originally, I took this information from: James D. Smart, *The Strange Silence of the Bible in the Church*. Philadelphia: Westminster Press, 1961, p. 64.

[5] Michael Molloy, *Experiencing the World's Religions*, 5th edition. New York: McGraw-Hill, 2010, p. 383.

CHAPTER 7: NEW TESTAMENT POTPOURRIE

[1] Elaine Pagels, *The Gnostic Gospels*, p. xvii.

[2] Ibid. p. xxiii.

[3] I use the plural (Bibles) because we don't have one uniform Bible for all Christian groups.

[4] Yes, I am very much aware (as I mentioned earlier) that some Christians will be very upset with these comments if I ignore what they perceive to be the guiding hand of God in the historical process (a function of the Holy Spirit). They will argue that although the process of Christian development may occasionally look chaotic, it is

always God-directed and turns out exactly as God intends. I leave it to the reader to decide whether such a faith-based approach to history flies in the face of the old adage: "If it looks like a duck, quacks like a duck, and walks like a duck, well . . . ? This is not to say that Christians are wrong. It only means that in this writing, I am approaching Christianity, not as a Christian, but as an historian. As humanly possible, I am trying to see Christianity from an "objective" position; that is, I am trying to apply the same rules of logic and scientific inquiry to Christianity as I do to the other major religions of the world. I believe it is hypocritical—and shortsighted—to apply those rules and standards to all other religions while excluding one's own faith from critical analysis on the basis of presumption and expediency (the Jesusgate approach).

[5] James M. Robinson, General Editor, *The Nag Hammadi Library In English*, 3rd Edition. New York: HarperCollins, 1990, p. 143.

[6] Ibid. p. 148.

[7] *The Other Gospels (Non-Canonical Gospel Texts)*, edited by Ron Cameron. Philadelphia: The Westminster Press, 1982. p. 125.

[8] *The Qur'an*, translated by Abdullah Yusuf Ali. New York: Tahrike Tarsile Qur'an, Inc., 6th US Edition, 2001, p. 75.

[9] Ron Cameron, *The Other Gospels*, p. 125.

[10] Whether or not Jesus knew Greek, as some scholars believe, makes little difference in this case because he would have taught in Aramaic, the common language of his people in Palestine.

[11] A.H. McNeile, *An Introduction to the Study of the New Testament*, 2nd Edition, Revised by CSC Williams. London: Oxford University Press, Amen House, 1953, p. 373.

[12] Bart D. Ehrman, *A Brief Introduction to the New Testament*. 2nd Edition, pp. 7-8.

[13] Raymond E. Brown, *An Introduction to the New Testament*. New York: Doubleday, 1997, p. 48.

[14] Bart D. Ehrman, *The New Testament: A Historical Introduction to the Early Christian Writings*, 3rd Edition, p. 484.

[15] Bart D. Ehrman, *A Brief Introduction to the New Testament*, 2nd Edition, p. 107.

[16] Ernie Bringas, *Going by the Book*, pp. 175-76.

[17] Robert M. Grant, *A Historical Introduction to the New Testament*. New York: Simon and Schuster, 1972, pp. 47-48.

[18] Although the opening verses of John's Gospel seem to equate Jesus (the Word) with God, they do not incorporate the Holy Spirit (the third party of the Trinity). However, 1 John does. Two other NT writers use Trinitarian language, although it is not yet a doctrine. Paul writes: "The grace of the Lord Jesus Christ, the love of God, and the communion of the Holy Spirit be with all of you" (2 Cor. 13:13). Matthew writes: "Go therefore and make disciples of all nations, baptizing them in the name of the Father, and of the Son and of the Holy Spirit" (28:19).

[19] Bruce M. Metzger, *Historical and Literary Studies*, pp. 101-02.

[20] Bart D. Ehrman, *Jesus, Interrupted*, p. 260.

[21] Bart D. Ehrman, *The New Testament: A Historical Introduction to the Early Christian Writings*, pp. 482-83.

[22] Ernie Bringas, *Going by the Book*, p. 186.

CHAPTER 8: WHO WROTE THE BOOK OF LOVE?
(Part 1)

[1] Placing the sun at the center of the solar system (heliocentric) as opposed to the geocentric model that places the earth at the center of the solar system.

[2] Saint Paul was a Jew, a Pharisee, a Roman citizen, and well educated. Following his dramatic conversion he became an early Christian missionary to the Gentiles (non-Jews) who started Christian communities outside of Palestine. He wrote many of the NT Epistles. His importance is such that he is often called "the second founder of Christianity." Christian tradition has Paul beheaded, ca. 67 AD, by the emperor Nero.

[3] Jarl Fossun and Philip Munoa, *Jesus and the Gospels*. Belmont, CA: Wadsworth, 2004, p. 92.

[4] Robert W. Funk and The Jesus Seminar, *The Acts of Jesus*. New York: HarperSanFrancisco, 1998, p. 1.

[5] Bart D. Ehrman, *A Brief Introduction to the New Testament*, 2nd Edition, p. 51.

CHAPTER 9: WHO WROTE THE BOOK OF LOVE?
(Part 2)

[1] Marla J. Selvidge, *Exploring the New Testament*, 2nd Edition, New Jersey: Prentice Hall, 2003, p. 111.

[2] William Barclay, *The Gospel of Matthew, Vol. 1*. Philadelphia: Westminster Press, 1958, p. xviii. (NOTE: As many as 678 verses appear in our newer translations of Mark.)

[3] John Dominic Crossan, *The Complete Gospels*. Santa Rosa, CA: Polebridge Press, 1994, p. 53.

[4] Scholars refer to this reliance by Matthew and Luke on the Q document, as the "double tradition."

[5] Scholars refer to this three Gospel agreement (where Matthew and Luke draw from Mark) as the "triple tradition" to distinguish it from the "double tradition" (where Matthew and Luke draw from Q).

[6] I. Howard Marshall, ed., *New Testament Interpretation: Essays on Principles and Methods*. Australia: The Paternoster Press, 1985, pp. 127-28. (Previously published by William B. Eerdmans) (NOTE: I have switched the order in which Marshall presents this material. He goes from Matthew to Mark whereas I move from Mark to Matthew; I do this because I want to show Mark's original writing before I show Matthew's editing of that writing.)

[7] Marla J. Selvidge, *Exploring the New Testament*, p. 53.

[8] Redaction criticism also seeks to determine the author's religious views as implied by his redaction. This "new" research procedure was developed following World War II.

[9] Sherman E. Johnson, *The Interpreter's Bible*, Vol. 7. Nashville: Abingdon Press, 1953, p. 234.

[10] *Steamboat Willie*, Wikipedia, the free encyclopedia.

[11] Within the context of this story, Matthew expands the scenario by introducing Peter's attempt—and failure—to walk on the water during the storm. This is not to be construed as negative behavior on Peter's part (such as Mark's "hardened hearts"), but as a natural survival instinct in the human character. Peter's fear is perfectly understandable.

[12] Hans Kung, *Theology for the Third Millennium*. New York: Doubleday, 1988, p. 287.

CHAPTER 10: HEEEEERE'S JOHNNY!

[1] James D.G. Dunn, *Did the First Christians Worship Jesus?: The New Testament Evidence.* Louisville: Westminster John Knox Press, 2010, p. 119.

[2] Robert W. Funk, Roy W. Hoover, and the Jesus Seminar, *The Five Gospels.* New York: Macmillan Publishing Company, 1993, p. 11.

[3] David L. Barr, *New Testament Story (An Introduction).* Belmont, CA: Wadsworth Cengage Learning, 2009, p. 396.

[4] James D.G. Dunn, *Did the First Christians Worship Jesus?: The New Testament Evidence,* p. 119.

[5] Robert A. Feuillet, *Introduction to the New Testament.* New York: Deselee Co., 1965, pp. 20, 31.

[6] Norman Perrin (1920-1976) was Associate Professor of New Testament, 1964-1976, University of Chicago Divinity School.

[7] Norman Perrin, *The New Testament: an Introduction,* 2nd edition under the general editorship of Robert Fern. New York: Harcourt Brace Jovanovich, 1982, pp. 52-53.

[8] Ibid. p. 249.

[9] Robert W. Funk, Roy W. Hoover, and the Jesus Seminar, *The Five Gospels,* p. 419.

[10] Stephen L. Harris, *The New Testament: A Student's Introduction,* Fifth Edition. New York: McGraw-Hill, 2006, p. 229.

[11] Ernie Bringas, *Going by the Book,* p. 190. The contradictions in the Gospel accounts of the Resurrection first drew serious attention through the publication in 1777 of *Fragments by an Anonymous Writer,* edited by Gotthold Ephraim Lessing. Actually, Lessing was drawing his information from an unpublished work by Herman Samuel Reimarus (1694-1768) who is credited by some for instigating the historian's search for the historical Jesus. I summarized most of this information from John Charlot's book, *New Testament Disunity,* pp. 80-81.

CHAPTER 11: PROPHECY AND JESUS (Part 1)

[1] One should note that Peter Stoner is a Professor of Science, not a biblical scholar.

[2] Matthew 1:22-23; 2:15; 2:17-18; 2:23; 4:14b-16; 8:17; 12:18-21; 13:35; 21:4-5; 27:9-10

[3] *The New Interpreters Bible.* Nashville: Abingdon Press, Volume VIII, 1995, p. 152.

[4] Ibid. p. 228.

[5] Babylon was a city of ancient Mesopotamia (present-day Iraq). Its ruins can be found in Al Hillah, Babil Province, about 55 miles south of Baghdad.

[6] Ramah was a city of ancient Israel about 5 miles north of Jerusalem.

[7] Rachel is the second and favorite wife of Jacob mentioned in the Book of Genesis.

[8] William Barclay, *The Gospel of Matthew, Vol. 1*, p. 28.

[9] Cathy Lynn Grossman, "Catholic bishops have kicked the 'booty' out of the Bible," *USA TODAY*, 3/1/2011.

[10] *The New Interpreter's Bible*, Volume VIII, p. 135.

[11] Ibid. p. 134.

[12] Ibid. pp. 135, 153, 310.

[13] Ibid. p. 154.

CHAPTER 12: PROPHECY AND JESUS (Part 2)

[1] John Dominic Crossan was professor of religious studies at DePaul University in Chicago; he co-founded the Jesus Seminar; today he is a major player in the field of biblical criticism.

[2] John Dominic Crossan, *Who Killed Jesus?* New York: HarperCollins Publishers, 1996, pp. 1-4.

[3] Bart D. Ehrman, *A Brief Introduction to the New Testament*, 2nd Edition, p. 157.

[4] John Dominic Crossan, *Who Killed Jesus"*, pp. 76 - 78.

[5] Take, for example, the Qur'an, the sacred text of the Muslims. The 114 suras (chapters) are not arranged with regard to chronology or even subject matter. With the exception of the opening prayer, they are arranged in sequence by the length of the chapter beginning with the longest sura and ending with the shortest. This type of format is highly unusual.

[6] The term Mormon is the term used to describe any member of The Church of Jesus Christ of the Latter Day Saints (the LDS Church).

[7] *The Book of Mormon.* Salt Lake City: Published by The Church of Jesus Christ of Latter-day Saints, 1981/1999, P, 1 of the Introduction.

[8] *The New Interpreter's Bible*, Vol. VIII, p. 516.

CHAPTER 13: THE BIRTH OF JESUS

[1] I have already noted some exceptions to this paucity of knowledge, e.g., the Jesus Seminar, some progressive ministers and churches, secular educational institutions, and so forth. Again, however, Jesusgaters continue to dominate the religious landscape.

[2] This assumption was initially challenged in 1971 at the first International Congress of Mithraic Studies. More recently, see: David Ulansey, *The Origins of the Mithraic Mysteries*. Oxford University Press revised paperback, 1991.

[3] *The Interpreter's Bible*, Vol. 1 – NT, p. 93.

[4] The Palestinian Jews—who spoke Aramaic—had their own translation of the Hebrew Bible, called the Targum (ca. first century AD). However, the majority of Jews lived outside of Palestine, and their language was Greek. They needed the Septuagint.

[5] *The Jewish Annotated New Testament*, Editors, Amy-Jill Levine and Marc Zvi Brettler. New York: Oxford University Press, 2010, p. 4.

[6] This was the famous tag line from one of American television's most creative police dramas (1958-63), *Naked City*.

[7] Henry Ansgar Kelly, *The Devil, Demonology and Witchcraft*, Revised Edition. Eugene, Oregon: Wipf & Stock Publishers, 2004, pp. 17, 25-26, 29. (Previously published by Doubleday.)

[8] Origen, *Against Celsus*, Book 1, Chapter 37.

[9] This belief was not universal and varied according to time and culture. For example, during the Paleolithic Age (ca. 35000-9000 BC) and Neolithic Age (ca. 9000-2000 BC), there is strong evidence to suggest that goddess culture was dominant and would have been woman-centered.

[10] This is not to imply that we are free of mythology in our present day. In fact, it is impossible to be myth free.

CHAPTER 14: THE DIVINITY OF JESUS (Part 1)

[1] Ernie Bringas, *Created Equal*, pp. 51-52.

[2] NOTE: Because of my educational responsibilities I did not perform with the touring Rip Chords (except when Phil and I started out at the very beginning; see: ripchords.info). For this particular summertime show, I simply observed from the wings. But it was a blast

anyway. (Unfortunately, this note accidentally failed to be included in the *Created Equal* publication.)

3 This is not to say that everyone in India has an obsolete mindset. In fact, some of our best and brightest engineers (as one example) come from India. Yet in certain parts of rural India, where the majority of Indians live, education is sorely lacking.

4 Mark C. Taylor, *Grave Matters*. Reaktion Books, 2004, p. 40.

5 This is an incredible line and I'd love to take credit for it but I picked it out of a 2002 Tom Cruise movie, *Minority Report*. Stephen Spielberg directed the film but I don't know who wrote that memorable line which I paraphrased a bit. I believe the original line was: "We do not choose our beliefs, our beliefs choose us."

6 This is not to say that "science" was totally absent. The beginnings of what we call science can be traced back to the ancient Greeks, hundreds of years before Jesus. But its impact was somewhat limited relative to its later development driven by the impetus of the Muslim's renowned "Baghdad's House of Wisdom" (ca. 760 AD), and Europe's Scientific Revolution that started ca. 1500s.

7 Hans W. Frei, *Theology and Narrative (Selected Essays)*, Edited by George Hunsinger and William C. Placher. Oxford: Oxford University Press, 1933, pp. 47-48.

Also: William G. Doty, *Contemporary New Testament Interpretation*. Englewood Cliffs, New Jersey: Prentice-Hall, 1972, p. 90.

Also: Rebecca Moore, *Voices of Christianity*, p. 85.

8 W.H.C. Frend, *The Early Church*, p. 5.

9 Although the Buddha (Siddhartha Gautama) was born a Hindu, he eventually broke away from Hinduism and founded, of course, the religion of Buddhism.

10 NOTE: In Hinduism, Jainism, and Theravada Buddhism, the word "heaven" is inappropriate, as they do not conceive of such a place.

11 *The New Oxford Annotated Bible*, pp. 9-10.

12 Joseph Campbell (1904-1989) was a prolific American author, the recipient of the Distinguished Scholar Award, Hofstra University, 1973. He also received the Melcher award for contribution to religion, 1976, for *The Mythic Image*.

13 Joseph Campbell, *Myths to Live By*. New York: Bantam, 1973, pp. 221-22.

[14] This is not to say that scientists don't have their blind spots, but for the most part, they definitely have a better grasp on reality (things as they really are).

[15] Bart D. Ehrman, *A Brief Introduction to The New Testament*, 2nd Edition, pp. 66, 157.

[16] Lewis M. Hopfe and Mark R. Woodward, *Religions of the World* (11th Edition), 2009, p. 264.

Howard Clark Kee, Franklin W. Young, and Karlfried Froehlich, *Understanding the New Testament*, 2nd Edition. Englewood Cliffs, NJ: Prentice-Hall, 1965, p. 35. Also: see Howard Clark Kee's, *The Beginnings of Christianity: An Introduction to the New Testament.* New York: T & T Clark International, 2005, pp. 28-35.

CHAPTER 15: THE DIVINITY OF JESUS (Part 2)

[1] The date ca. 44 AD is extrapolated from Acts 12:1 where Herod Aggripa 1 (10 BC – 44 AD) is mentioned. Also, the term *Christians* (according to *The New Oxford Annotated Bible,* 3rd edition, p. 206 NT) is a Latin word meaning "partisans [supporters] of Christ." The word also appears in Acts 26:28, and 1 Peter 4:16. According to some sources, Ignatius of Antioch made the earliest recorded use of the term *Christianity* around 100 AD.

[2] W.H.C. Frend, *The Early Church*, p. 27.

[3] Alan Richardson, Editor, *A Theological Word Book of the Bible.* New York: The Macmillan Publishing Co., 1950, p. 46.

[4] Ibid. p. 131.

[5] Howard Clark Kee, Franklin W. Young, and Karlfried Froehlich, *Understanding the New Testament*, 2d Edition, p. 201.

[6] Norman Perrin, *The New Testament: an Introduction*, p. 84.

[7] Howard Clark Kee, Franklin W. Young, and Karlfried Froehlich, *Understanding the New Testament*, p. 201.

[8] *The New Oxford Annotated Bible*, p. 330NT.

[9] Be aware that many scholars today do not believe that Colossians came from Paul's hand. They consider the work to have been written one or two decades after his death, perhaps by one of his disciples.

CHAPTER 16: EPILOGUE

[1] Richard Dawkins, *The God Delusion*. New York: Houghton Mifflin Company, 2008, p. 51.

[2] In 2008 I was fortunate to catch a 1946 movie classic called *Sister Kenny*, staring Rosalind Russell. This memorable line caught my attention (Brackets mine). *Sister Kenny* is the life story of Elizabeth Kenny (1880-1952), a physical therapist who revolutionized the treatment for polio in spite of skeptical doctors. As a note of interest, the actress Rosalind Russell was a personal friend of Kenny.

[3] Ernie Bringas, *Going by the Book*, pp. 166-70.

[4] John S. Dunne, *The Way of All the Earth*. New York: Macmillan Publishing Co., 1972, p. 114.

[5] 194 Carl R. Rogers, *On Becoming a Person*. Boston: Houghton Mifflin Co., 1961, p. 27.

[6] Kahlil Gibran (1883-1931) was a Lebanese poet, philosopher, and artist. He is best known for his classic masterpiece, *The Prophet*, published in 1923 and still in bookstores today.

APPENDIX A

[1] Torah is a Hebrew word that means "guidance" or "direction." Traditionally, it refers to God's Law (allegedly given to Moses) that appears in the first five books of the Old Testament—Genesis, Exodus, Leviticus, Numbers, and Deuteronomy. (Torah can also signify all Jewish literature and teaching.)

[2] Evolution is no longer a "theory" in the popular understanding of that word. It is a well-grounded (but imperfect) scientific principle as to how life developed. It continues to undergo further refinement as new knowledge is acquired.

APPENDIX B

[1] Robert E. Van Voorst, *Reading the New Testament Today*. Belmont, CA: Thompson Wadsworth, 2005, p. 449.

[2] Marla J. Selvidge, *Exploring the New Testament*, p. 189.

[3] Bart Ehrman, *The New Testament: A Historical Introduction to the Early Christian Writings*, pp. 394, 401-03.

[4] Ibid. p. 484.

APPENDIX C

[1] Although Paleo-Hebrew was present up until the early part of the second century, it was used primarily only by learned scribes.

[3] Zebedee, according to Matthew 4:21, was the father of the disciples James and John.

[4] Bart D. Ehrman, *A Brief Introduction to the New Testament*, 2nd Edition, p. 125.

[5] 205 Raymond, E. Brown, *An Introduction to the New Testament*, pp. 368-69.

[6] Ehrman, *A Brief Introduction*, 2nd Edition, p. 125.

[7] Bart D. Ehrman, *Lost Christianities*, p. 172.

[8] Clement of Alexandria (ca. 150-213 AD) was the first notable scholar of the Church of Alexandria, Egypt.

[9] Jarl Fossum and Philip Munoa, *Jesus and the Gospels*. Belmont, CA: Wadsworth, 2004, p. 90.

[10] Ibid.

[11] *The New Oxford Annotated Bible*, p. 394NT.

[12] Robert W. Funk, Roy W. Hoover, and the Jesus Seminar, *The Five Gospels*, p. 20.

[13] Jarl Fossum and Philip Munoa, *Jesus and the Gospels*, p. 91.

[14] It is almost universally agreed by biblical scholars that the Gospel of Luke and the Book of Acts (The Acts of the Apostles) were composed by the same person, ergo, Luke-Acts.

[15] Marla J. Selvidge, *Exploring the New Testament*, p. 109.

APPENDIX D

[1] David S. Noss, *A History of the World's Religions*, Twelfth Edition. New Jersey: Prentice Hall, 2009, pp. 42-43. There is also an expanded version in the 13th Edition, 2012, pp. 36-37.

[2] *Revised Standard Version*, (Genesis 8:6-12), p. 276.

DIRECTORY OF THE 75
SCHOLARS UTILIZED
(Only if bio info was available)

Karen Armstrong a former Roman Catholic nun is a British author and commentator who is the author of twelve books on comparative religion. Armstrong first rose to prominence in 1993 with her international best seller, *A History of God: The 4000-Year Quest of Judaism, Christianity and Islam.*

Walter Bauer (1877-1960) was an eminent German scholar of massive knowledge and comprehension. His Greek dictionary (often updated now) remains the standard tool for students who study New Testament Greek, the first language in which the NT was written.

Joseph Cullen Ayer, Jr. (1866-1944) was a Protestant Episcopalian. He was educated at Harvard University and the universities of Berlin, Halle, and Leipsic (Ph.D., 1893), and at the Episcopal Theological School in Cambridge, Massachusetts.

William Barclay (1907-1978) was an author, radio and television presenter, Church of Scotland minister, and Professor of Divinity and Biblical Criticism at the University of Glasgow.

David L. Barr is Professor of Religion at Wright State University, Dayton, Ohio.

Marcus J. Borg is an American Biblical scholar and author. He holds a Ph.D. degree from Oxford University and is Hundere Distinguished

Professor of Religion and Culture at Oregon State University from which he retired in 2007. Borg has been national chair of the Historical Jesus Section of the Society of Biblical Literature, co-chair of its International New Testament Program Committee and president of the Anglican Association of Biblical Scholars. He is a fellow of the Jesus Seminar.

Marc Zvi Brettler is an American Bible scholar. He earned his B.A., M.A., and Ph.D. from Brandeis University. He is the Dora Golding Professor of Biblical Studies and chair of the Department of Near Eastern and Judaic Studies at Brandeis University. Brettler's main areas of research are religious metaphors and the Bible, biblical historical texts, and women and the Bible. In 2004 Brettler won the National Jewish Book Award for *The Jewish Study Bible*.

Raymond E. Brown, (1928-1998), was an author, an American Roman Catholic priest, and a major biblical scholar. He earned his Ph.D. at the Johns Hopkins University. Brown was professor emeritus at the prestigious Protestant Union Theological Seminary (UTS) in New York where he taught for 29 years. He was the first Roman Catholic professor to gain tenure there.

Ron Cameron received his B.A. in Philosophy and Religion from Western Kentucky University, and his Ph.D. in the Study of Religion from Harvard University. He is Professor of Religion at Wesleyan University. He has also taught at Harvard Divinity School.

Joseph Campbell (1904-1989) was a prolific American author, the recipient of the Distinguished Scholar Award from Hofstra University. He also received the Melcher award (contribution to religion) for his book, *The Mythic Image*.

John Charlot teaches Hawaiian and Polynesian religions as well as New Testament and Religion and Art at the University of Hawaii at Manoa.

Harvey Gallagher Cox, Jr., is one of the preeminent theologians in the U.S. Cox attended the University of Pennsylvania and obtained a B.A. degree with honors in history. He went on to earn a B.D. degree from the Yale University Divinity School, and a Ph.D. degree in the history and philosophy of religion from Harvard University. He served as Hollis Research Professor of Divinity at the Harvard Divinity School, until his retirement in 2009.

Keith Crim is a freelance editor and former professor of philosophy at Virginia Commonwealth University in Richmond, Virginia. He is the general editor of *Dictionary of Living Religions* and *The Perennial Dictionary of World Religions*.

John Dominic Crossan is an Irish-American religious New Testament world-class scholar and former Catholic priest. He earned his Ph.D. at Maynooth College, the Irish national seminary. He has authored several books and is best known for co-founding the Jesus Seminar with Robert Funk in 1985. He is considered a major figure in the field of biblical scholarship. He is also a member of the Society of Biblical Literature (SBL).

Richard Dawkins received his M.A. and Ph.D. from Oxford University. He has taught zoology at the University of California at Berkeley and at Oxford University, and was Oxford's Professor for Public Understanding from 1995 until 2008. Dawkins is an atheist. He is an evolutionary biologist and prolific writer. Among his previous books are *The Ancestor's Tale, The Selfish Gene,* and *The Blind Watchmaker*. His 2006 book, *The God Delusion*, has sold more than two million copies.

William G. Doty is a prolific writer, translator, and editor who published fourteen books and over seventy essays in a wide range of journals including religious studies, anthropology, psychology, classics, and art criticism. He served from 1987-1994 as the national coordinator for the yearly American Academy of Religion competition for the best book in the field.

James D.G. Dunn is one of the world's top New Testament scholars. Dunn has an M.A. and B.D. from the University of Glasgow and a Ph.D. and D.D. from the University of Cambridge. He is Lightfoot Professor of Divinity Emeritus at the University of Durham in England. He is a prolific writer on Christianity.

John S. Dunne is a well-known prolific writer and is Professor of Theology at the University of Notre Dame.

Bart D. Ehrman received both his Masters of Divinity and Ph.D. from Princeton Theological Seminary. He is one of the world's renowned New Testament scholars. He is the James A. Gray Distinguished Professor at the University of North Carolina at Chapel Hill where he has served as both the Director of Graduate Studies and the Chair of the Department of Religious Studies. He has published extensively in the fields of New Testament and Early Christianity, having written or edited twenty-four books, numerous scholarly articles, and dozens of book reviews. He has authored four New York Times bestsellers. Among his fields of scholarly expertise are the historical Jesus, the early Christian apocrypha, the apostolic fathers, and the manuscript tradition of the New Testament.

Hans W. Frei went to the graduate school at Yale Divinity School in 1947, and began a lengthy doctoral dissertation under H. Richard Niebuhr, on Karl Barth's early doctrine of Revelation. He completed his thesis in 1956 and was promoted to Professor of Theology. A year later, he returned to Yale Divinity School as Assistant Professor of Religious Studies.

Timothy Freke is a British author of books on religion and perhaps is best known for his books, co-authored with Peter Gandy, which advocate a Gnostic understanding of early Christianity.

William Hugh Clifford Frend (1916 - 2005) Professor Frend was an English ecclesiastical historian, archaeologist, author, and Anglican priest.

Karlfried Froehlich was Professor of Church History at Princeton Theological Seminary before retiring. He currently serves at Princeton as the Henry III Guest Lecturer in Theology and Communications.

Robert W. Funk (1926 – 2005) was an American biblical scholar, and co-founder of the Jesus Seminar and the nonprofit Westar Institute. Funk received his bachelor's of divinity and master's degrees from Butler University, a Ph.D. from Vanderbilt University and was a Guggenheim

Fellow and a Senior Fulbright Scholar. He taught at the American School of Oriental Research in Jerusalem, was chairman of the graduate department of religion at Vanderbilt University and executive secretary of the Society of Biblical Literature.

Peter Gandy is a British author who focuses on mysticism, particular the mystery religions. He holds an M.A. in classical civilization and is known mainly for his books co-authored with Timothy Freke.

Blake R. Grangaard is Professor of Religion at Heidelberg University, Ohio. He earned his B.A. from St. Olaf College, his M.Div. from Luther Theological Seminary and his Ph.D. from Union Theological Seminary in Virginia. He was a church pastor for almost 10 years before turning to academia. He has been at Heidelberg since 1996.

Robert M. Grant is professor of New Testament at the University of Chicago. He is a foremost NT scholar. His books include *Gnosticism*, *The Earliest Lives of Jesus*, and *The Secret Sayings of Jesus*.

Kahlil Gibran (1883-1931) was a Lebanese poet, philosopher, and artist. He is best known for his classic masterpiece, *The Prophet*, published in 1923 and still in bookstores today.

Stephen L. Harris is Professor Emeritus of Humanities and Religious Studies at California State University, Sacramento. He served there ten years as department chair and was named a Woodrow Wilson Fellow. He received his M.A. and Ph.D. degrees from Cornell University. Harris is a member of the American Academy of Religion, a fellow at the Westar Institute, and has authored several books on religion, some of which are used in introductory university courses.

Charles W. Hedrick is Distinguished Emeritus Professor of Religious Studies at Southwest Missouri State University. He was a member of the international team (UNESCO) of scholars who worked for several years in Cairo, Egypt, reconstructing and translating the Nag Hammadi Codices and later excavated at the site of the Nag Hammadi discovery. He is a distinguished author, translator, and teacher in the academic study of religion.

Lewis M. Hopfe (1935-1992) received his B.A. in religious studies from Baylor University, an M.Div. from Sowthwestern Baptist Theological Seminary, and his Ph.D. in Old Testament studies from Boston University. His academic legacy is a college textbook, *Religions of the World.*

George Hunsinger is an ordained Presbyterian minister and the Hazel Thompson McCord Professor of Systematic Theology at Princeton Theological Seminary and a leading expert on the eminent scholar Karl Barth (pronounced "Bart").

Sherman E. Johnson (d. 1993) was a graduate of Seabury Western and of the University of Chicago, from which he had his Ph.D. He taught a Yale Divinity School and played a major role in the founding of the Graduate Theological Union in Berkeley, and for twenty years was Dean at the Church Divinity School of the Pacific.

Paul Johnson is an English journalist, historian, speechwriter and author. He was educated at the Jesuit independent school Stonyhurst College, and Magdalen College, Oxford. A prolific writer, he has written over forty books and contributed to numerous magazines and newspapers.

Henry Kamen is a British historian. He earned his Ph.D. at the University of Oxford. He subsequently taught at various universities in Spain and in the United States (University of Wisconsin). Since his retirement in 2002, he has continued lecturing and writing, and lives currently in Spain and in the United States.

Howard Clark Kee is William Goodwin Aurelio Professor of Biblical Studies Emeritus at Boston University and Visiting Faculty at the University of Pennsylvania. Kee's publications include the first edition of *The Cambridge Companion to the Bible, Beginnings of Christianity: Introduction to the New Testament* (2005), *Understanding the New Testament* (5th ed.), and *Jesus in History* (3rd ed.).

Henry Ansgar Kelly is an Emeritus Distinguished Professor at UCLA. His expertise is in Medieval and Renaissance Literature and History; Biblical Studies; Ecclesiastical History and Theology.

Hans Kung is a Swiss Catholic priest, theologian, and prolific author. Because he has challenged the doctrine of papal infallibility the Vatican rescinded his authority to teach Catholic theology. He had to leave the Catholic faculty at the University of Tubingen, but remained as a professor of ecumenical theology, serving as an emeritus professor since 1996. Although Küng is not officially allowed to teach Catholic theology, neither his bishop nor the Holy See has revoked his priestly faculties.

Eugene N. Lane first studied at the University of Princeton. He received his M.A. and Ph.D. from Yale University. After that, he was professor from 1962 to 1966 at the University of Virginia, and from 1966 to 2000 at the University of Missouri. His main interest was the study of ancient religion, especially the oriental cults in the Roman Empire.

John H. Leith (1919–2002) received his Ph.D. from Yale University. He was an important Presbyterian theologian and ordained minister who was the Pemberton Professor of Theology at Union Theological Seminary in Virginia from 1959 to 1990. He authored at least 18 books and countless essays on Christianity.

Gotthold Ephraim Lessing (1729–1781) was a German writer, philosopher, dramatist, publicist, and art critic, and one of the most outstanding representatives of the Enlightenment era. His plays and theoretical writings substantially influenced the development of German literature.

Amy-Jill Levine is E. Rhodes and Leona B. Carpenter Professor of New Tetament Studies at Vanderbilt University Divinity School, Department of Religious Studies, and Graduate Department of Religion. She holds an M.A. and Ph.D. from Duke University. Levine has been awarded grants from the Mellon Foundation, the National Endowment for the Humanities, and the American Council of Learned Societies.

I. Howard Marshall is Professor Emeritus of New Testament Exegesis at the University of Aberdeen, Scotland, where he also received his Ph.D. He was formerly the chair of the Tyndale Fellowship for Biblical and Theological Research; he was also president of the British New Testament Society and chair of the Fellowship of European Evangelical

Theologians. He is the author of numerous publications, including 2005 Gold Medallion Book Award winner *New Testament Theology*.

Bruce Metzger (1914–2007) received his Th.B. (Bachelor of Theology) from Princeton University. He was a professor at Princeton Theological Seminary and Bible editor who served on the board of the American Bible Society and United Bible Societies. He was a scholar of Greek New Testament, New Testament Textual Criticism, and wrote prolifically on these subjects. He was recognized as a world-class scholar.

Michael Molloy received his MA from St. John's University, and his Ph.D. from the University of Hawaii. He has focused on Jewish, Christian, Hindu, and Buddhist mysticism. He is best known for his college textbook, *Experiencing the World's Religions*.

Rebecca Moore, Ph.D. is an associate professor in the Department of Religious Studies at San Diego State University, where she teaches courses in Christianity, New Testament, and Religion in America. She has published on the subject of Christian and Jewish Dialogue, with an emphasis on medieval biblical exegesis. She also writes and publishes in the field of new religions in America.

Philip Munoa received his MA and Ph.D. from Michigan University and teaches Religious Studies, New Testament, at Hope College. He has authored several writings, including a textbook on the New Testament.

Walter Nigg Walter Nigg studied philosophy and Protestant theology at the universities of Gottingen , Leipzig and Zurich He was an Adjunct Professor of Church History in Zurich.

David S. Noss (1920–2010) earned a Ph.D. in Religion and the Arts from the University of Chicago Divinity School. Dr. Noss joined the Religion and Philosophy Department of Heidelberg College in 1950. He is well known for his authorship of *A History of the World's Religions*, a textbook used on college campuses throughout the U.S.

David P. Nystrom received his Ph.D. from the University of California at Davis. He is the Sr. Vice President at Biola University. He is a specialist in Roman social history and in the New Testament. He has authored dozens of articles and two books, including *The History of Christianity*.

John A. O'Brien (1893–1980) was Professor of Theology at the University of Notre Dame. He was a scholar and author.

Elaine Pagels received her Ph.D. from Harvard University. She has a B.A. and M.A. from Stanford University. She is the Harrington Spear Paine Professor of Religion at Princeton University. The recipient of a MacArthur Fellowship, she has authored several books and is best known for her studies and writing on the Gnostic Gospels. *Revelations* is her most recent offering.

Jaroslav Pelikan (1923-2006) received his Ph.D. at the University of Chicago. He was a scholar in the history of Christianity, Christian theology and medieval intellectual history. He joined Yale University in 1962 as the Titus Street Professor of Ecclesiastical History and in 1972 was named Sterling Professor of History. Awards include the Graduate School's 1979 Wilbur Cross Medal and the Medieval Academy of America's 1985 Haskins Medal.

Norman Perrin (1920-1976) was Associate Professor of New Testament, at the University of Chicago Divinity School. Professor Perrin was an author and internationally known for his work on Redaction Criticism of the New Testament.

William C. Placher (1948-2008) was a distinguished professor of philosophy and religion at Wabash College in Crawfordsville, Indiana. He earned his M.A. and Ph.D. from Yale University. He was the author of 13 books.

Herman Samuel Reimarus (1694-1768) was a German philosopher and writer of the Enlightenment. He supported the concept of Deism, the belief in the existence of a supreme being, specifically of a creator who does not intervene in the universe. Some historians' credit him with initiating the investigation of the historical Jesus.

Alan Richardson (1905-75), formerly Dean of York, Professor of Christian Theology at the University of Nottingham and Canon of Durham Cathedral.

James M. Robinson received his D.Theol (Summa cum Laude), at the University of Basel, Switzerland (in Contemporary Theology, supervisor Karl Barth). His Th.D was earned at Princeton Theological Seminary. He is Professor Emeritus of Religion at Claremont Graduate University, in California. He is a member of the Jesus Seminar and arguably the most prominent Q and Nag Hammadi library scholar of the 20th century.

Carl R. Rogers (1902 – 1987) obtained his M.A. and a Ph.D. from Teachers College, Columbia University. He was an influential American psychologist and is widely considered to be one of the founding fathers of psychotherapy research and was honored for his pioneering work with the Award for Distinguished Scientific Contributions by the American Psychological Association.

Marla J. Selvidge, Ph.D., is Professor and Director of the Center for Religious Studies at the University of Central Missouri. She is the 1999 winner of the William H. Byler Distinguished Faculty Award, and has published both nationally and internationally in the fields of biblical studies, world religions, peace studies, and feminist issues.

James D. Smart (1906-1982) received his Ph.D. from the University of Toronto. The Reverend Dr. James Dick Smart was an internationally renowned writer, Christian educator, theologian, and Presbyterian pastor. He was a noted scholar, and professor at the prestigious Union Theological Seminary (UTS) in New York.

John Shelby Spong is a retired American Bishop of the Episcopal Church. He was a Phi Beta Kappa graduate of the University of North Carolina at Chapel Hill, and received his Master of Divinity degree from the Episcopal Theological Seminary in Alexandria, Virginia. He has written many books and has held visiting positions and given lectures at major American theological institutions, most prominently at the Harvard Divinity School. He retired in 2000.

Mark C. Taylor received his Ph.D. from Harvard University. He is the Cluett Professor of Humanities at Williams College, Williamstown, Massachusetts. He is a philosopher of religion and cultural critic who has published more than twenty books on theology, philosophy, art and architecture, media, technology, economics, and the natural sciences.

Franklin W. Young received his Ph.D. from Duke University. Young became professor of New Testament at the Episcopal Seminary of the Southwest. He later served on the faculty at Princeton; he was director of graduate studies in religion and then chair of department of religion. Thereafter, Young returned to Duke Divinity School and served as professor of New Testament and patristic studies until 1970, when he was awarded the Amos Ragan Kearns endowed professorship. Young served as director of graduate studies in religion at Duke for six years.

L. Michael White received his Ph.D. and master of divinity degrees from Yale University. He is an American Biblical scholar and director of the Institute for the Study of Antiquity and Christian Origins at the University of Texas at Austin. He is the author or co-author of seven books, twenty-six articles, and editor of four volumes and collected essays.

CSC Williams (ca. 1906 – 1962) was a Welsh Anglican priest and university lecturer. Williams was educated at Clifton College and Jesus College, Oxford, where he obtained a first-class degree in theology. He was also University Lecturer in the New Testament and published various books on the Old and New Testaments.

Mark R. Woodward is associate professor of religious studies ate Arizona State University. He received his Ph.D. in anthropology from the University of Illinois and also studied at the Divinity School at the University of Chicago. His research specializations include religion and modernity and religion and politics. He is the co-author of a college text, *Religions of the World.*

Phil Zuckerman is Professor of Sociology at Pitzer College, Claremont, California. He received his B.A., M.A., and Ph.D. from the University of Oregon.

INDEX

97, 105-06, 112, 115, 121,
131, 137, 148, 150, 156, 172,
194-95, 233, 249, 252, 255,
285, 291; defined, XI-XII;
XVII
Biblical authority, II, 44, 91, 115,
275-76
Biblical scholar, defined, 31
Biblical scholarship, XII, XVIII,
6, 44, 82, 150, 194 (see also,
biblical criticism)
Biblical science, XII, 260 (see also,
biblical criticism)
Biblical studies XII, 24, 82, 231,
292, 296, 300, (see also, bibli-
cal criticism)
Biology, 249; Virgin Birth, 32,
199, 212-13
Bishop Dionysius, 64
Bishop Hosius, 64
Bishop Ridley, 20
Bonanza, 37
Borg, Marcus J., 277; bio, 33, 291-
92
Brown, Raymond E., 98, 269, 281,
290; bio, 292

C

California Sound, 40-41,
Caligula, Roman emperor, 223
Calvin, John, 19, 276
Campbell, Joseph, 225, 287; bio,
292
Canon, defined, 20; 86-91, 93, 95,
109-10, 300; Buddhist, 115
Celsus, 49-52, 286
Chalcedonian Creed, 66-67
Christ, defined, 170; XV, 19, 32,
57, 60-61, 66, 72, 99, 103,149,
154, 185, 229-30, 234,

236-37, 240-43, 247, 264,
271, 275, 282, 285, 288
Christian Jew (Jewish Christians),
156, 170, 175, 177, 226-28,
234-35, 237-240, 243, 246,
270, 298
Christology, defined, 56-57; 59,
61-62, 67-68, 71, 83, 132,
142, 231, 240, 242, 246-47
Church and State, 17, 81
Church Fathers, 51-52, 79, 96, 99,
211
Circumcision (the Jewish law),
238, 246; mythology, 225
Codex (Codices), defined, 86; 93,
96, 295
Codex Sinaiticus, 93, 98, 110
Codex Vaticanus, 93, 98, 110
Constantine (Roman emperor),
52, 62-65, 67-70, 228, 232,
247, 279
Copernicus, Nicolaus, 77-78, 115,
221
Coptic, the language, 86, 92, 96,
108; the church, 86, 110
Council of Antioch, 64; city of,
234, 288
Council of Chalcedon, 62, 65, 68,
70-71, 78; creed of, 65-67,
104, 218, 228, 247
Council of Nicea, (location; creed
of) 59, 62-65, 67-68, 70-72,
104, 144, 218, 226, 228, 232,
247
Council of Trent, 79
Covenant, (between Abraham and
God), 238
Criticism (see biblical criticism)
Crossan, John Dominic, 171-72,
176, 178, 180-81, 277, 283,
285; bio, 293

ABOUT THE AUTHOR

Presently, as an adjunct faculty member, Ernie Bringas teaches Religious Studies at Glendale Community College in Arizona. Under their auspices, he previously taught these classes at Arizona State University.

Ernie received his B.A. at the California State University, Long Beach. His graduate studies led to a Master of Divinity degree from United Theological Seminary, Dayton, Ohio, in 1966. Further religious studies were briefly pursued at the Pacific School of Religion, Berkeley, California.

After graduating from seminary, Ernie was ordained as a minister of the United Methodist Church. He served the Church for almost twenty years before venturing into academic studies,

During the early 1960s, while pursuing his university and seminary education, Ernie and his partner Phil Stewart founded a rock group that came to be known as the Rip Chords. The group, recording for Columbia Records, placed five hit singles on Billboard's Hot 100 singles chart, 1962-65 (see: ripchords.info).

Related Titles

If you enjoyed *Jesusgate*, you may also enjoy other
Rainbow Ridge titles. Read more about them at
www.rainbowridgebooks.com

The Cosmic Internet: Explanations from the Other Side
by Frank DeMarco

Conversations with Jesus: An Intimate Journey
by Alexis Eldridge

Dialogue with the Devil: Enlightenment for the Unwilling
by Yves Patak

The Divine Mother Speaks: The Healing of the Human Heart
by Rashmi Khilnani

Difficult People: A Gateway to Enlightenment
by Lisette Larkins

When Do I See God: Finding the Path to Heaven
by Jeff Ianniello

Dance of the Electric Hummingbird
by Patricia Walker

Coming Full Circle: Ancient Teachings for a Modern World
by Lynn Andrews

Thank Your Wicked Parents
by Richard Bach

Afterlife Conversations with Hemingway:
A Dialogue on His Life, His Work, and the Myth
by Frank DeMarco

The Buddha Speaks: To the Buddha Nature Within
by Rashmi Khilnani

Consciousness: Bridging the Gap Between Conventional Science
and the New Super Science of Quantum Mechanics
by Eva Herr

Messiah's Handbook: Reminders for the Advanced Soul
by Richard Bach

Blue Sky, White Clouds
by Eliezer Sobel

Rainbow Ridge Books publishes spiritual and metaphysical titles, and is distributed by Square One Publishers in Garden City Park, New York.

To contact authors and editors, peruse our titles, and see submission guidelines, please visit our website at:

www.rainbowridgebooks.com

For orders and catalogs, please call toll-free:
(877) 900-BOOK